Kaplan Foundations: ACT® & SAT® Prep

Math and Science

K12 LEARNING SERVICES

Acknowledgments

Special thanks to those who made this book possible including Laura Aitcheson, Becky Berthiaume, Michael Boothroyd, Matthew Callan, Potoula Chresomales, Marilyn Engle, Kate Fisher, Adam Hinz, Kate Hurley, Brandon Jones, Rebecca Knauer, Celina Lasota, James Radkins, Justin Starr, Bob Verini, Devon Wible, Daniel Wittich, and many others who contributed materials and advice.

Published by Kaplan Publishing, a division of Kaplan, Inc.
750 Third Avenue
New York, NY 10017

Printed in the United States of America

10 9 8 7 6 5 4 3 2 1

ISBN-13: 978-1-62523-344-8

Table of Contents

UNIT THREE: PROBLEM SOLVING & DATA ANALYSIS

UNIT FOUR: GEOMETRY

PART TWO: SCIENCE

UNIT FIVE: SCIENCE

PART THREE: MATH AND SCIENCE PROGRESS CHECKS

PART ONE

Math

UNIT ONE

Introductory Algebra

IN THIS UNIT, YOU WILL LEARN HOW TO:

1. Apply the Kaplan Method for Math
2. Add and subtract integers and fractions
3. Perform the order of operations
4. Solve linear equations
5. Graph linear equations
6. Solve and graph inequalities
7. Graph systems of equations
8. Solve systems of equations
9. Translate English into math
10. Solve word problems with equations and inequalities

CHAPTER 1

The Kaplan Method for Math

CHAPTER OBJECTIVES

By the end of this chapter, you will be able to:

1. Utilize the Kaplan Method for Math to formulate a plan and solve questions
2. Identify and apply multiple strategies for checking solutions

Many introductory algebra questions are designed to test your ability to:

- Perform the order of operations
- Solve, understand, and graph linear equations and inequalities
- Solve, understand, and graph systems of equations
- Translate English into math
- Solve word problems using equations and inequalities

✔ Helpful Hint

Use the Kaplan Method for Math on every applicable question throughout this course so that it becomes second nature; it will increase your efficiency and accuracy.

THE KAPLAN METHOD FOR MATH

Step 1: Read the question, identifying and organizing important information as you go

- **What information am I given?** Look in the question stem and in the answer choices for the info you need.
- **Separate the question from the context.** Cross out any info you don't need to solve the question.
- **How are the answer choices different?** The answer choices can help you choose the best method for solving the question.
- **Should I label or draw a diagram?** Sketch a diagram if you need one. If a figure is provided, label it with info from the question.

Step 2: Choose the best strategy to answer the question

- **Look for patterns.** Before you start time-consuming math, check for shortcuts.
- **Pick numbers or use straightforward math.** You can pick numbers when questions that describe relationships between quantities don't provide specific values (like percentages).

Step 3: Check that you answered the *right* question

- Review the question stem.
- Check units of measurement.
- Double-check your work.

✓ Helpful Hint

Questions may ask you for quantities like $x + 1$ or the product of x and y. Be careful on these questions! They often include tempting answer choices that correspond to the value of x or y individually. Take a moment at the end of every question to make sure you're answering the right question.

Step 1: READ the question, IDENTIFYING and ORGANIZING important information as you go

A farmer's market sells watermelons, cantaloupe, and honeydew for \$0.40 per pound. On Mondays, all melons are sold at a 20% discount. The market also sells avocados for \$0.35 each. Which equation represents the total cost, c, if a customer buys five avocados and a watermelon weighing p pounds on a Monday?

A) $c = 0.2p + 0.35$

B) $c = 0.32p + 1.75$

C) $c = 0.4p + 0.35$

D) $c = 0.4p + 1.75$

- **What information am I given?** Look in the question stem and answer choices for the info you need.

- **Separate the question from the context.** Cross out any info you don't need to solve the question.

- **How are the answer choices different?** The answer choices can help you choose the best method for solving the question.

- **Should I label or draw a diagram?** Sketch a diagram if you need one. If a figure is provided, label it with info from the question.

Step 2: CHOOSE the best strategy to answer the question

A farmer's market sells watermelons, cantaloupe, and honeydew for $0.40 per pound. On Mondays, all melons are available at a 20% discount. The market also sells avocados for $0.35 each. Which equation represents the total cost, *c*, if a customer buys five avocados and a watermelon weighing *p* pounds on a Monday?

A) $c = 0.2p + 0.35$

B) $c = 0.32p + 1.75$

C) $c = 0.4p + 0.35$

D) $c = 0.4p + 1.75$

- **Look for patterns.** Before you start time-consuming math, check for shortcuts.

  ____

  ____

- **Pick numbers or use straightforward math.** You can pick numbers when questions that describe relationships between quantities don't provide specific values (like percentages).

  ____

  ____

✓ Helpful Hint

You won't earn any extra points for solving a question the hard way, so be sure to use the easiest method possible!

Step 3: CHECK that you answered the *right* question

- Review the question stem.
- Check units of measurement.
- Double-check your work.

A farmer's market sells watermelons, cantaloupe, and honeydew for $0.40 per pound. On Mondays, all melons are available at a 20% discount. The market also sells avocados for $0.35 each. Which equation represents the total cost, *c*, if a customer buys five avocados and a watermelon weighing *p* pounds on a Monday?

A) $c = 0.2p + 0.35$

B) $c = 0.32p + 1.75$

C) $c = 0.4p + 0.35$

D) $c = 0.4p + 1.75$

This worked solution would resemble the following:

A farmer's market sells watermelons, cantaloupe, and honeydew for $0.40 per pound. On Mondays, all melons are available at a 20% discount. The market also sells avocados for $0.35 each. Which equation represents the total cost, c, if a customer buys five avocados and a watermelon weighing p pounds on a Monday?

A) $c = 0.2p + 0.35$

B) $c = 0.32p + 1.75$

C) $c = 0.4p + 0.35$

D) $c = 0.4p + 1.75$

Picking Numbers:

$p = 100$

$0.40 per pound minus 20% discount (which means paying only 80%) plus 5 avocados for $0.35 each

$0.40(100) - 0.40 \times 0.2(100) + 5(0.35)$
$40 - 8 + 1.75$
33.75

A) $c = 0.2p + 0.35$
$c = 0.2(100) + 0.35$
$c = 20 + 0.35$
$c = 20.35$

B) $c = 0.32p + 1.75$
$c = 0.32(100) + 1.75$
$c = 32 + 1.75$
$c = 33.75$ ✓

C) $c = 0.4p + 0.35$
$c = 0.4(100) + 0.35$
$c = 40 + 0.35$
$c = 40.35$

D) $c = 0.4p + 1.75$
$c = 0.4(100) + 1.75$
$c = 40 + 1.75$
$c = 41.75$

Straightforward math:

$0.40 per pound minus 20% discount (which means paying only 80%) plus 5 avocados for $0.35 each

$0.40p - 0.40 \times 0.2p + 5(0.35)$
$0.40p - 0.08p + 1.75$
$0.32p + 1.75$

PRACTICE

Use the Kaplan Method to answer the following questions. Use the hints provided as needed.

$$n = 25 + 5T$$

1. The equation above is used to model the relationship between the number of popsicles, n, sold per day at a snack bar and the average daily temperature, T, in degrees Fahrenheit. Which of the following best describes the meaning of the 5 in the equation?

   A) For every increase of 5°F, one more popsicle will be sold.

   B) For every decrease of 5°F, one more popsicle will be sold.

   C) For every increase of 1°F, five more popsicles will be sold.

   D) For every decrease of 1°F, five more popsicles will be sold.

hint *You can use either straightforward math or you can pick numbers to solve. Because T is temperature, you can pick 100 and then 101 to see what happens to n. Then match the relationship with an answer choice.*

2. Which of the following is equivalent to $(x - y)\left(\frac{5}{6}\right)$?

   A) $\left(\frac{5x}{6}\right) - y$

   B) $\left(\frac{5}{6}\right) - xy$

   C) $\frac{5x - 5y}{6x - 6y}$

   D) $\frac{5x - 5y}{6}$

hint *Picking numbers is a great way to solve this question. Remember to avoid picking the numbers 0 and 1 because they have special properties.*

3. Luis has $3\frac{1}{3}$ yards of ribbon to use for two separate presents, one of which is very large. If Luis uses $2\frac{1}{2}$ yards to decorate the larger present, which of the following represents the number of yards of ribbon, r, that Luis will have left to use for the second present?

   A) $3\frac{1}{3} - 2\frac{1}{2}$

   B) $3\frac{1}{3}r - 2\frac{1}{2}$

   C) $3\frac{1}{3} - 2\frac{1}{2}r$

   D) $3\frac{1}{3}r - 2\frac{1}{2}r$

hint *You can't pick numbers for this question, but you can solve for the amount of ribbon left for the second present and then match the number to the answer choice that will provide the same answer.*

Use the Kaplan Method to answer the following multiple-choice questions on your own.

$$20s + p = 125$$

1. A high school drama department is running a promotion in which a number of free tickets are given away for each of the four performances of a popular musical. The equation above can be used to model the number of free passes, p, that remain to be given away s shows after the promotion began. How many passes remain after 2 shows?

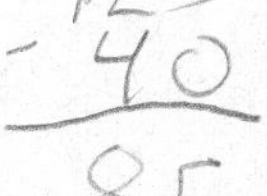

A) 6.15

B) 45

C) 85

D) 105

2. Tony is mixing concrete for a playset installation. The ratio of concrete mix to water is 3:4. Tony added $\frac{1}{2}$ quart of water to a wheelbarrow filled with concrete mix. He had already poured $\frac{1}{4}$ quart of water into the wheelbarrow. If Tony needs to add $1\frac{1}{2}$ quarts of water in total, how many quarts does he still need to add to the concrete mixture?

A) $\frac{1}{6}$

B) $\frac{1}{4}$

C) $\frac{1}{2}$

D) $\frac{3}{4}$

3. Liv is hanging a picture on the wall. She first hung it 71 inches above the ground, but then decided it was too low, so she raised it 6 inches. Which of the following represents the number of inches, i, Liv hung the picture above the ground?

A) $6 + i$

B) $71 - i$

C) $71 + 6$

D) $71 + 6i$

Use the Kaplan Method to answer the following multiple-choice questions for homework.

1. An animal shelter specializing in re-homing cats rescues approximately 200 local strays every year. Last year, 11 cats at the animal shelter each had a litter of kittens. Four cats had 5 kittens each, and the other cats had 4 kittens each. Which of the following represents the number of kittens, k, that were born at the animal shelter last year?

   A) $k = 200 - 4(5) + 7(4)$

   B) $k = 4(5) + 4(11 - 4)$

   C) $k = 200 + 4(5) + 7(4)$

   D) $k = 4(5) - 4(11 - 4)$

2. Which of the following is equivalent to $(s + 7)\left(\frac{4}{t}\right)$?

   A) $\left(\frac{4s}{t}\right) + 7$

   B) $\left(\frac{4s + 7}{t}\right) + st$

   C) $\frac{4s + 28}{t}$

   D) $\frac{4s + 28}{st + 7t}$

3. Stefani earns $900 every month at her work study job in the college admissions office. If she uses 35 percent of what's left of her paycheck after taxes, p, to pay her bills, 30 percent for books, $130 for personal expenses, and saves the rest, which of the following represents the amount of money, m, she is able to save each month?

   A) $m = p - 0.65p - 130$

   B) $m = p + 0.30p - 130$

   C) $m = p + 0.35p + 130$

   D) $m = p - 0.65p + 130$

The following questions are similar to what you would encounter on a college admissions test such as the SAT or ACT. Apply the Kaplan Method for Math to answer the following questions.

1. Jackson works at a tire store. He gets paid \$90 for a day's work, plus a commission of \$16 for each tire he sells. Which equation represents the relationship between one day of Jackson's pay, y, and the number of tires he sells, x?

   A) $x = 16y + 90$

   B) $x = 90y + 16$

   C) $y = 16x + 90$

   D) $y = 90x + 16$

Price of One Canister	Projected Number of Canisters Sold
\$0.75	10,000
\$0.80	9,000
\$0.85	8,000
\$0.90	7,000
\$0.95	6,000
\$1.00	5,000

2. Which of the following equations best describes the relationship shown in the table, where n indicates the number of canisters sold and p represents the price in dollars of one canister?

   A) $n = -20{,}000p + 25{,}000$

   B) $n = -200p + 250$

   C) $n = 200p + 250$

   D) $n = 20{,}000p + 25{,}000$

CHAPTER 2

Adding and Subtracting Integers & Fractions

CHAPTER OBJECTIVES

By the end of this chapter, you will be able to:

1. Combine positive and negative integers
2. Combine unlike fractions
3. Answer real-world questions involving integers and fractions

THE KAPLAN METHOD FOR MATH

Step 1: Read the question, identifying and organizing important information as you go

- What information am I given?
- Separate the question from the context.
- How are the answer choices written?
- Should you label or draw a diagram?

Step 2: Choose the best strategy to answer the question

- Look for patterns.
- Pick numbers or use straightforward math.

Step 3: Check that you answered the *right* question

- Review the question stem.
- Check units of measurement.
- Double-check your work.

2

INTEGERS

An **integer** is a whole number or the negative of a whole number; zero is also an integer that is neither positive nor negative. Zero is considered an even number because it sits between two odd numbers.

A **positive integer** is an integer that is greater than zero.

A **negative integer** is an integer that is less than zero.

On a number line, **negative integers** are to the left of zero, and **positive integers** are to the right of zero.

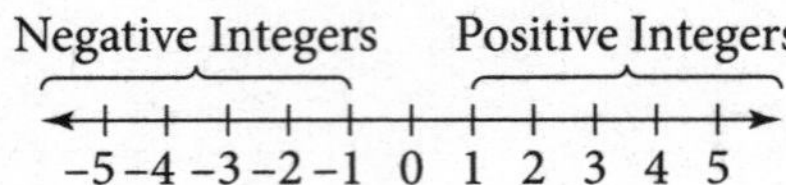

Identifying Integers

When working with numbers, you'll want to remember that the "+" or "–" directly in front of a number is attached to the number and acts as its sign. Mathematical expressions are combinations of positive and/or negative terms.

What are the two integers being combined in the expression −10 + 8? ________________

Sometimes an expression will begin with a number that has no sign in front of it, such as the "3" in the expression 3 – 5.

When there is no sign, the number is automatically **positive.**

You can rewrite the expression 3 – 5 as addition: 3 + (– 5).

A. Attaching a single sign to each number, what integers are being combined in the expression 9 – 31? ________________

B. Rewrite the expression 9 – 31 as addition and combine. ________________

Other expressions may contain a double sign, such as "– (–7)" in the expression –12 – (–7) or "+ (–21)" in the expression 6 + (–21).

> Whenever you see a double sign, employ the rules for multiplying positives (+) and negatives (–) to decide which sign to use.

In the expression –14 – (–3), subtracting –3 is the same as adding 3. The expression can be rewritten as –14 + [–1(–3)]. When you multiply –1 by –3, you get 3. Therefore, –14 – (–3) = –14 + 3, which equals –11.

In the expression –12 – (–7), the integers being combined are –12 and 7.

A. Attaching a single sign to each number, what integers are being combined in the expression 20 – (–11)? ________________

B. Rewrite the expression 9 – 6 as addition, and identify the integers being combined. ________________

Combining Integers with the Same Sign

> When you combine two numbers with the same sign, you get more of the same type, whether positive or negative.

Just as mixing apples with apples makes more apples, combining positives with positives makes more positives, and combining negatives with negatives makes more negatives.

A. What operation does the word "combining" suggest? ________________

B. What would be the result of combining 3 apples and 4 apples? ________________

C. What would be the result of combining 5 cups of sugar and 13 cups of sugar? ________________

D. What would be the result of combining 8 and 3? ________________

E. What would be the result of combining –14 and –11? ________________

Mathematicians use the word *simplify* to indicate combining like terms.

A. Simplify the expression 20 + 11. ________________

B. Simplify the expression –14 – 21. ________________

2

Combining Integers with Different Signs

To combine numbers with different signs, identify the larger number (the number that is farthest from 0 on the number line), subtract the smaller number from the larger number, and apply the sign of the larger number to your final answer.

Follow the prompts below to simplify the expression 2 – 13.

Identify the larger number (the number that is farthest from 0 on the number line).

____

Subtract the smaller number from the larger number. ____________________

Apply the sign of the larger number to your final answer. ____________________

Try It Out! **Complete the following sample question.**

Two bicyclists were traveling through hilly terrain. During their ride, they started at an elevation of 500 feet and climbed 1,000 feet, then descended 275 feet. What was the final elevation for the riders?

A) 225

B) 725

C) 1,225

D) 1,725

Step 1: Identify the signs of the numbers in the question
+500, +1,000, −275

Step 2: Identify the operations needed
Add the positive and negative integers starting with the beginning elevation: $500 + (1{,}000) + (-275)$

Step 3: Evaluate the expression
$500 + 1{,}000 - 275 = 1{,}225$

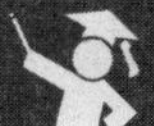

This worked solution would resemble the following:

Two bicyclists were traveling through hilly terrain. During their ride, they started at an elevation of 500 feet and climbed 1,000 feet, then descended 275 feet. What was the final elevation for the riders?

A) 225

B) 725

C) 1,225

D) 1,725

Straightforward math:

$500 + 1{,}000 - 275 = 1{,}225$

Use the Kaplan Method to answer the following questions.

1. Simplify 14 – 3.
   A. Rewrite the expression as addition. ____________________
   B. Take the larger number and note its sign. ____________________
   C. Subtract the smaller number from the larger number. ____________________
   D. Write the simplified expression, applying the correct sign. ____________________

2. Simplify –14 – (–4).
   A. Rewrite the expression as addition. ____________________
   B. Identify the larger number (the number that is farthest from 0 on the number line).
   ____
   C. Subtract the smaller number from the larger number. ____________________
   D. Write the simplified expression, applying the correct sign. ____________________

Use the Kaplan Method to answer the following questions on your own.

1. What is the simplified value of positive 43 combined with negative 56?
2. Simplify each of the following expressions:

   27 + (–35)

   14 – (–27)

3. The red team and the blue team are having a tug-of-war. At first, the red team pulls the blue team forward 2 feet, but the blue team wins the contest by countering with a 4-foot pull in the opposite direction. What is the total number of feet traveled?

FRACTIONS

A **simple fraction** is a number in the form $\frac{a}{b}$, where a and b are integers and b is not zero; fractions are used to name parts of a whole object or parts of a whole collection of objects.

A **numerator** is the number of equal parts being considered when a whole is divided into equal parts—in the fraction $\frac{a}{b}$, a is the numerator.

A **denominator** is the number of equal parts into which the whole or group is divided—in the fraction $\frac{a}{b}$, b is the denominator.

Finding a Common Denominator

Fractions with different denominators are called *unlike* fractions, and you can't combine unlike fractions until you rewrite them using a common denominator. This denominator has to be a **multiple** of the denominator of every fraction in the expression. In other words, it must be a **common multiple** of the denominators. When adding and subtracting fractions, most people find it easiest to use the lowest common multiple of the denominators, also known as the **least common multiple** (LCM).

Follow the prompts below to find the LCM of 2 and 3.

Starting with 2, make a list of the first six multiples of 2. ______________________

Starting with 3, make a list of the first six multiples of 3. ______________________

Write down all the numbers that appear in both lists above, and circle the lowest number.

____

What is the LCM of 2 and 3? ______

Using the LCM to Combine Unlike Fractions

To combine unlike fractions such as $\frac{1}{2}$ and $\frac{3}{5}$, you need to find a common denominator.

Follow the prompts below to find the LCM of 2 and 5.

Starting with 2, make a list of the first six multiples of 2. ______________________

Starting with 5, make a list of the first six multiples of 5. ______________________

Write down all the numbers that appear in both lists above, and circle the lowest number.

____

What is the LCM of 2 and 5? ______________________

Write the LCM into the denominator of the empty fraction below.

$\frac{1}{2} = \frac{\quad}{\quad}$

By what number do you need to multiply 2 to make 10? ______________________

Multiply the entire fraction of $\frac{1}{2}$ by $\frac{5}{5}$ to find your new fraction. Write this fraction into the empty space above.

> **✔ Helpful Hint**
>
> **You can multiply any mathematical expression by the number 1 without changing the value of the expression. The number 1 can be written in a variety of ways, including $\frac{5}{5}$ and $\frac{2}{2}$.**

Now you've got a fraction equivalent to $\frac{1}{2}$ but with a denominator of 10. You can follow the same approach to rewrite $\frac{3}{5}$ with a denominator of 10.

$\frac{3}{5} = \frac{\quad}{\quad}$

By what number do you need to multiply 5 to make 10? ______________________

Multiply the entire fraction of $\frac{3}{5}$ by $\frac{2}{2}$ to find your new fraction. Write this fraction in the empty space above.

Now you're ready to combine your like fractions: $\frac{1}{2} + \frac{3}{5} = \frac{5}{10} + \frac{6}{10} = \frac{11}{10} = 1\frac{1}{10}$

2

> **✔ Helpful Hint**
>
> Many standardized tests such as the SAT require you to convert your final answer to a decimal or an improper fraction. For example, $1\frac{1}{4}$ is equivalent to 1.25 and also to $\frac{5}{4}$. Each test will tell you which equivalents are acceptable to use when answering student-produced response questions.

From start to finish, the mathematical calculations required to combine $\frac{1}{2}$ and $\frac{3}{5}$ are as follows:

$$\frac{1}{2}+\frac{3}{5}=\left(\frac{1}{2}\times\frac{5}{5}\right)+\left(\frac{3}{5}\times\frac{2}{2}\right)=\frac{5}{10}+\frac{6}{10}=\frac{11}{10}=1\frac{1}{10}$$

> **✔ Helpful Hint**
>
> Combining unlike fractions can also be expressed algebraically as
>
> $$\frac{a}{b}+\frac{c}{d}=\left(\frac{a}{b}\times\frac{d}{d}\right)+\left(\frac{c}{d}\times\frac{b}{b}\right)=\frac{a\times d}{b\times d}+\frac{c\times b}{b\times d}=\frac{ad+cb}{bd}$$

Using Common Factors to Calculate LCM

A. When you're adding and subtracting fractions with large numbers in the denominators, you can break the denominators into their prime factors.

Follow the prompts below to calculate LCM by using common factors.

Add $\frac{7}{15}+\frac{11}{18}$.

Break the denominators into their prime factors: $15 = 3 \times 5$ *and* $18 = 3 \times 3 \times 2$

Identify any shared prime factors. With 15 and 18, 3 is a shared prime factor. Take the shared prime factor, and multiply it with all of the other prime factors: LCM = $3(2 \times 3 \times 5) = 90$.

Now determine what each denominator must be multiplied by in order to equal the LCM:
$15 \times 6 = 90$ *and* $18 \times 5 = 90$

Rewrite the fractions with the lowest common denominator:

$$\left(\frac{7}{15}\times\frac{6}{6}\right)+\left(\frac{11}{18}\times\frac{5}{5}\right)=\frac{42}{90}+\frac{55}{90}=\frac{97}{90}=1\frac{7}{90}$$

B. Sometimes one fraction already uses the LCM as its denominator. In that case, you only need to rewrite the *other* fraction.

Follow the prompts below to rewrite just one of the two fractions.

Add $\frac{3}{4} + \frac{5}{12}$.

What is the LCM of 4 and 12? ______________________

Find the fraction equivalent to $\frac{3}{4}$ that uses the LCM as its denominator. ______________________

Rewrite the expression using fractions with the lowest common denominator. ______________________

Find the sum and simplify your answer. ______________________

Try It Out! **Complete the following sample question.**

Samantha keeps track of the extra hours she spends studying Chinese each week. Over a 4-week period leading up to a test, in weeks 1–4 she studied $6\frac{1}{4}$, $5\frac{2}{3}$, $7\frac{1}{6}$, and $8\frac{1}{2}$ hours, respectively. How many extra hours did Samantha study in all?

A) $26\frac{7}{12}$

B) $26\frac{5}{6}$

C) $27\frac{7}{12}$

D) $27\frac{5}{6}$

Step 1: Determine the operations

Translate "how many" into "add the numbers"

Step 2: Find the common denominator by finding the LCM

Break the denominators into their smallest factors:

$4 = 2 \times 2$ $6 = 3 \times 2$

$3 = 3 \times 1$ $2 = 2 \times 1$

The LCM must have room for all of those factors:

$$LCM = 2 \times 2 \times 3 = 12$$

Now determine what each denominator must be multiplied by in order to equal the LCM:

$4 \times 3 = 12 \quad 6 \times 2 = 12$

$3 \times 4 = 12 \quad 2 \times 6 = 12$

Rewrite the fractions with the lowest common denominator:

$$\left(6\frac{1}{4} \times \frac{3}{3}\right) + \left(5\frac{2}{3} \times \frac{4}{4}\right) + \left(7\frac{1}{6} \times \frac{2}{2}\right) + \left(8\frac{1}{2} \times \frac{6}{6}\right)$$

Step 3: Evaluate the expression

$$\left(6\frac{3}{12}\right) + \left(5\frac{8}{12}\right) + \left(7\frac{2}{12}\right) + \left(8\frac{6}{12}\right) = 26\frac{19}{12} = 27\frac{7}{12}$$

This worked solution would resemble the following:

Samantha keeps track of the extra hours she spends studying Chinese each week. Over a 4-week period leading up to a test, in weeks 1–4 she studied $6\frac{1}{4}$, $5\frac{2}{3}$, $7\frac{1}{6}$, and $8\frac{1}{2}$ hours, respectively. How many extra hours did Samantha study in all?

A) $26\frac{7}{12}$

B) $26\frac{5}{6}$

C) $27\frac{7}{12}$

D) $27\frac{5}{6}$

Straightforward math:

$$\left(6\frac{3}{12}\right) + \left(5\frac{8}{12}\right) + \left(7\frac{2}{12}\right) + \left(8\frac{6}{12}\right) = 26\frac{19}{12} = 27\frac{7}{12}$$

Use the Kaplan Method to answer the following questions.

Find the lowest common denominator of $\frac{11}{12}$ and $\frac{3}{4}$.

Starting with 12, make a list of the first six multiples of 12. ______________________

Starting with 4, make a list of the first six multiples of 4. ______________________

Write down all the numbers that appear in both lists above, and circle the lowest number.

____

What is the LCM of 12 and 4? ______________________

What is the lowest common denominator of $\frac{11}{12}$ and $\frac{3}{4}$? ______________________

Why is it important to begin with the original denominator when making a list of multiples?

____

____

2

Use the Kaplan Method to answer the following questions on your own.

1. Add $\frac{1}{6} + \frac{7}{10}$ and express your answer in simplest form. ________________

2. Subtract $\frac{3}{7} - \frac{4}{21}$ and express your answer in simplest form. ________________

3. Alex is cooking chili, and she wants to follow her grandmother's recipe as closely as possible. If Alex combines $\frac{2}{3}$ tablespoons of cumin, $\frac{1}{4}$ tablespoon of chili powder, and $\frac{1}{2}$ tablespoon of oregano, how many tablespoons of spices did Alex add to her chili in all? Write your answer as an improper fraction. ________________

Use the Kaplan Method to answer the following questions for homework.

INTEGERS

1. What is the simplified value of negative 12 combined with negative 20?
2. What is the simplified value of positive 30 combined with negative 50?
3. Simplify each expression:

   $-31 + -2$

   $-20 + 25$

   $22 - (-33)$

4. In chemistry class, Kobe conducts an experiment in which he combines chemicals that have opposite effects. Each drop of acid solution will subtract 1 from the pH value, while each drop of base solution will add 1 to the pH value. What will the net effect on the pH be after he combines 3 drops of acid solution and 5 drops of base solution?

FRACTIONS

1. What is the lowest common denominator that could be used to add $\frac{4}{9} + \frac{5}{6}$?
2. Simplify $\frac{1}{3} + \frac{1}{4}$.
3. Simplify $\frac{8}{11} - \frac{1}{5}$.
4. Lou cuts his own hair using automatic hair clippers that are set to $\frac{1}{2}$ inch. For the summer, he changes the setting to $\frac{3}{8}$ inches. What is the difference between the two settings?

The following questions are similar to what you would encounter on a college admissions test such as the SAT or ACT. Apply the Kaplan Method and your knowledge of integers and fractions to answer the following questions.

1. A contractor is installing solar panels on a flat roof of an industrial plant. In order to properly secure each panel, the contractor must install base-and-post mounts into holes drilled into the roof. If the contractor drills a hole that is $2\frac{3}{8}$ inches deep and installs one base-and-post mount, which has a total height of $5\frac{1}{6}$ inches, into the hole, how many inches of the base-and-post mount extend above the roof?

   A) $2\frac{1}{4}$

   B) $2\frac{19}{24}$

   C) $7\frac{1}{6}$

   D) $7\frac{13}{24}$

2. A media library specialist is creating a seasonal exhibit. He has 117 older editions already, and he puts in a purchase order for 56 new editions. If the library agrees to order all but 19 of the new edition titles in the purchase order, and library patrons then borrow 27 of the new editions, how many new editions were not borrowed?

   A) 10

   B) 37

   C) 127

   D) 154

CHAPTER 3

Order of Operations

3

CHAPTER OBJECTIVES

By the end of this chapter, you will be able to:

1. Add, subtract, multiply, divide, and use exponents in the correct order for any mathematical expression
2. Apply what you've learned about order of operations to simplify expressions

THE KAPLAN METHOD FOR MATH

Step 1: Read the question, identifying and organizing important information as you go

- What information am I given?
- Separate the question from the context.
- How are the answer choices written?
- Should you label or draw a diagram?

Step 2: Choose the best strategy to answer the question

- Look for patterns.
- Pick numbers or use straightforward math.

Step 3: Check that you answered the *right* question

- Review the question stem.
- Check units of measurement.
- Double-check your work.

3

ORDER OF OPERATIONS

In math, an **operation** is any action you perform on a number. Addition, subtraction, multiplication, and division are all operations. Raising a number to a "power" is also an operation. When you raise a number to a power you notate this operation with an **exponent**. An exponent tells you how many times to multiply a number by itself. In the expression 3^2, the number 3 is "raised to the 2nd power." The number 3 is the **base** and 2 is the **exponent**. Raising 3 to the 2nd power means you will multiply 3 by itself 2 times: $3^2 = 3 \times 3 = 9$.

✓ Helpful Hint

Raising a base to the 2nd power is called "squaring" the number. This term comes from geometry. To find the area of a square, you multiply the base and the height. Because a square has four equal sides, the base and the height are equal. Therefore, the formula for the area is simply the length of any one side of the square raised to the 2nd power. *Area of a square = base × height = side × side =* $side^2$

PEMDAS is the order in which you perform operations in math expressions. **PEMDAS** stands for:

P **Parentheses**

E **Exponents**

M **Multiplication**

D **Division**

A **Addition**

S **Subtraction**

ANSWERING ORDER OF OPERATIONS QUESTIONS

You can perform the order of operations with the same approach:

Step 1: Perform operations within parentheses. If you have an expression such as $4 \times (7 - (8 \div 2))$, simplify the operations inside the *innermost* parentheses first:

$$4 \times (7 - (8 \div 2)) = 4 \times (7 - 4)$$

Then perform the operation within the remaining parentheses:

$$4 \times (7 - 4) = 4 \times 3$$

And, finally, simplify:

$$4 \times 3 = 12$$

Step 2: Apply exponent powers to numbers or expressions.

Step 3: Multiply and divide. Multiplication and division are the same type of operation, so they are both part of the third step. If an expression includes both multiplication and division, move left to right, multiplying and/or dividing as you go.

Step 4: Add and subtract. The fourth step includes both addition and subtraction because they are similar operations (just like multiplication and division). Apply addition and subtraction left to right just as you would multiplication and division.

Try It Out! **Work through the following sample question.**

Simplify $4 \div 4 + 12 - 6 \times 3 + (7 + 4 \times 2) + (2 + 3)^2$.

Step 1: Perform operations within parentheses. You have two sets of parentheses, so move left to right.

First set of parentheses:

$4 \div 4 + 12 - 6 \times 3 + (7 + 4 \times 2) + (2 + 3)^2$

$4 \div 4 + 12 - 6 \times 3 + (7 + 8) + (2 + 3)^2$

$4 \div 4 + 12 - 6 \times 3 + (15) + (2 + 3)^2$

Second set of parentheses:

$4 \div 4 + 12 - 6 \times 3 + 15 + (2 + 3)^2$

$4 \div 4 + 12 - 6 \times 3 + 15 + 5^2$

Step 2: Apply exponent powers to numbers or expressions.

$4 \div 4 + 12 - 6 \times 3 + 15 + 5^2$

$4 \div 4 + 12 - 6 \times 3 + 15 + 25$

Step 3: Multiply and divide. Move left to right as you simplify.

$4 \div 4 + 12 - 6 \times 3 + 15 + 25$

$1 + 12 - 6 \times 3 + 15 + 25$

$1 + 12 - 18 + 15 + 25$

Step 4: Add and subtract.

$1 + 12 - 18 + 15 + 25 = 35$

VARIABLES

In addition to numbers, expressions can also contain **variables**. In algebra, variables are letters that represent unknown values. You cannot add or subtract variables and numbers together because you don't know the specific values that the variables represent. Numbers and variables are called "unlike terms":

$$x + 4$$

While you can't perform addition or subtraction between a variable and a number, you *can* perform multiplication and division. When you **multiply** a variable by a number, you simply put that number in front of the variable:

$$2 \bullet x = 2x$$

Similarly, when you **divide** a variable by a number, you get:

$$x \div 2 = \frac{x}{2}$$

You can also divide a number by a variable:

$$2 \div x = \frac{2}{x}$$

If an expression includes both a variable and parentheses, use the distributive property to simplify:

$$(2 + x) \bullet 4$$

$$(2 \bullet 4) + (x \bullet 4)$$

$$(8) + (4x)$$

$$8 + 4x$$

3

Try It Out! **Work through the following sample question.**

Simplify $x \bullet 5 - 12 \div (1+3)$.

Step 1: Perform operations within parentheses.

$x \bullet 5 - 12 \div (1+3)$

$x \bullet 5 - 12 \div (4)$

Step 2: Apply exponent powers to numbers or expressions. Because there are no exponents, you can move right onto the next step.

Step 3: Multiply and divide. Move left to right as you simplify.

$x \bullet 5 - 12 \div 4$

$5x - 12 \div 4$

$5x - 3$

Step 4: Add and subtract. Because you can't add numbers and variables, the expression is fully simplified as $5x - 3$.

Use the Kaplan Method to answer the following questions. Use the hints provided as needed.

1. Simplify $9 \times 8 \div 4 + 13 - 12 \div 2$.

   A) 13

   B) 18

   C) 25

   D) 29

hint *Because there are no parentheses or exponents, go straight to Multiplication/Division.*

2. Simplify $3^2 \times 8 + 4$.

   A) 42

   B) 52

   C) 76

   D) 108

hint *As you follow **PEMDAS** don't forget the **E**.*

3. Simplify $(4^2 \div 8) \bullet (18 \bullet (3-2)) - x$.

   A) $18 - x$

   B) $36 - x$

   C) $36x$

   D) $-18x$

hint *Perform operations inside the innermost parentheses first. Then the next innermost parentheses, and so on, until you've completed the **P** in **PEMDAS**. Remember, you can't add or subtract numbers and variables together—they are unlike terms.*

Use the Kaplan Method to answer the following questions on your own.

1. Simplify $17 + 2 \times 7 - 4 + 3 \times 6$.

   A) 25

   B) 45

   C) 91

   D) 792

2. Simplify $3(7 - 9) + 4 \times 5$.

   A) -10

   B) 14

   C) 26

   D) 50

3. Simplify $(3^3 \div 9) \bullet (7 \bullet (-5x + 2x))$.

   A) $-63x$

   B) $-3x$

   C) $63x + 3$

   D) $103 + x$

Use the Kaplan Method to answer the following questions for homework.

1. Simplify $(13-4) \bullet x \div 4$.

   A) $\frac{9x}{4}$

   B) $13x$

   C) $\frac{13x}{4}$

   D) $\frac{9}{4}$

2. Simplify $4 \times 1 + 8 \div 2^2 \times (14 + 5 \times 2)$.

   A) 16

   B) 28

   C) 46

   D) 52

3. Simplify $(3+2) \bullet x - 12$.

   A) $x - 7$

   B) $x + 17$

   C) $5x - 12$

   D) $5x - 60$

The following questions are similar to what you would encounter on a college admissions test such as the SAT or ACT. Apply the Kaplan Method and your knowledge of the order of operations to answer the following questions.

1. Simplify $(22 \div 2) \bullet 4 + x \div 3 - 19$.

   A) $44 + \frac{x}{-16}$

   B) $\frac{11}{4} + x - 16$

   C) $25 + \frac{x}{3}$

   D) $44 + \frac{x}{3}$

2. Simplify $(3 \bullet (x + 2)) \bullet 4 - 12$.

   A) $12x - 4$

   B) $12x + 12$

   C) $-24x - 16$

   D) $-24x - 42$

CHAPTER 4

Single-Variable Linear Equations

CHAPTER OBJECTIVES

By the end of this chapter, you will be able to:

1. Solve one-variable linear equations
2. Solve absolute-value equations

THE KAPLAN METHOD FOR MATH

Step 1: Read the question, identifying and organizing important information as you go

- What information am I given?
- Separate the question from the context.
- How are the answer choices written?
- Should you label or draw a diagram?

Step 2: Choose the best strategy to answer the question

- Look for patterns.
- Pick numbers or use straightforward math.

Step 3: Check that you answered the *right* question

- Review the question stem.
- Check units of measurement.
- Double-check your work.

4

EQUATIONS

An **equation** is formed by placing an equal sign between two numerical or variable expressions, called **sides** of the equation. There are four properties of equalities that will help you to solve equations.

If a, b, and c are real numbers, and $a = b$, then:

Addition Property: $a + c = b + c$ and $c + a = c + b$

Subtraction Property: $a - c = b - c$

Multiplication Property: $ca = cb$ and $ac = bc$

Division Property: $\frac{a}{c} = \frac{b}{c}$

Each property demonstrates that you must "do the same thing to both sides." If you add c on the left side, you must add c on the right side, which is the **Cardinal Rule of Equations**.

Picking numbers is not only helpful in solving questions, but also in understanding math concepts such as the properties above. If $a = 4$, $b = \frac{8}{2}$, and $c = 2$, then:

Addition Property: $4 + 2 = \frac{8}{2} + 2$ and $2 + 4 = 2 + \frac{8}{2}$

Subtraction Property: $4 - 2 = \frac{8}{2} - 2$

Multiplication Property: $2(4) = 2\left(\frac{8}{2}\right)$ and $4(2) = \left(\frac{8}{2}\right)(2)$

Division Property: $\frac{4}{2} = \frac{\frac{8}{2}}{2}$

In every equation above, the **Cardinal Rule of Equations** was followed from adding 2 to both sides all the way to dividing by 2 on both sides.

SOLVING ONE-VARIABLE EQUATIONS

You can solve one-variable equations with the same approach:

Step 1: Combine like terms (follow the order of operations)

Step 2: Isolate the variable

Step 3: Simplify

Try It Out! **Complete the following sample questions.**

1. $8x - 5 + 2x = 15$

   Step 1: Combine like terms ______________________________

   Step 2: Isolate the variable ______________________________

   Step 3: Simplify ______________________________

2. $7(w - 3) + 17 = 3$

   Step 1: Combine like terms (use the order of operations first) ______________________________

   Step 2: Isolate the variable ______________________________

   Step 3: Simplify ______________________________

Try It Out! **Work through the following multiple-choice question.**

In any triangle, the sum of the measures of the angles is 180°. In ΔABC, $\angle A$ is 17° and $\angle B$ is 54°. What is the degree measure of $\angle C$?

A) 37°

B) 38°

C) 71°

D) 109°

You can translate the information in the question stem into math: $17 + 54 + c = 180$.

Step 1: Combine like terms

$17 + 54 + c = 180$

$71 + c = 180$

Step 2: Isolate the variable

$71 + c = 180$

$-71 \qquad -71$

Step 3: Simplify

$c = 180 - 71$

$c = 109$

This worked solution would resemble the following:

In any triangle, the sum of the measures of the angles is 180°. In ΔABC, $\angle A$ is 17° and $\angle B$ is 54°. What is the degree measure of $\angle C$?

A) 37°

B) 38°

C) 71°

D) 109°

Straightforward math:

$$17 + 54 + c = 180$$

$$71 + c = 180$$

$$-71 \qquad -71$$

$$c = 109$$

Double-check:

$17 + 54 + 109 = 180$ ✓

SOLVING ONE-VARIABLE EQUATIONS WITH ABSOLUTE VALUE

The **absolute value** of a number is its distance from zero on the number line. Distance is always a positive number or zero, so the absolute value of a number is *always* a positive number or zero.

The numbers 2 and –2 have the same absolute value because they are both 2 units away from zero on the number line:

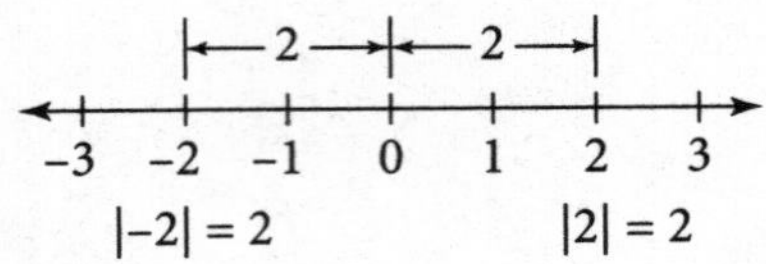

4

When absolute-value equations include a variable such as *x*, you have to write two separate equations to account for the fact that there are not just one but **two** numbers *x* units away from 0.

You can approach every absolute-value one-variable equation with the same approach:

Step 1: Isolate everything within the absolute-value sign on one side of the equation

Step 2: Remove the absolute-value sign and rewrite as two equations

Step 3: Within each equation:

- Combine like terms (follow the order of operations)
- Isolate the variable
- Simplify

Try It Out! **Complete the following sample questions.**

1. $|x + 1| = 3$

Remove the absolute-value sign and rewrite as two equations.

	Equation 1	Equation 2
Combine like terms		
Isolate the variable		
Simplify		

2. $|7 - y| - 2 = 2$

Isolate the absolute-value portion, remove the absolute-value sign, and rewrite as two equations.

	Equation 1	Equation 2
Combine like terms		
Isolate the variable		
Simplify		

Try It Out! **Complete the following multiple-choice question.**

A power strip is utilized to prevent the loss of electronic-device programming by electrical surges. If the power strip is designed to allow 97 volts, plus or minus 19 volts, which value satisfies the following equation?

$|97 - x| = 19$

A) −78

B) −19

C) 97

D) 116

Remove the absolute-value sign and rewrite as two equations:

	Equation 1	Equation 2
Combine like terms		
Isolate the variable		
Simplify		

This worked solution would resemble the following:

A power strip is utilized to prevent the loss of electronic-device programming by electrical surges. If the power strip is designed to allow 97 volts, plus or minus 19 volts, which value satisfies the following equation?

$|97 - x| = 19$

A) −78

B) −19

C) 97

D) 116

4

Straightforward math:

$97 - x = 19$	$97 - x = -19$
$-97 \quad -97$	$-97 \quad -97$
$\underline{-x} = \underline{-78}$	$\underline{-x} = \underline{-116}$
$-1 \quad -1$	$-1 \quad -1$
$x = 78$	$x = 116$

Double-check:

97 volts + 19 volts = 116 volts ✓

Use the Kaplan Method to answer the following questions. Use the hints provided as needed.

1. What is the value of x that satisfies the equation $2x + 4 = \dfrac{5x + 3}{6}$?

   A) −4

   B) −3

   C) 3

   D) 4

hint *Avoid working with fractions by multiplying both sides by 6.*

2. If $\dfrac{7 + x}{12 + x} = \dfrac{2}{3}$, what is the value of x?

   A) −8

   B) −3

   C) 3

   D) 8

hint *Cross-multiply first. Then distribute the 3 on the left and the 2 on the right in the equation 3(7 + x) = 2(12 + x).*

3. If $y < 0$ and $\left|\dfrac{y+4}{3}\right| = 5$, what is the value of y?

   A) −19

   B) −11

   C) 15

   D) 19

hint *Remember to solve for the positive and negative values on the right side of the equation.*

PERFORM

Use the Kaplan Method to answer the following questions on your own.

1. In any quadrilateral, the sum of the measures of the angles is 360°. In quadrilateral *ABCD*, $\angle A$ is 25°, $\angle B$ is 72°, and $\angle C$ is 113°. What is the degree measure of $\angle D$?

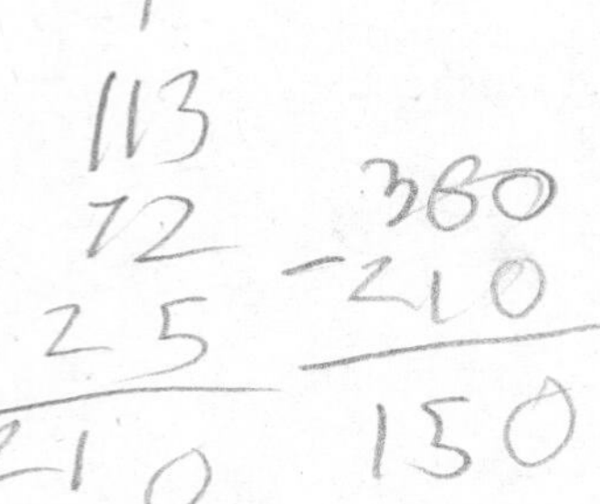

   A) 30°
   B) 150°
   C) 190°
   D) 210°

4

2. For what value of *k* does $21 = \frac{k}{6} - 9$?
   A) 72
   B) 117
   C) 180
   D) 450

3. What is one possible value of *a* if $|(3a+2)-4(a-2)| = 7$?
   A) −13
   B) −3
   C) 1
   D) 17

Use the Kaplan Method to answer the following questions for homework.

1. A car traveled at an average speed of 68 miles per hour for 3 hours and at an average speed of 42 miles per hour for an additional 2 hours. What is the total distance, in miles, that the car traveled?

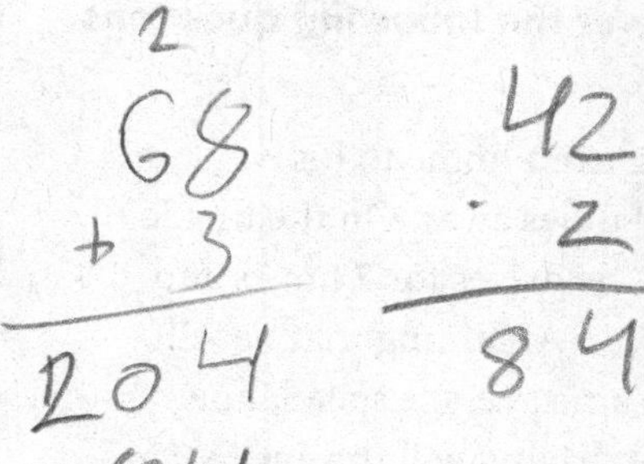

A) 84

B) 204

C) 275

D) 288

2. If $\frac{7+x}{9+x} = \frac{1}{2}$, what is the value of x?

A) −11

B) −5

C) 5

D) 11

3. If $t > 0$, for what value of t does

$$42 = \left|\frac{75}{t}\right| + 27?$$

A) 2

B) 3

C) 5

D) 11

The following questions are similar to what you would encounter on a college admissions test such as the SAT or ACT. Apply the Kaplan Method and your knowledge of single-variable equations to answer the following questions.

1. Jay is traveling from home to his university 780 miles away. On the first leg of his journey, he drives for 7 hours and travels 420 miles. Assuming that he will maintain the same average speed, how many hours of driving will the entire trip take?

4

A) 6

B) 7

C) 13

D) 20

2. For what value of x does $-6x - |4 - 9| + x = 20$?

A) −5

B) −4

C) 4

D) 5

CHAPTER 5

Solving & Graphing Linear Equations

CHAPTER OBJECTIVES

By the end of this chapter, you will be able to:

1. Calculate the slope of a line using two points
2. Write equations in slope-intercept form
3. Graph linear equations in the coordinate plane

THE KAPLAN METHOD FOR MATH

Step 1: Read the question, identifying and organizing important information as you go

- What information am I given?
- Separate the question from the context.
- How are the answer choices written?
- Should you label or draw a diagram?

Step 2: Choose the best strategy to answer the question

- Look for patterns.
- Pick numbers or use straightforward math.

Step 3: Check that you answered the *right* question

- Review the question stem.
- Check units of measurement.
- Double-check your work.

5

THE COORDINATE PLANE

Every point on the coordinate plane can be uniquely identified by a pair of signed numerical coordinates that define the perpendicular distance from the *x*-axis and the *y*-axis. These coordinates are called an *ordered pair* and are written in the form (*x*, *y*).

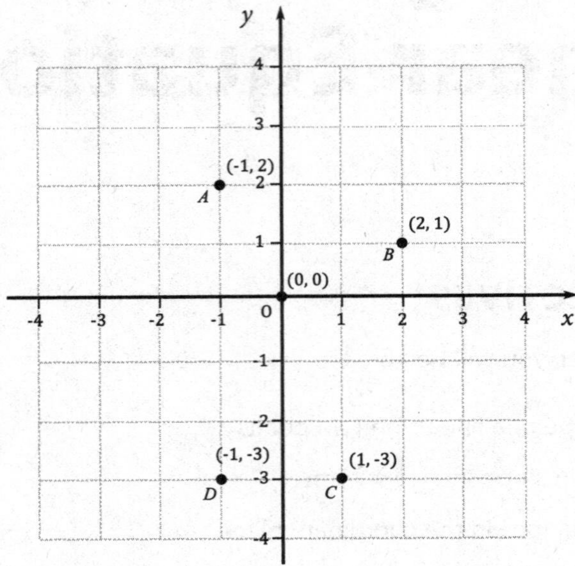

Slope

The *slope* is a ratio that expresses the amount of $\frac{\text{change in } y}{\text{change in } x}$ between any two points on the *xy*-plane. The symbol for slope is m, and the formula for slope is:

$$m = \frac{y_2 - y_1}{x_2 - x_1}$$

Use the formula to calculate the slope between:

A. Points *C* and *B*: $m = \frac{1-(-3)}{2-(1)} = \frac{1+3}{2-1} = 4$. Because *y* changes +4 units for each +1 unit change in *x*, the slope is **positive**.

B. Points *A* and *B*: $m = \frac{1-(2)}{2-(-1)} = \frac{1-2}{2+1} = \frac{-1}{3}$. Because *y* changes −1 unit for each +3 unit change in *x*, the slope is **negative**.

C. Points *D* and *C*: $m = \frac{-3-(-3)}{1-(-1)} = \frac{-3+3}{1+1} = \frac{0}{2} = 0$. Because *y* changes 0 units for all changes in *x*, the slope is **zero**. (Zero divided by any number is zero.)

D. Points *A* and *D*: $m = \frac{2-(-3)}{-1-(-1)} = \frac{2+3}{-1+1} = \frac{5}{0} =$ *undefined*. Because for all changes in *y*, there are 0 changes in *x*, the slope is **undefined**. (Any number divided by zero is undefined.)

Slope-Intercept Equation

The *slope-intercept* equation for a line is written in the form $y = mx + b$, in which y is the y-coordinate, m is the slope, x is the x-coordinate, and b is the y-intercept. The y-intercept is the point where the line crosses the y-axis: (0, b).

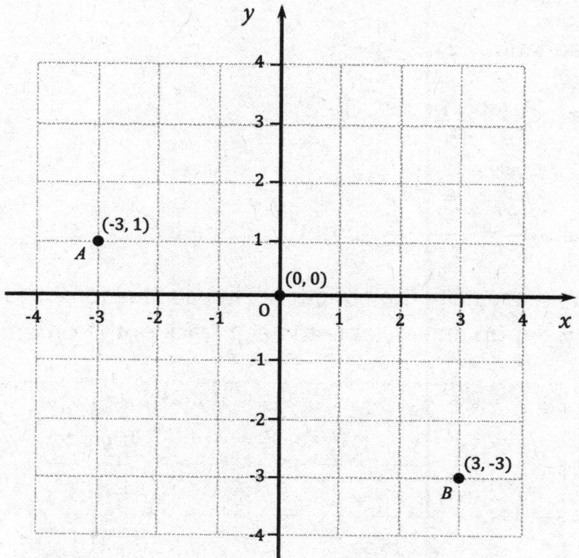

Try It Out! **Complete the following sample questions.**

What is the slope of a line that passes through points A and B? ________________

What is the y-intercept of a line that passes through points A and B? ________________

GRAPHING A LINEAR EQUATION

Try It Out! **Follow the steps to practice graphing linear equations.**

Step 1: Rewrite the following equation in slope-intercept form. Use the Cardinal Rule of Equations to solve for *y* in terms of *x*:

Graph the following equation: $2y - 4x - 3 = 1$

Isolate *y*: $2y - 4x + 4x - 3 + 3 = 1 + 4x + 3$

Combine like terms: $2y = 4x + 4$

Divide both sides by 2: $\frac{2y}{2} = \frac{(4x+4)}{2}$ to get $y = 2x + 2$

Step 2: Find ordered pairs that satisfy the equation. Plug a value for *x* into the equation to find the corresponding value for *y*. Set up an *x–y* table to keep track of the ordered pairs:

x	$2x+2$	*y*	ordered pairs (x, y)
–1	$2(-1)+2$	0	(–1, 0)
0	$2(0)+2$	2	(0, 2)
1	$2(1)+2$	4	(1, 4)

Step 3: Plot the points and connect them with a line.

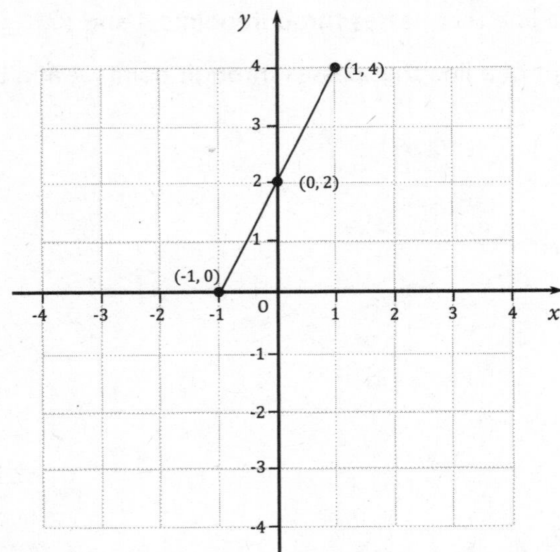

✔ Helpful Hint

An equation for a line is no different than any other equation. Follow the Cardinal Rule of Equations and the order of operations.

Try It Out! **Work through the following multiple-choice question.**

What is the y-intercept of a line that has a slope of 4 and crosses the x-axis at $x = 3$?

A) −12

B) −3

C) 3

D) 12

At the y-intercept, $x = 0$, and the ordered pair is $(0, b)$. When a line crosses the x-axis, $y = 0$, and the ordered pair is $(x, 0)$. Write the equation of a line in *slope-intercept* form, and substitute the values given in the question stem.

$y = 4x + b$

Substitute: $0 = 4(3) + b$

Multiply 4(3) and isolate b: $0 - 12 = 12 - 12 + b$

Simplify: $b = -12$. Choice (A) is correct.

This worked solution would resemble the following:

What is the y-intercept of a line that has a slope of 4 and crosses the x-axis at $x = 3$?

A) −12

B) −3

C) 3

D) 12

Straightforward math:

$y = 4x + b$

$0 = 4(3) + b$

$0 = 12 + b$

$-12 \quad -12$

$-12 = b$

5

Use the Kaplan Method to answer the following questions. Use the hints provided as needed.

1. What is the slope of the line in the *xy*-plane with the ordered pairs (–4, 2) and (–2, –6) in its solution set?

   A) –4

   B) $-\frac{1}{4}$

   C) $\frac{1}{4}$

   D) 4

hint *Use the slope formula* $m = \frac{y_2 - y_1}{x_2 - x_1}$ *to answer this question. Use parentheses to help keep your signs straight.*

2. Which of the following statements best describes the line of the following equation?

   $$3y + x - 7 = 5$$

   A) A line with a negative slope $m = -3$ and a *y*-intercept $y = -4$

   B) A line with a negative slope $m = -\frac{1}{3}$ and a *y*-intercept $y = 4$

   C) A line with a positive slope $m = \frac{1}{3}$ and a *y*-intercept $y = -12$

   D) A line with a positive slope $m = 3$ and a *y*-intercept $y = 12$

hint *Treat a linear equation like any other equation. Rearrange the equation using the Cardinal Rule of Equations to solve for y in terms of x.*

3. What is the slope of the line in the *xy*-plane with the ordered pairs (–4, 2) and (–2, 2) in its solution set?

   A) Positive

   B) Negative

   C) Zero

   D) Undefined

hint *A positive slope moves up and to the right. A negative slope moves down and to the right. A zero slope is parallel to the x-axis. An undefined slope is parallel to the y-axis.*

5

Use the Kaplan Method to answer the following questions on your own.

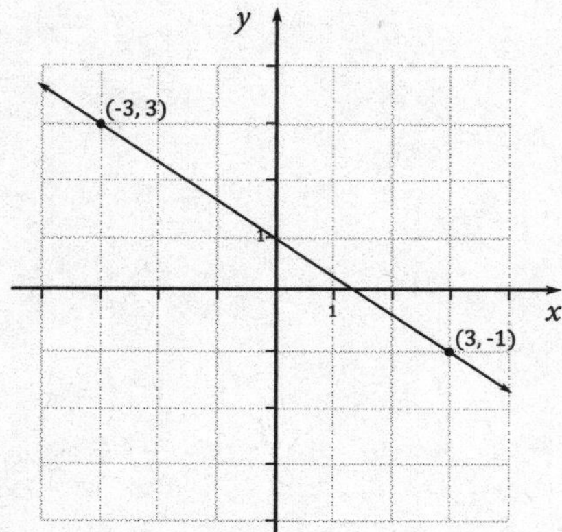

1. Which equation best represents the line above?

A) $y = -\frac{2}{3}x + 1$

B) $y = -\frac{3}{2}x - 1$

C) $y = -\frac{2}{3}x - 1$

D) $y = -\frac{3}{2}x + 1$

2. What is the slope of the line in the *xy*-plane with the ordered pairs $(-7, 3)$ and $(-1, 15)$ in its solution set?

A) -2

B) $-\frac{1}{2}$

C) $\frac{1}{2}$

D) 2

3. In following equation, what is the value of y when $x = 3$?

$$5y - 6x + 3 = -10$$

A) $-\frac{31}{5}$

B) -1

C) 1

D) $\frac{31}{5}$

Use the Kaplan Method to answer the following questions for homework.

1. If the following table of values were plotted as a graph on the *xy*-plane, what is the equation of the line?

x	y
−2	1
0	2
2	3

A) $y = -2x - 2$

B) $y = -2x + 2$

C) $y = -\frac{1}{2}x - 2$

D) $y = \frac{1}{2}x + 2$

2. What is the *y*-intercept of the line in the *xy*-plane with the ordered pairs (1, 21) and (4, 42) in its solution set?

A) 0

B) 7

C) 9

D) 14

3. Line *l* has a slope of −2 and the ordered pair (2, 3) is in its solution set. Which of the following ordered pairs is also in the solution set of the equation for line *l*?

A) (2, 1)

B) (3, 0)

C) (6, −5)

D) (8, −7)

The following questions are similar to what you would encounter on a college admissions test such as the SAT or ACT. Apply the Kaplan Method and your knowledge of linear equations to answer the following questions.

1. Point A is to be graphed in a quadrant, not on the axis of the xy-plane below.

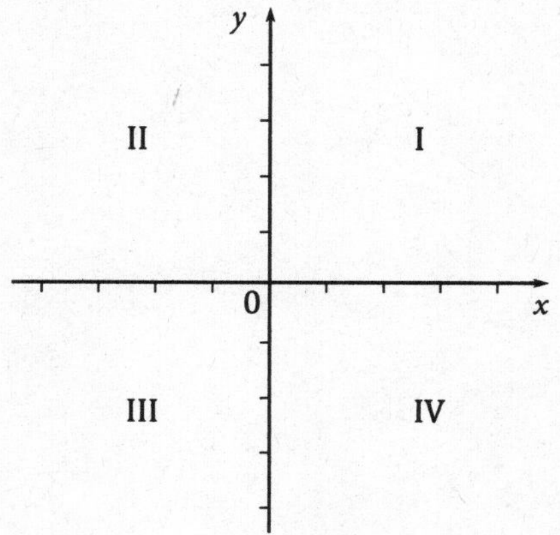

If the ordered pair representing Point A is to have opposite signs, then Point A must be located in

A) Quadrant II only.

B) Quadrant IV only.

C) Quadrants I or III only.

D) Quadrants II or IV only.

t	g
1	8.5
2	12.0
3	15.5
4	19.0

2. Which of the following equations best describes the relationship shown in the table above, where t indicates the number of hours a pump is operating to fill a tank, and g represents the number of gallons in the tank? (Assume a constant output from the pump.)

A) $g = 3.5t + 5$

B) $g = 3.5t$

C) $g = 8.5t - 5$

D) $g = 8.5t$

5

CHAPTER 6

Solving & Graphing Inequalities

CHAPTER OBJECTIVES

By the end of this chapter, you will be able to:

1. Simplify inequality expressions
2. Graph inequalities on a number line

THE KAPLAN METHOD FOR MATH

6

Step 1: Read the question, identifying and organizing important information as you go

- What information am I given?
- Separate the question from the context.
- How are the answer choices written?
- Should you label or draw a diagram?

Step 2: Choose the best strategy to answer the question

- Look for patterns.
- Pick numbers or use straightforward math.

Step 3: Check that you answered the *right* question

- Review the question stem.
- Check units of measurement.
- Double-check your work.

INEQUALITIES

A number line shows relationships among real numbers.

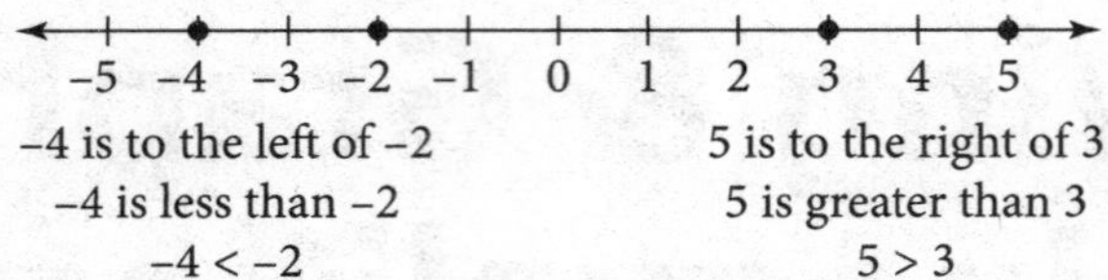

A value of a variable may be unknown, but you may know that it's greater than, less than, or equal to another number. For example, $x \geq 3$ means "x is greater than or equal to 3."

An inequality is formed by placing an inequality symbol ($>, <, \leq, \geq$) between numerical or variable expressions called **sides** of the inequality.

Graphing One-Variable Inequalities

To graph a one-variable inequality on a number line, fill in the dot for $\leq$ and $\geq$ symbols. Do NOT fill in the dot for expressions that use $>$ and $<$.

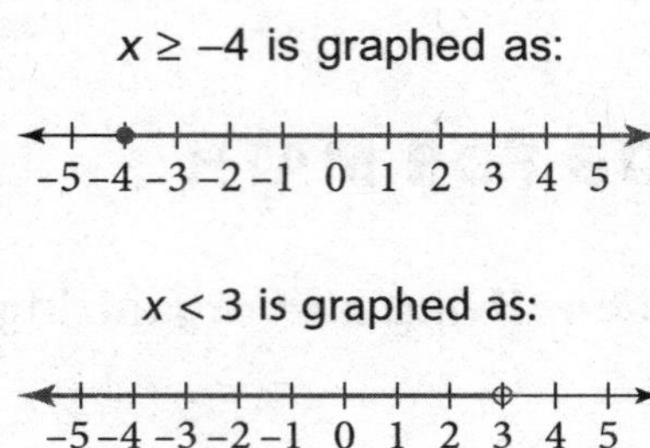

Properties of Inequalities

The Addition and Subtraction Properties for equations and inequalities are *exactly the same.* If a, b, and c are real numbers, and $a = b$, then the following applies for equations. If x, y, and z are real numbers, and $x > y$, the following applies for inequalities.

	Equations	Inequalities
Addition Property	$a + c = b + c$ and $c + a = c + b$	$x + z > y + z$ and $z + x > z + y$
Subtraction Property	$a - c = b - c$	$x - z > y - z$

Multiplication and division, however, can be much different.

	Equations	Inequalities
	When multiplying or dividing by a **POSITIVE** value, the properties are the **same** for equations and inequalities.	
Multiplication Property	$2a = 2b$ and $a(2) = b(2)$	$a(2) > b(2)$ and $2a > 2b$
Division Property	$\frac{a}{2} = \frac{b}{2}$	$\frac{a}{2} \geq \frac{b}{2}$
	When multiplying or dividing by a **NEGATIVE** value, the properties are **NOT the same** for equations and inequalities. When you multiply or divide by a negative number, you must reverse the direction of the inequality sign.	
Multiplication Property	$-2a = -2b$ and $a(-2) = b(-2)$	If $a > b$, then $a(-2) < b(-2)$ If $a > b$, then $-2a < -2b$
Division Property	$\frac{a}{-2} = \frac{b}{-2}$	If $a \geq b$, then $\frac{a}{-2} \leq \frac{b}{-2}$

While there may be a few differences between equations and inequalities, one rule that remains is the **Cardinal Rule of Equations**: do the same thing to both sides. Whatever you do to the left side of an inequality, you must do to the right side of an inequality.

Solving One-Variable Inequalities

You can solve each one-variable inequality with the same approach:

Step 1: Combine like terms (follow the order of operations)

Step 2: Isolate the variable

Step 3: Simplify

Try It Out! **Complete the following sample questions.**

1. If $8 - 2b \geq 4 - b$, what is the value of b?

   Step 1: Combine like terms ____________________

   Step 2: Isolate the variable ____________________

   Step 3: Simplify ____________________

2. If $2(x - 4) \leq 6$, what is the value of x?

   Step 1: Combine like terms ____________________

   Step 2: Isolate the variable ____________________

   Step 3: Simplify ____________________

Work through the following multiple-choice question.

Rajesh wants to rent a car for his business trip. With his corporate discount, the rental costs $125 a week plus $0.15 a mile. Using the inequality below, what is the furthest Rajesh can travel if he wants to spend $200 or less?

$125 + 0.15m \leq 200$

A) 500

B) 550

C) 675

D) 800

Isolate the variable and simplify:

$$125 + 0.15m \leq 200$$

$$-125 \qquad\qquad -125$$

$$\frac{0.15m}{0.15} \leq \frac{75}{0.15}$$

$$m \leq 500$$

This worked solution would resemble the following:

Rajesh wants to rent a car for his business trip. With his corporate discount, the rental costs \$125 a week plus \$0.15 a mile. Using the inequality below, what is the furthest Rajesh can travel if he wants to spend \$200 or less?

$125 + 0.15m \leq 200$

A) 500

B) 550

C) 675

D) 800

Straightforward math:

$125 + 0.15m \leq 200$

$-125 \qquad\qquad -125$

$\frac{0.15m}{0.15} \leq \frac{75}{0.15}$

$m \leq 500$

6

Double-check:

$125 + 0.15(500) \leq 200$

$125 + 75 \leq 200$

$200 \leq 200$ ✓

SOLVING ONE-VARIABLE INEQUALITIES WITH ABSOLUTE VALUE

Chapter 4 introduced **absolute value**; the absolute value of a number is its distance from 0 on the number line. Distance is always a positive number or 0, so the absolute value of a number is also *always* a positive number or 0. Just as you write two separate equations to solve absolute-value expressions that include a variable such as x, you have to write two separate inequalities to solve so that you account for the fact that there are not just one but *two* ranges of values x units away from 0. Make sure to "flip" the inequality sign for the negative equation.

You can solve absolute-value one-variable inequalities with the same approach:

Step 1: Isolate everything within the absolute-value sign on one side of the equation

Step 2: Remove the absolute-value sign and rewrite as two inequalities

Step 3: Within each inequality:

- Combine like terms (follow the order of operations)
- Isolate the variable
- Simplify

Try It Out! **Complete the following sample questions.** 6

1. $|1-2x| \geq 11$

Remove the absolute-value sign and rewrite as two inequalities.

	Inequality 1	Inequality 2
Step 1: Combine like terms		
Step 2: Isolate the variable		
Step 3: Simplify		

2. $|2y+10|-2 \leq 2$

Isolate the absolute-value portion, remove the absolute-value sign, and rewrite as two equations.

	Inequality 1	Inequality 2
Step 1: Combine like terms		
Step 2: Isolate the variable		
Step 3: Simplify		

Try It Out! **Complete the following multiple-choice question.**

The ideal diameter for the piston of a particular automobile is 4 inches. The actual diameter can vary from the ideal diameter by at most 0.15 inches. Using the inequality below, find the range of acceptable diameters for the piston.

$|x - 4| \leq 0.15$

A) $-4.15 \leq x \leq 4.15$

B) $-3.85 \leq x \leq 4.15$

C) $0.15 \leq x \leq 4.15$

D) $3.85 \leq x \leq 4.15$

Remove the absolute-value sign and rewrite as two inequalities:

	Inequality 1	Inequality 2
Combine like terms		
Isolate the variable		
Simplify		

6

This worked solution would resemble the following:

The ideal diameter for the piston of a particular automobile is 4 inches. The actual diameter can vary from the ideal diameter by at most 0.15 inches. Using the inequality below, find the range of acceptable diameters for the piston.

$|x - 4| \leq 0.15$

A) $-4.15 \leq x \leq 4.15$

B) $-3.85 \leq x \leq 4.15$

C) $0.15 \leq x \leq 4.15$

D) $3.85 \leq x \leq 4.15$

Straightforward math:

$x - 4 \leq 0.15$ $\quad$ $x - 4 \geq -0.15$

$+4 \quad +4$ $\quad$ $+4 \quad +4$

$x \leq 4.15$ $\quad$ $x \geq 3.85$

Double-check:

$|4.15 - 4| \leq 0.15$ $\quad$ $|3.85 - 4| \leq 0.15$

$|0.15| \leq 0.15$ $\quad$ $|-0.15| \leq 0.15$

$0.15 \leq 0.15$ ✓ $\quad$ $0.15 \leq 0.15$ ✓

Use the Kaplan Method to answer the following questions. Use the hints provided as needed.

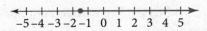

−5 −4 −3 −2 −1 0 1 2 3 4 5

1. The number line above represents which of the following inequalities?

   A) $x < -1.5$

   B) $x \leq -1.5$

   C) $x \geq -1.5$

   D) $x > -1.5$

hint *Check to see if the dot is filled in or not filled in. Then determine if the number line indicates "greater than" or "less than."*

2. Which of the following inequalities defines the solution set for the inequality $9 \leq \frac{y}{-2}$?

   A) $y \geq -18$

   B) $y \leq -18$

   C) $y \geq -4.5$

   D) $y \leq -4.5$

hint *Reverse the direction of the inequality sign if you multiply or divide by a negative number.*

3. If $|2x + 6| \leq 8$, which inequality expresses all of the possible values for x?

   A) $-7 < x < 1$

   B) $-7 \leq x \leq 1$

   C) $-1 < x < 7$

   D) $-1 \leq x \leq 7$

hint *Write two separate inequalities to solve for all possible values.*

Use the Kaplan Method to answer the following questions on your own.

1. If $-4x - 7 < 13$, which of the following is NOT a value of x?

   A) −5

   B) 10

   C) 15

   D) 21

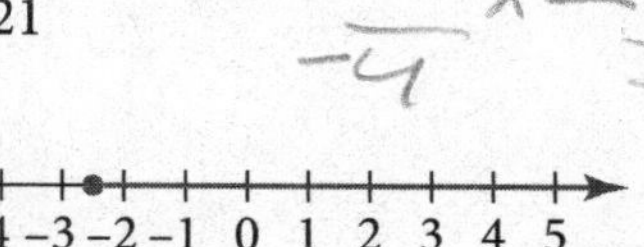

2. Which of the following numbers is NOT included in the inequality on the number line above?

   A) −3

   B) −2.5

   C) 2

   D) 2.5

3. Which of the following inequalities defines the solution set for the inequality $|4x - 11| < 9$?

   A) $\frac{1}{2} > x > 5$

   B) $\frac{1}{2} \geq x \geq 5$

   C) $\frac{1}{2} < x < 5$

   D) $\frac{1}{2} \leq x \leq 5$

Use the Kaplan Method to answer the following questions for homework.

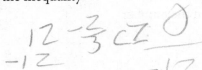

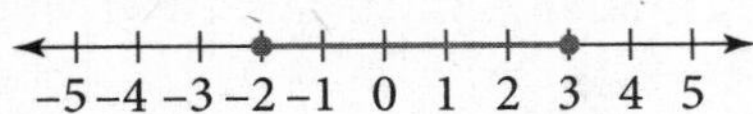

1. The number line above represents which of the following inequalities?

   A) $-2 > x > 3$

   B) $-2 \leq x \leq 3$

   C) $-2 \geq x \geq 3$

   D) $-2 < x < 3$

2. Which of the following inequalities defines the solution set for the inequality $12 - \frac{2}{3}c \geq 0$?

   A) $c \geq -18$

   B) $c \leq -18$

   C) $c \geq 18$

   D) $c \leq 18$

3. Which of the following inequalities defines the solution set for the inequality $|25x + 2| < 7$?

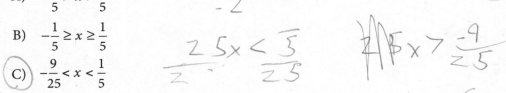

   A) $-\frac{1}{5} > x > \frac{1}{5}$

   B) $-\frac{1}{5} \geq x \geq \frac{1}{5}$

   C) $-\frac{9}{25} < x < \frac{1}{5}$

   D) $-\frac{9}{25} \geq x \geq \frac{1}{5}$

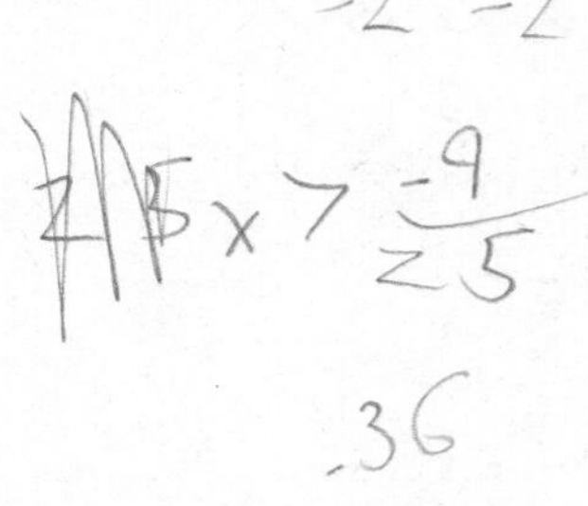

The following questions are similar to what you would encounter on a college admissions test such as the SAT or ACT. Apply the Kaplan Method and your knowledge of linear inequalities to answer the following questions.

1. To cut a lawn, Valentina charges a fee of \$25 for her equipment and \$10 per hour spent cutting a lawn. Iker charges a fee of \$20 for his equipment and \$12 per hour spent cutting a lawn. If h represents the number of hours spent cutting a lawn, what are all the values of h for which Valentina's total charge is greater than Iker's total charge?

   A) $h > 2$

   B) $h \leq 2$

   C) $h \geq 2.5$

   D) $h < 2.5$

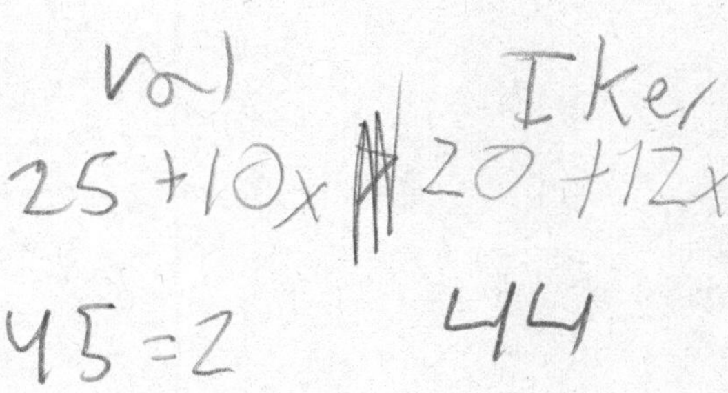

2. If $-1 \leq y \leq 5$, which inequality expresses the same possible values for y?

   A) $|y - 1| \leq 5$

   B) $|y + 1| \leq 5$

   C) $|y - 2| \leq 3$

   D) $|y + 2| \leq 3$

CHAPTER 7

Graphing Systems of Equations

CHAPTER OBJECTIVES

By the end of this chapter, you will be able to:

1. Graph systems of equations
2. Solve systems of linear equations using graphing
3. Identify a system of equations represented by a graph

THE KAPLAN METHOD FOR MATH

Step 1: Read the question, identifying and organizing important information as you go

- What information am I given?
- Separate the question from the context.
- How are the answer choices written?
- Should you label or draw a diagram?

Step 2: Choose the best strategy to answer the question

- Look for patterns.
- Pick numbers or use straightforward math.

Step 3: Check that you answered the *right* question

- Review the question stem.
- Check units of measurement.
- Double-check your work.

GRAPHING SYSTEMS OF EQUATIONS

Two or more equations that have the same variables form a system of equations. To graphically solve, you must find all ordered pairs (x, y) that make *both* equations true.

- If the lines **intersect**, there is only **one solution**.
- If the lines **are parallel**, there is **no solution**.
- If the lines **are equivalent**, there are **infinitely many solutions**.

You can graph each system of equations with the same approach:

Step 1: Rewrite each equation in $y = mx + b$ form.

Step 2: Set up an x–y table for each question.

Step 3: Graph the equations in the same coordinate plane.

Try It Out! **Complete the following sample questions.**

1. Solve the system by graphing:

$x - y = 3$

$2x + y = 3$

Step 1: Rewrite each equation in $y = mx + b$ form.

$x - y = 3$ $-x \quad -x$ $\underline{-y} = \underline{-x + 3}$ $-1 \quad -1$ $y = x - 3$	$2x + y = 3$ $-2x \quad -2x$ $y = -2x + 3$

Step 2: Set up an *x*–*y* table for each equation.

x	**x − 3**	*y*	**ordered pairs (*x*, *y*)**
–1	(–1) – 3	–4	(–1, –4)
0	(0) – 3	–3	(0, –3)
1	(1) – 3	–2	(1, –2)

x	**–2x + 3**	*y*	**ordered pairs (*x*, *y*)**
–1	–2(–1) + 3	5	(–1, 5)
0	–2(0) + 3	3	(0, 3)
1	–2(1) + 3	1	(1, 1)

Step 3: Graph the equations ($y = x - 3$) and ($y = -2x + 3$) in the same coordinate plane.

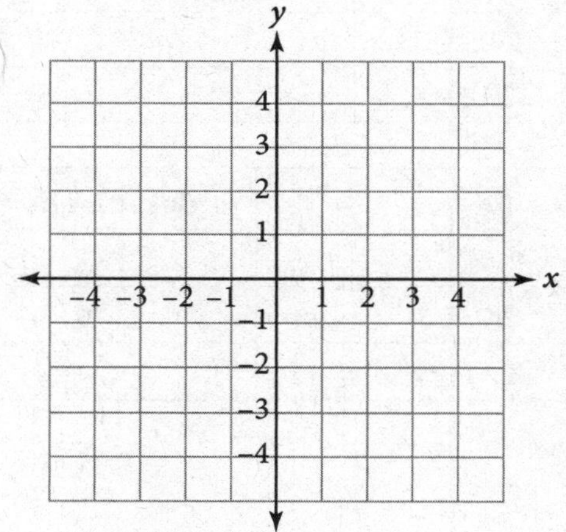

What is the intersection point? ________________

You can double-check the solution by substituting the values into each equation.

$x - y = 3$ $\qquad$ $2x + y = 3$

2. Solve the system by graphing:

$2x - y = -3$

$2x - y = 1$

Step 1: Rewrite each equation in $y = mx + b$ form.

$2x - y = -3$	$2x - y = 1$
$-2x \quad -2x$	$-2x \quad -2x$
$\underline{-y} = \underline{-2x - 3}$	$\underline{-y} = \underline{-2x + 1}$
$-1 \quad -1$	$-1 \quad -1$
$y = 2x + 3$	$y = 2x - 1$

Step 2: Set up an *x–y* table for each equation.

x	**2x + 3**	**y**	**ordered pairs (x, y)**
–1	2(–1) + 3	1	(–1, 1)
0	2(0) + 3	3	(0, 3)
1	2(1) + 3	5	(1, 5)

x	**2x – 1**	**y**	**ordered pairs (x, y)**
–1	2(–1) – 1	–3	(–1, –3)
0	2(0) – 1	–1	(0, –1)
1	2(1) – 1	1	(1, 1)

Step 3: Graph the equations ($y = 2x + 3$) and ($y = 2x - 1$) in the same coordinate plane.

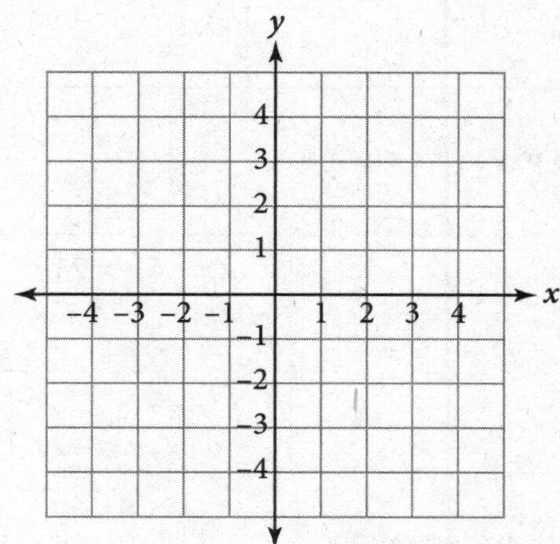

Will the lines intersect? _______________

What is the solution? _______________

3. Solve the system by graphing:

$$6x + 3y = 12$$
$$12x + 6y = 24$$

Step 1: Rewrite each equation in $y = mx + b$ form.

$6x + 3y = 12$ $-6x \quad -6x$ $\frac{3y}{3} = \frac{-6x + 12}{3}$ $y = -2x + 4$	$12x + 6y = 24$ $-12x \quad -12x$ $\frac{6y}{6} = \frac{-12x + 24}{6}$ $y = -2x + 4$

Step 2: Set up an x–y table for each equation.

x	**−2x + 4**	**y**	**ordered pairs (x, y)**
−1	−2(−1) + 4	6	(−1, 6)
0	−2(0) + 4	4	(0, 4)
1	−2(1) + 4	2	(1, 2)

x	**−2x + 4**	**y**	**ordered pairs (x, y)**
−1	−2(−1) + 4	6	(−1, 6)
0	−2(0) + 4	4	(0, 4)
1	−2(1) + 4	2	(1, 2)

7

Step 3: Graph the equations $(y = -2x + 4)$ and $(y = -2x + 4)$ in the same coordinate plane.

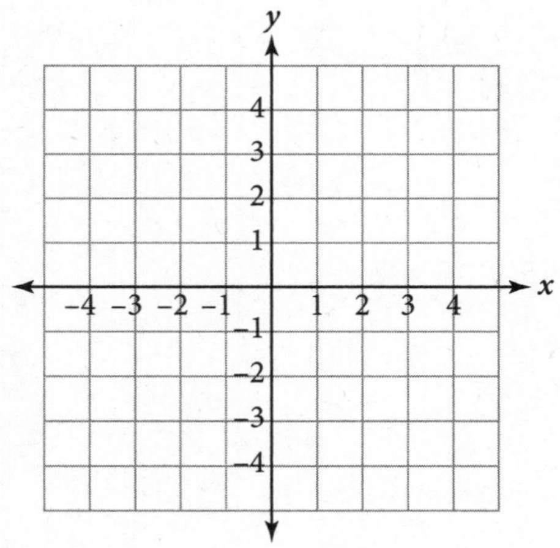

What is the solution? ________________

Use the Kaplan Method to answer the following questions. Use the hints provided as needed.

1. Which of the following system of equations has the ordered pair (3, –2) as its solution?

   A) $2x + y = 8$ and $x - y = 1$

   B) $x + 2y = -8$ and $x - y = -1$

   C) $2x + y = 8$ and $x + y = -1$

   D) $2x - y = 8$ and $x + y = 1$

hint *Plug the information in the question stem into the answer choices.*

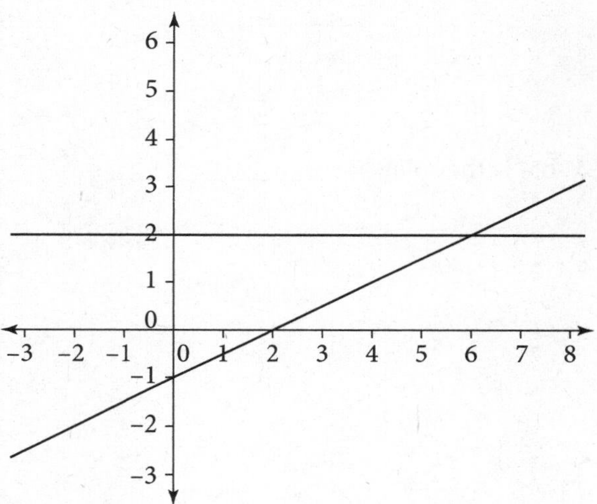

2. The graph above plots the equations $y + 1 = \frac{1}{2}x$ and $y = 2$. Which ordered pair (x, y) represents the point of intersection?

   A) (0, –1)

   B) (0, 2)

   C) (2, 6)

   D) (6, 2)

hint *Save time by using the graph provided to determine the point of intersection.*

3. Solve the system by graphing:

$$y = \frac{3}{2}x$$

$$y = -\frac{1}{2}x + 4$$

x	$\frac{3}{2}x$	y	ordered pairs (x, y)
–1			
0			
1			

x	$-\frac{1}{2}x + 4$	y	ordered pairs (x, y)
–1			
0			
1			

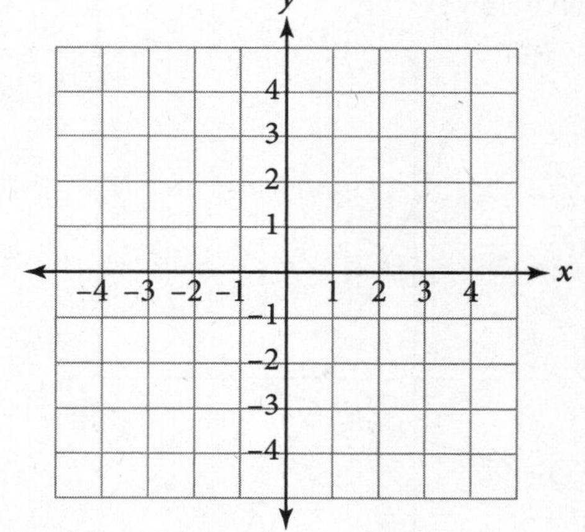

What is the intersection point? ____________

hint *Double-check your work by plugging the point of intersection back into each equation.*

7

Use the Kaplan Method to answer the following questions on your own.

1. Solve the system by graphing:

$y = \frac{1}{2}x + 1$

$4x - 8y = -8$

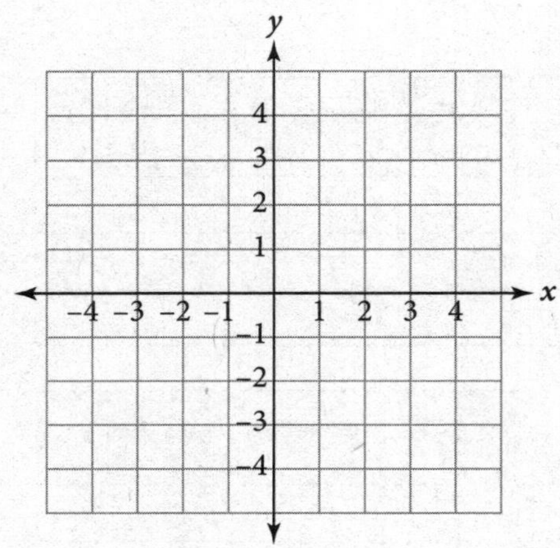

What is the solution? ________________

2. Which is true of the system of equations in the graph below?

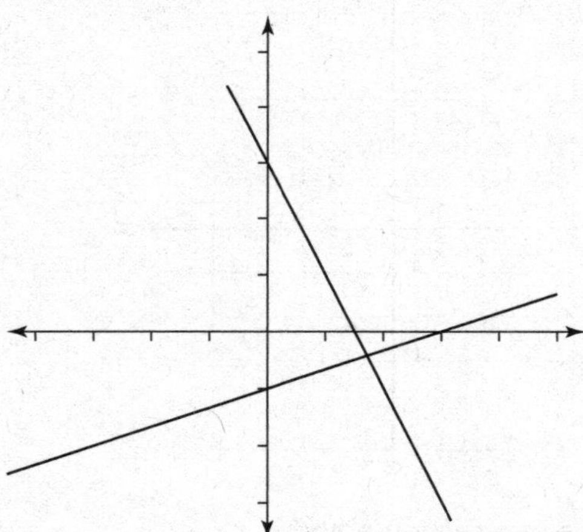

A) The system has no solutions.
B) The system has infinitely many solutions.
C) The system has one solution.
D) The system has two solutions.

3. Solve the system by graphing:

$6x + 4y = 2$

$2y + 3x = 1$

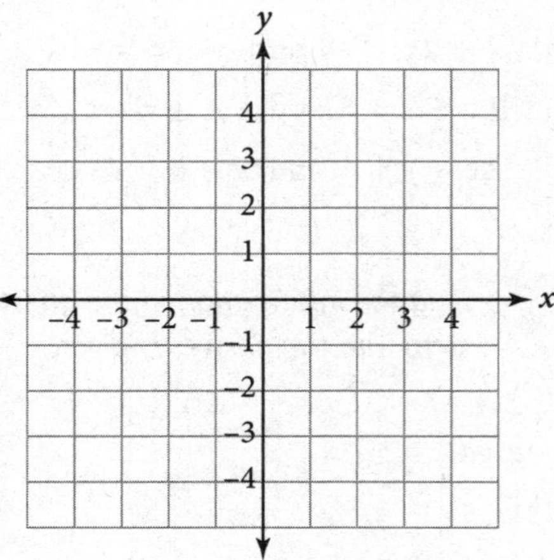

What is the solution? ________________

7

Use the Kaplan Method to answer the following questions for homework.

1. The system of equations in the graph below has

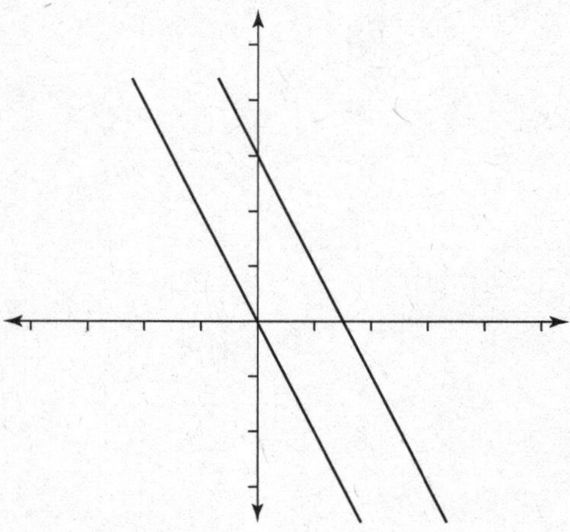

A) no solutions.

B) infinitely many solutions.

C) one solution.

D) two solutions.

2. Solve the system by graphing:

$-2x + y = -1$

$x + y = 5$

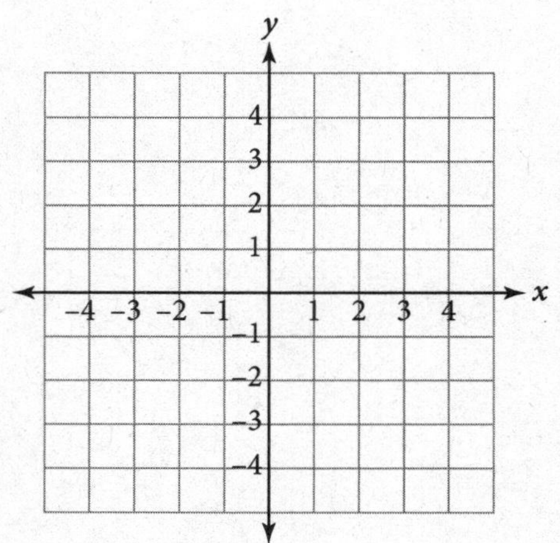

What is the solution? _______________

3. Solve the system by graphing:

$y - 2x = -5$

$y - x = -3$

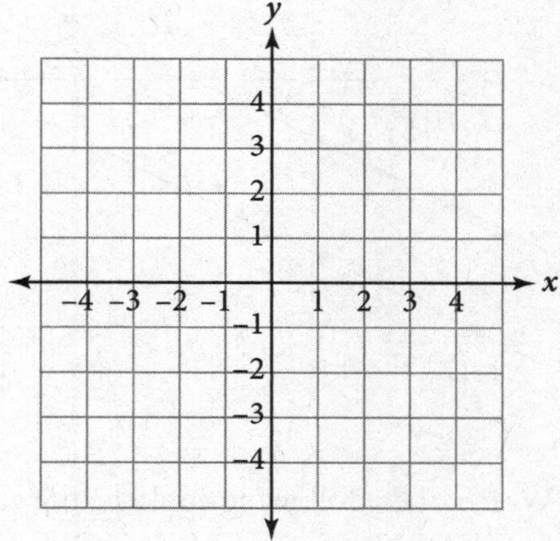

What is the solution? _______________

7

The following questions are similar to what you would encounter on a college admissions test such as the SAT or ACT. Apply the Kaplan Method and your knowledge of systems of equations to answer the following questions.

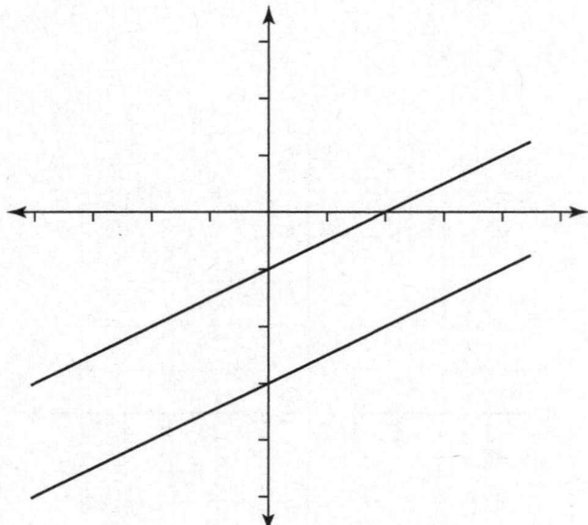

1. Which of the following could be the equations of the lines graphed above?

   A) $y = 2x - 3$ and $y = \frac{1}{2}x - 6$

   B) $y = 2x - 3$ and $y = 2x - 6$

   C) $y = -2x + 3$ and $y = -\frac{1}{2}x + 6$

   D) $y = \frac{1}{2}x - 3$ and $y = \frac{1}{2}x - 6$

2. Which of the following systems of equations has no solution?

A)

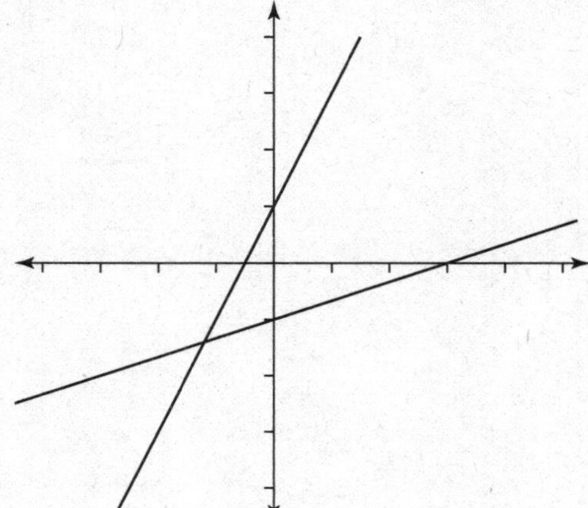

C)

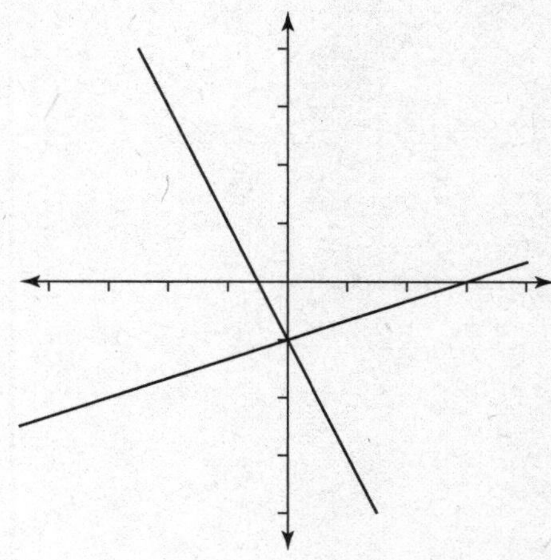

B)

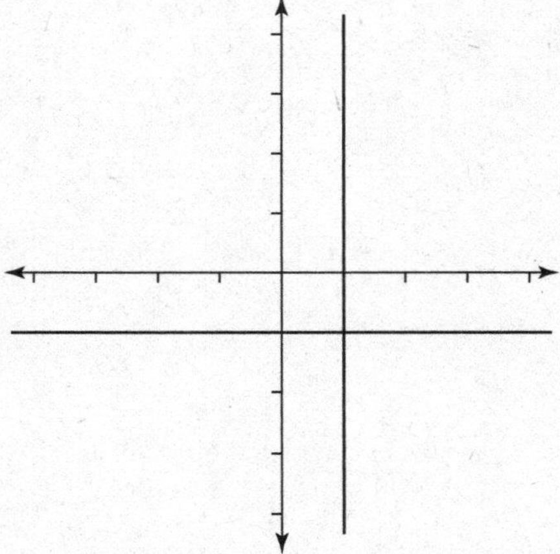

D)

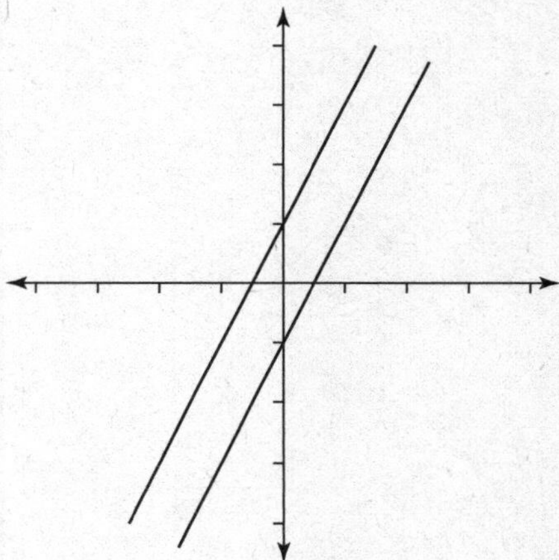

CHAPTER 8

Solving Systems of Equations

CHAPTER OBJECTIVES

By the end of this chapter, you will be able to:

1. Solve systems of equations using substitution
2. Solve systems of equations using combination

THE KAPLAN METHOD FOR MATH

Step 1: Read the question, identifying and organizing important information as you go

- What information am I given?
- Separate the question from the context.
- How are the answer choices written?
- Should you label or draw a diagram?

Step 2: Choose the best strategy to answer the question

- Look for patterns.
- Pick numbers or use straightforward math.

Step 3: Check that you answered the *right* question

- Review the question stem.
- Check units of measurement.
- Double-check your work.

SOLVING SYSTEMS OF EQUATIONS: SUBSTITUTION AND COMBINATION

The two main methods for solving a system of linear equations are **substitution** and **combination** (sometimes referred to as linear elimination).

Substitution is the most straightforward method for solving equations, and it can be applied in every situation. Unfortunately, it is often the longer and more time-consuming route for solving systems of equations as well. To use substitution, solve the easier of the two equations for one variable, then substitute that result into the other equation.

Try It Out! **Work through the following multiple-choice question using substitution.**

Xavier is the placekicker for his college football team. Each field goal, *f*, scored 3 points, and each point after a touchdown, *t*, scored 1 point, for a season total of 70 points. The following equations represent the total number of points Xavier scored as well as the total number of times Xavier kicked. If Xavier kicked 38 times and never missed, how many field goals did he kick last season?

$3f + t = 70$

$f + t = 38$

A) 16

B) 22

C) 32

D) 38

Step 1: Isolate *t* in the second equation

$f + t = 38$

$-f \qquad -f$

$t = 38 - f$

Step 2: Substitute 38 – *f* into the first equation

$3f + (38 - f) = 70$

Step 3: Solve for *f*

$3f + 38 - f = 70$

$2f + 38 = 70$

$-38 \quad -38$

$2f = 32$

$f = 16$

✓ Helpful Hint

Take time to choose which variable to isolate. If you are solving to find the value of just one variable, isolate the opposite variable. That way, you'll save yourself time when you substitute the expression into the other equation. (Isolating *t* in the second equation made it possible to quickly solve for *f*.)

Combination involves adding the two equations together to eliminate a variable. Often, one or both of the equations are multiplied by a constant before they are added together. Combination is almost always the better technique to use to solve a system of equations when the question only asks you for the value of one of the variables, but even when a question asks you for both variables, combination is often faster than substitution.

Try It Out! **Work through the following multiple-choice question using combination.**

Xavier is the placekicker for his college football team. Each field goal, *f*, scored 3 points and each point after a touchdown, *t*, scored 1 point, for a season total of 70 points. The following equations represent the total number of points Xavier scored as well as the total number of times Xavier kicked. If Xavier kicked 38 times and never missed, how many field goals did he kick last season?

$3f + t = 70$

$f + t = 38$

A) 16

B) 22

C) 32

D) 38

Step 1: Stack the equations

$3f + t = 70$

$f + t = 38$

Step 2: Multiply the second equation by –1

$3f + t = 70$

$-1[f + t = 38]$

8

Step 3: Combine (add) the two equations

$$\begin{array}{r} 3f + t = 70 \\ + \quad -f + -t = -38 \\ \hline 2f = 32 \end{array}$$

Step 4: Isolate the variable

$f = 16$

✓ Helpful Hint

Most students prefer substitution, but standardized test questions are often designed to be quickly solved with combination. Learning how to use combination can save both time and energy.

This worked solution would resemble the following:

Xavier is the placekicker for his college football team. Each field goal, *f*, scored 3 points, and each point after a touchdown, *t*, scored 1 point, for a season total of 70 points. The following equations represent the total number of points Xavier scored as well as the total number of times Xavier kicked. If Xavier kicked 38 times and never missed, how many field goals did he kick last season?

$f + t = 38$

$3f + t = 70$

A) 16

B) 22

C) 32

D) 38

8

Straightforward math:

$3f + t = 70$

$-1[f + t = 38]$

$$\begin{array}{r} 3f + t = 70 \\ + \quad -f + -t = -38 \\ \hline 2f = 32 \\ f = 16 \end{array}$$

REMINDERS

Systems of Equations: No Solution

Most systems of equations have one solution. Occasionally, a system of equations will have no solution, which means that the two equations do not intersect. If the equations are both linear and they do not intersect, they must have parallel slopes.

Systems of Equations: Infinite Solutions

In addition to one solution and no solution, systems of equations may have an infinite number of solutions if the equations represent the same line.

PRACTICE

Use the Kaplan Method to answer the following questions. Use the hints provided as needed.

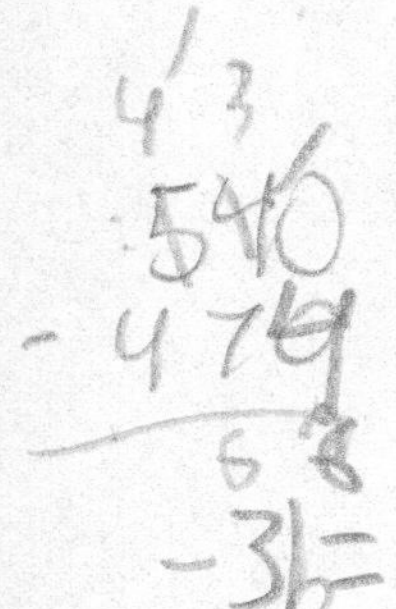

1. At a restaurant, a bowl of soup, b, costs \$7, and a salad, s, costs \$10. The equations below represent the number of items sold as well as the corresponding revenue. How much of each item did the restaurant sell?

$$b + s = 54$$
$$\$7b + \$10s = \$474$$

A) 32 bowls of soup; 22 salads
B) 28 bowls of soup; 26 salads
C) 26 bowls of soup; 28 salads
D) 22 bowls of soup; 32 salads

hint *Either combination or substitution will work well with this question.*

2. If $y = x + 3$ and $-3y = 3$, which of the following points represents the solution to the system of equations?

A) (–5, –4)
B) (–4, –1)
C) (1, 5)
D) (1, –1)

hint *Substitution is a great way to solve this question. Be sure to distribute the negative signs correctly as you solve.*

✔ Helpful Hint

System of equation questions may ask you for the answer in terms of an (x, y) ordered pair. Be on the lookout for answers that reverse the values or negate the values. For example, if the correct answer is (–2, 3), trap answers would include (3, –2), (2, –3), and (–2, –3).

3. If $y = \frac{2}{3}x$ and $x + 6y = 30$, what is the value of x?

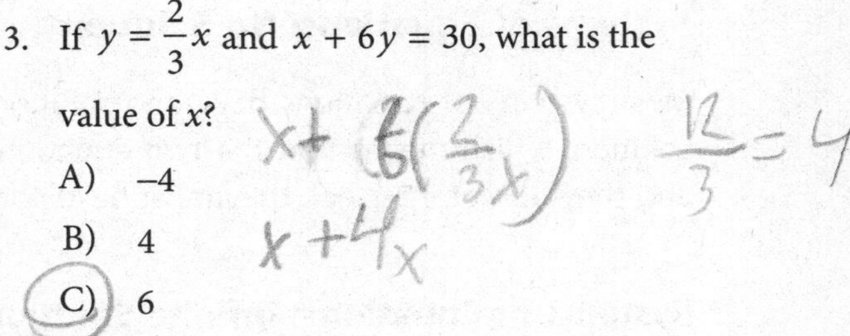

A) –4
B) 4
C) 6
D) 24

hint *You can use substitution to solve. It's helpful to rewrite 6 as $\frac{6}{1}$ before you multiply by $\frac{2}{3}$x.*

8

Use the Kaplan Method to answer the following questions on your own.

1. There are 26 times as many students in Lincoln High School as teachers. When all the teachers and students are seated in the 900-seat school auditorium, only 9 seats are unoccupied. The equations below represent the ratio of teachers to students as well as the total number of seats the teachers and students occupy in the auditorium. How many teachers are at Lincoln High?

$$26t = s$$

$$s + t = 900 - 9$$

A) 33
B) 45
C) 85
D) 105

2. The equations below show that a carrot, c, has 13 calories more than a celery stalk, s, and that seven carrots and nine celery stalks have 203 calories. How many calories are in each vegetable?

$$c = s + 13$$

$$7c + 9s = 203$$

A) 20 calories in a carrot; 7 calories in celery
B) 76 calories in a carrot; 63 calories in celery
C) 9 calories in a carrot; 22 calories in celery
D) 20 calories in a carrot; 33 calories in celery

3. If $3x - 2y = 4$ and $2x + y = 5$, what is the value of y?

A) −2
B) 0
C) 1
D) 2

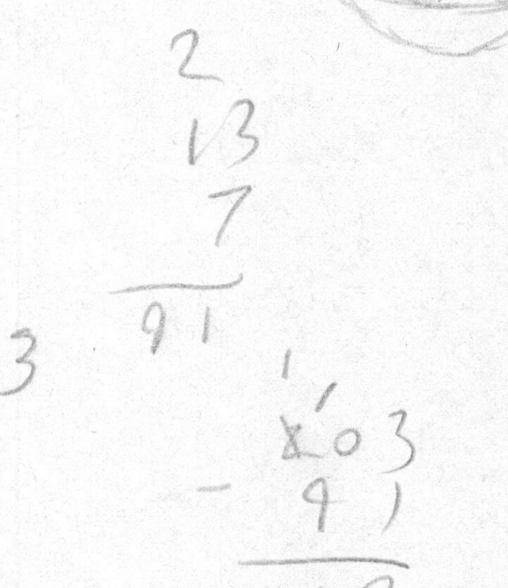

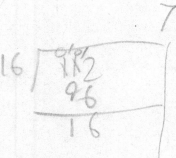

HOMEWORK

Use the Kaplan Method to answer the following questions for homework.

1. If $3r + 2s = 24$ and $r + s = 12$, what is the value of $r + 2$?

   A) -4
   B) 0
   C) 2
   D) 8

2. If $y = 2x$ and $5x - y = 30$, what is the value of y?

   A) 2
   B) 5
   C) 10
   D) 20

3. If $y = x - 1$ and $-4y = -12$, which of the following points represents the solution to the system of equations?

   A) $(-4, -3)$
   B) $(4, 3)$
   C) $(-5, 3)$
   D) $(5, -3)$

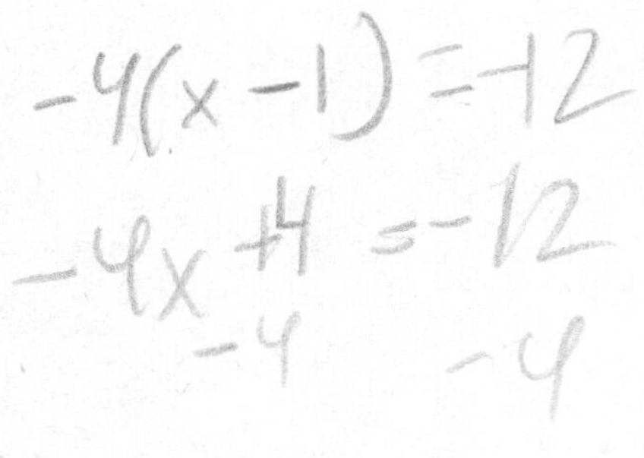

The following questions are similar to what you would encounter on a college admissions test such as the SAT or ACT. Apply the Kaplan Method and your knowledge of systems of equations to answer the following questions.

1. For what value of a would the following system of equations have no solution?

   $4y = 28x + 16$
   $y = ax + 7$

   A) 4
   B) 7
   C) 16
   D) 28

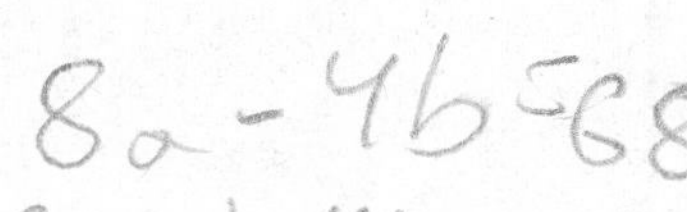

2. If $2a - b = 17$ and $3a + 4b = -13$, what is the value of $a + b$?

   A) -2
   B) 2
   C) 5
   D) 12

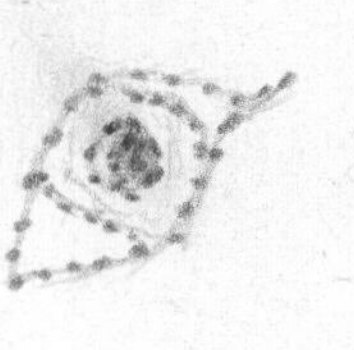

CHAPTER 9

Translating English into Math

CHAPTER OBJECTIVES

By the end of this chapter, you will be able to:

1. Identify common English phrases that represent mathematical concepts
2. Translate any word problem into a mathematical expression, equation, or inequality

THE KAPLAN METHOD FOR MATH

Step 1: Read the question, identifying and organizing important information as you go

- What information am I given?
- Separate the question from the context.
- How are the answer choices written?
- Should you label or draw a diagram?

Step 2: Choose the best strategy to answer the question

- Look for patterns.
- Pick numbers or use straightforward math.

Step 3: Check that you answered the *right* question

- Review the question stem.
- Check units of measurement.
- Double-check your work.

COMMON TRANSLATIONS

Mathematical ideas can be expressed in a number of ways using the English language. The following table shows some of the most common phrases and mathematical equivalents.

Translation Table	
English	**Math**
equals, is, equivalent to, was, will be, has, costs, adds up to, the same as, as much as	$=$
plus, added, sum, combined, total, increased, more than	$+$
minus, subtracted from, smaller than, less than, fewer, decreased by, difference between	$-$
times, of, multiplied by, product of, twice, double, by	$\times$
divided by, per, out of, each, ratio, quotient	$\div$
a number, how much, how many, what	x, n, etc.

Addition

A. You have four cards in your hand. You draw cards until you've **increased** your number of cards by three. How many cards do you have now? $4 + 3 = 7$

B. Frankie was famished by the time he sat down to eat dinner. He first grabbed one chicken leg, but then **added** four more to his plate. How many chicken legs did Frankie have on his plate? $1 + 4 = 5$

C. On Monday, Grant collected empty aluminum cans from his neighbors. On Tuesday, Tilden collected empty glass bottles from local restaurants. On Wednesday, the boys **combined** what they had collected and delivered the items to the recycling center. **Together**, they had 142 items to recycle. How many items did they have to recycle **together**? $c + b = 142$

D. What does $4x$ **plus** $7x$ equal? $4x + 7x = 11x$

E. Jake has 13 questions to complete for homework. You have 4 **more than** Jake. How many questions do you have to complete for homework? __________

F. What is the **sum** of $\sqrt[3]{64}$ and 19? __________

G. Naja's portion of a term paper is seven pages long. Cooper's portion of a term paper is six pages long. How many pages do they have in **total**? __________

9

Subtraction

A. Five **minus** four equals one. $5 - 4 = 1$

B. How much **smaller than** 23 is 7? $23 - 7 = 16$

C. Eight **less than** 14 equals six. $14 - 8 = 6$

D. The **difference between** seven and four is three. $7 - 4 = 3$

E. Ten **decreased by** five is five. ___________

F. You have three **fewer** pets than Candice. Candice has eight pets. Therefore, you have five pets. ___________

G. If 17 is **subtracted from** 26, the answer is 9. ___________

Multiplication

A. The **product of** 12 and 10 yields 120. $12 \times 10 = 120$

B. 42 **multiplied by** two equals 84. $42 \times 2 = 84$

C. 27 **times** 3 is 81. $27 \times 3 = 81$

D. 20 percent **of** 100 is 20. $0.20 \times 100 = 20$

E. **Twice** 13 is 26. ___________

F. 114 is **double** 57. ___________

G. A yard that is 15 feet **by** 20 feet has an area of 300 feet. ___________

Division

A. 18 **divided by** three equals six. $18 \div 3 = 6$

B. 100 **divided by** five is 20. $100 \div 5 = 20$

C. The **quotient** of 40 and 10 is four. $40 \div 10 = 4$

> ✔ **Helpful Hint**
>
> **After the word "quotient," the first number listed gets divided by the second number listed. The quotient of a and $b = \frac{a}{b}$.**

D. Five **out of** ten equals one-half. ______________

E. The **ratio of** 10 to 60 is one-sixth. ______________

9

✔ Helpful Hint

After the word "ratio," the first number listed gets divided by the second number listed. The ratio of a to $b = \frac{a}{b}$.

F. A fighter jet travels 500 miles **per** every 30 minutes. What is its speed in miles per hour? ________

Convert minutes to hours to get the right answer in miles per **hour**.

$$30 \text{ minutes} \times \frac{1 \text{ hour}}{60 \text{ minutes}} = \frac{30}{60} \text{ hours} = \frac{1}{2} \text{ hour} = 0.5 \text{ hour}$$

Perform the division operation, and the answer will be in the correct units (miles per hour).

✔ Helpful Hint

A percent is literally a number "per" "cent." Because "cent" means 100 (think money and coins), percent literally means "divided by 100."

Algebraic Terms

A. 75 is 25% of what **number**? $75 = 0.25x$

B. **How much** money does Samir have if he has $23 more than Hudson and together they have $122? $s + (s - 23) = 122$

C. **How many** quarters are in 15 dollars? ________

D. **What is the perimeter** of a rectangle with a length of 4 and a height of 6? ________

Complex Expressions

Questions may ask you to translate phrases that contain more than just one or two mathematical operations. Translate one operation at a time, and write down each component as you work from left to right.

A. 50 percent **of** six **times** four is 12. $0.50 \times 6 \times 4 = 12$

B. Rashida plans to buy a $30 shirt. If she uses a coupon for $5 **off** and has to pay 7 **percent** sales tax, how much will she pay in all? $(30 - 5)1.07 = 26.75$

C. A number whose **product** with 9 is the same as its **sum** with 56. ________

Try It Out! **Translate English to math to solve the following multiple-choice question.**

A car traveled at an average speed of 60 miles per hour for four hours and consumed fuel at a rate of 34 miles per gallon. Approximately how many gallons of fuel did the car use for the entire four-hour trip?

A) 3

B) 7

C) 138

D) 206

60 miles per hour for 4 hours = 60 mph × 4 hrs = 240 miles

240 miles ÷ 34 mpg = 7.06 gallons

This worked solution would resemble the following:

A car traveled at an average speed of 60 miles per hour for four hours and consumed fuel at a rate of 34 miles per gallon. Approximately how many gallons of fuel did the car use for the entire four-hour trip?

A) 3

B) 7

C) 138

D) 206

Straightforward math:

$60 \times 4 = 240$

$240 \div 34 = 7.06 \approx 7$

PRACTICE

Use the Kaplan Method to answer the following questions. Use the hints provided as needed.

1. 17 less than 42 is what number?

   Math: ____________________

   Answer: ____________________

hint *The phrase "less than" indicates that you should subtract.*

2. Five plus 29 yields what number?

   Math: ____________________

   Answer: ____________________

hint *"Yields" is another way of saying "equals."*

3. Jenn has 21 fewer homework problems to do than Danika. Danika has 25 math problems to do. Kamila has four more problems than both Danika and Jenn combined. How many problems does Kamila have to do?

   Math: ____________________

   Answer: ____________________

hint *Solve for the number of math problems Jenn has to complete before calculating Kamila's homework problems.*

4. What number do you get when you divide 49 by seven and add 10?

   Math: ____________________

   Answer: ____________________

hint *Remember to follow order of operations. Write out the operations in math form, and then use PEMDAS to determine which operation happens first.*

Use the Kaplan Method to answer the following questions on your own.

1. An unknown number is five less than the product of seven and four.

   Math: ____________________

   Answer: ____________________

2. The product of 21 and seven yields what number?

   Math: ____________________

   Answer: ____________________

3. There are 32 mice and nine gophers living in the farm fields. What is the quotient of mice and gophers?

   Math: ____________________

   Answer: ____________________

4. Rehan brought 12 books to the donation drive. Dylan brought eight more than twice as many books as Rehan. What is the difference between Rehan's number of books and Dylan's number of books?

   Math: ____________________

   Answer: ____________________

Use the Kaplan Method to answer the following questions for homework.

1. The ratio of 76 to 19 is what number?

   Math: ____________________

   Answer: ____________________

2. Melody sold her bike for three times the price she paid for it. When she bought it, she paid $60. What is the difference between the amount she sold it for and the amount she paid for it originally?

   Math: ____________________

   Answer: ____________________

3. Eight fewer than five times 19 gives you what number?

   A) 33
   B) 57
   C) 87
   D) 103

4. On Beach Cleanup Day, Jacqueline collected twice as many pieces of trash as her teacher. Her teacher collected 58 pieces of trash. Combined, they picked up how many pieces of trash?

   A) 84
   B) 116
   C) 174
   D) 232

The following questions are similar to what you would encounter on a college admissions test such as the SAT or ACT. Apply the Kaplan Method and your knowledge of translating English into math to answer the following questions.

1. Harry is half his brother's age. His brother is 28 years younger than their Aunt Jenny, who is five years older than Harry and his brother's dad. Their dad is 31 years old. How old is Harry?

   A) 2

   B) 4

   C) 8

   D) 12

2. The product of 129 and the sum of eight and the difference between 12 and three is what number?

   A) 439

   B) 1,032

   C) 2,193

   D) 12,384

9

CHAPTER 10

Solving Word Problems with Equations and Inequalities

CHAPTER OBJECTIVES

By the end of this chapter, you will be able to:

1. Solve equation word problems
2. Solve inequality word problems
3. Interpret the meaning of the slope and the *y*-intercept from a graph given a real-world scenario

THE KAPLAN METHOD FOR MATH

Step 1: Read the question, identifying and organizing important information as you go

- What information am I given?
- Separate the question from the context.
- How are the answer choices written?
- Should you label or draw a diagram?

Step 2: Choose the best strategy to answer the question

- Look for patterns.
- Pick numbers or use straightforward math.

Step 3: Check that you answered the *right* question

- Review the question stem.
- Check units of measurement.
- Double-check your work.

10

WORD PROBLEMS

Whether you are working with equations or inequalities, you will need to translate English into math. The following table, which was introduced in chapter 9, includes common phrases and their mathematical equivalents.

Translation Table	
English	**Math**
equals, is, equivalent to, was, will be, has, costs, adds up to, the same as, as much as	=
plus, added, sum, combined, total, increased, more than	+
minus, subtracted from, smaller than, less than, fewer, decreased by, difference between	−
times, of, multiplied by, product of, twice, double, by	×
divided by, per, out of, each, ratio, quotient	÷
a number, how much, how many, what	*x*, *n*, etc.

Equation Word Problems

Equation word problems require you to translate English into math and then solve for a specific value. You can solve equation word problems with the same approach:

Step 1: Define variables with appropriate letters.

Step 2: Translate phrases into math.

Step 3: Determine which value the question asks you to solve for and in what units.

Step 4: Set up an equation and solve.

Try It Out! **Work through the following sample question.**

If Tom reads for 2 hours each day, how many hours does he read each week?

Step 1: Define variables with appropriate letters.

d for the number of days, *h* for hours, *w* for week, and *t* for time reading

Step 2: Translate phrases into math.

$2\frac{h}{d}$ for *2 hours each day*

$7\frac{d}{w}$ for *days Tom reads each week*

t for *how many hours each week*

Step 3: Determine which value the question asks you to solve for and in what units.

Solve for *t*:

$$t = \frac{\text{hours}}{\text{week}}$$

Step 4: Set up an equation and solve.

$$t = 2\frac{h}{d} \times 7\frac{d}{w} = (2 \times 7)\frac{hd}{dw}$$

$$t = 14\frac{h}{w}$$

Inequality Word Problems

Approach inequality word problems the same way you would approach equation word problems, except solve for the range of values that satisfies the inequality.

Try It Out! **Work through the following sample question.**

If Melody practices the violin for a minimum of 3 hours per day and a maximum of 4 and a half hours per day for six days each week, which inequality defines the range of possible hours Melody practices each week?

Step 1: Define variables with appropriate letters.

d for the number of days, *h* for hours, *w* for week, and *t* for time practicing

Step 2: Translate phrases into math.

$3\frac{h}{d}$ for a minimum of 3 hours each day and $4.5\frac{h}{d}$ for a maximum of 4 and a half hours per day

$6\frac{d}{w}$ for days Melody practices each week

t for how many hours each week

Step 3: Determine which value the question asks you to solve for and in what units.

Solve for a range of possible *t*:

$$t = \frac{\text{hours}}{\text{week}}$$

Step 4: Set up an inequality and solve.

$$t \geq 3\frac{h}{d} \times 6\frac{d}{w} \text{ and } t \leq 4.5\frac{h}{d} \times 6\frac{d}{w}$$

$$18\frac{h}{w} \leq t \leq 27\frac{h}{w}$$

Slope and *y*-Intercept Word Problems

These word problems will combine the description of a real-world scenario with its graphical representation. You will be asked to determine the meaning of the slope and the meaning of the *y*-intercept. Use the labels on the axes to determine these meanings. The **slope** will be the amount of change in the data plotted on the *y*-axis over the amount of change in the data plotted on the *x*-axis. The ***y*-intercept** will be the quantity of the data plotted on the *y*-axis that you started with.

You can solve equation word problems with the same approach:

Step 1: Determine what the *y*-axis represents.

Step 2: Determine what the *x*-axis represents.

Step 3: Identify the units and meaning of the slope.

Step 4: Determine what the *y*-intercept represents.

Try It Out! **Work through the following sample question.**

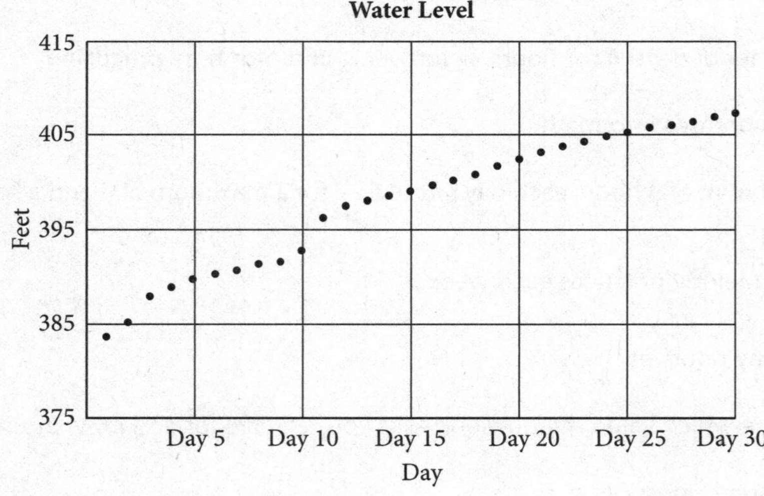

The graph above shows the daily water level, in feet, for a reservoir in northern California. What do the slope and the *y*-intercept most likely represent?

✔ **Helpful Hint**

Do not spend time calculating the slope or the *y*-intercept. Focus only on the information you need to answer the question.

Step 1: Determine what the *y*-axis represents.

Water level in feet

Step 2: Determine what the *x*-axis represents.

The day

Step 3: Identify the units and meaning of the slope.

If the slope of a line is $\frac{\text{change in } y}{\text{change in } x}$, the units of the slope are $\frac{\text{feet}}{\text{day}}$.

The slope means the rate at which the water level is changing.

Step 4: Determine what the *y*-intercept represents.

The *y*-intercept represents how much "*y*" was already present when the measuring started, which in this case is the water level in feet already in the reservoir on the first day of measuring.

Try It Out! **Work through the following multiple-choice question.**

A bicyclist is riding on a section of road that drops in elevation by 2 meters for every 100 meters along the length of the road. If the road is at 1,000 meters when it begins to drop, and the bicyclist is traveling at 4 meters per second, what is the elevation 200 seconds after the road begins to descend?

A) 996

B) 984

C) 960

D) 840

Step 1: Define variables with appropriate letters.

Meters = m, Time = s, Rate = $\frac{m}{s}$

Step 2: Translate phrases into math.

Elevation at start: 1,000 m

Drop means *subtract*

Rate of elevation change: $\frac{2\,m}{100\,m}$

Bicyclist's rate: $4\frac{m}{s}$

Time: $200\,s$

Steps 3 and 4: Determine which value the question asks you to solve for and in what units. Then, set up an equation and solve.

Solve for the new elevation in meters by subtracting the change in elevation from the beginning elevation:

1,000 *m* – *change in elevation*

Solve for the change in elevation by calculating how far the cyclist rides in 200 seconds:

$$4\frac{m}{s} \times 200\,s = 800\,m$$

Multiply that by the rate of change for the elevation:

$$800\,m \times \frac{2\,m}{100\,m} = 16\,m$$

Plug that into the expression above:

$$1{,}000\,m - 16\,m = 984\,m$$

This worked solution would resemble the following:

A bicyclist is riding on a section of road that drops in elevation by 2 meters for every 100 meters along the length of the road. If the road is at 1,000 meters when it begins to drop, and the bicyclist is traveling at 4 meters per second, what is the elevation 200 seconds after the road begins to descend?

A) 996

B) 984

C) 960

D) 840

Straightforward math:

$$4\frac{m}{s} \times 200\,s = 800\,m$$

$$800\,m \times \frac{2\,m}{100\,m} = 16\,m$$

$$1{,}000\,m - 16\,m = 984\,m$$

Use the Kaplan Method to answer the following questions. Use the hints provided as needed.

1. The monthly overhead at Carla's bicycle repair shop consists of $1,000 for rent, $25 for insurance, $35 for advertising, $90 for self-employment tax, and $100 for utilities. If she charges $25 per hour for her repair labor, how many hours per month must Carla work to pay the overhead on her shop?

   A) 30

   B) 40

   C) 50

   D) 60

hint *Break the sentences into small phrases and translate them into math.*

2. Alyssa is buying new tires for her car. If tires that fit her car range in price from $79 plus 8% sales tax per tire to $105 plus 8% sales tax per tire, what is the least and greatest amounts she can pay for her tires?

   A) $252.80 to $336.00

   B) $316.00 to $420.00

   C) $322.32 to $428.40

   D) $341.28 to $453.60

hint *Set this up as an inequality:*
4(lowest cost tire) + sales tax
≤ Total cost ≤ 4(greatest cost tire)
+ sales tax

3. Amanda teaches a coding class on the weekend at the local community college. The college charges her a flat fee for the computer lab plus a per computer rental rate for each computer used. If Amanda's total costs, as a function of the number of computers used, were plotted on a graph, what would the y-intercept represent?

   A) The computer rental rate

   B) The fee for the computer lab

   C) The total number of computers rented

   D) The average cost per student

hint *The y-intercept represents the amount of y before any change in x. What must Amanda pay even before she enrolls any students?*

Use the Kaplan Method to answer the following questions on your own.

1. Joelle plans to install solar panels in her home to provide her electricity. Currently, her home consumes 48 kWh (kilowatt hours) per day. The sunlight striking her home each day averages 6 kWh per meter squared and the solar panels are able to convert 15% of the sunlight into electricity. How many square meters of solar panels does Joelle need?

A) 9.5

B) 12

C) 43.2

D) 53.3

2. Jamal's greenhouse must maintain a temperature between 58°F and 82°F for optimal plant growth. He can set his temperature monitor in 5°F increments to send him an alert if the temperature is too low or too high. What settings should Jamal use to protect his plants?

A) ≤ 55°F or ≥ 85°F

B) ≥ 55°F or ≤ 85°F

C) ≤ 60°F or ≥ 80°F

D) ≥ 60°F or ≤ 80°F

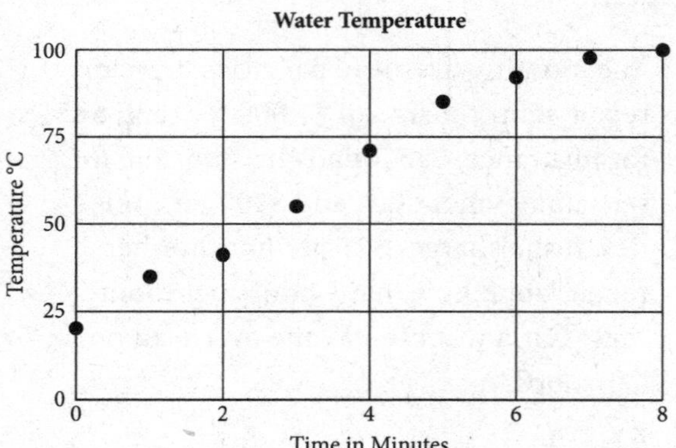

3. The figure above shows the temperature of water over time as it is heated. What does the y-intercept represent?

A) The temperature of the water before it was heated

B) The rate at which the water warmed

C) The freezing point of water

D) The length of time the water was heated

Use the Kaplan Method to answer the following questions for homework.

1. A packaging machine fills an average of 72 bags per minute. Each bag requires 12 inches of packaging film. Which equation expresses the number of feet needed per hour?

A) $\left(72\frac{\text{bags}}{\text{minute}} \times 60\frac{\text{minutes}}{\text{hour}}\right) \times \left(12\frac{\text{inches}}{\text{bag}} \times 12\frac{\text{inches}}{\text{foot}}\right)$

B) $\left(72\frac{\text{bags}}{\text{minute}} \times 60\frac{\text{minutes}}{\text{hour}}\right) \times \left(12\frac{\text{inches}}{\text{bag}} \times \frac{1 \text{ foot}}{12 \text{ inches}}\right)$

C) $\dfrac{\left(72\frac{\text{bags}}{\text{minute}} \times 60\frac{\text{minutes}}{\text{hour}}\right)}{\left(12\frac{\text{inches}}{\text{bag}} \times 12\frac{\text{inches}}{\text{foot}}\right)}$

D) $\dfrac{\left(72\frac{\text{bags}}{\text{minute}}\right)}{\left(60\frac{\text{minutes}}{\text{hour}}\right)} \times \left(12\frac{\text{inches}}{\text{bag}} \times 12\frac{\text{inches}}{\text{foot}}\right)$

2. Ben's robotics team wants to order T-shirts before the robotics competition. A local silk screener will print the shirts for \$5 per shirt with a minimum of 5 shirts. If the team has saved \$43 for the shirts, which inequality expresses the number of shirts, s, Ben's team can order?

A) $5 < s \leq 9$

B) $5 \leq s \leq 8$

C) $5 > s > 9$

D) $5 \geq s \geq 8$

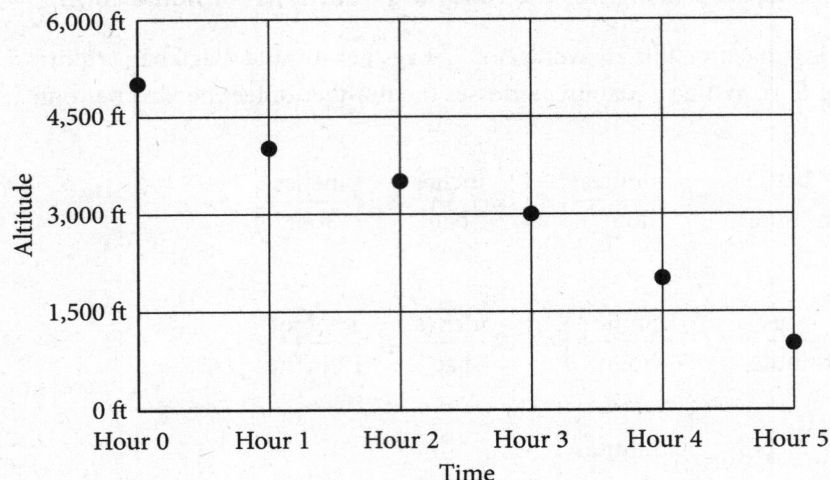

3. The figure above tracks the descent by two hikers to their campsite. What does the slope of the line represent?

   A) The altitude when they began to descend

   B) The time when they began to descend

   C) The rate of their descent

   D) The total time they descended

The following questions are similar to what you would encounter on a college admissions test such as the SAT or ACT. Apply the Kaplan Method and your knowledge of word problems to answer the following questions.

1. A freight company charges a flat fee of \$9.00 for insurance and \$3.00 per pound to ship a package. If it costs \$60.00 to ship a package, how many pounds does the package weigh?

   A) 5

   B) 12

   C) 17

   D) 20

2. Franklin pumps water from his well to his storage tank. The pump starts when there are 50 gallons in the tank and stops when there are 500 gallons in the tank. If the length of time it takes to fill the pump varies between 3 and 5 hours, which inequality expresses the rate, r, in gallons per hour at which the pump fills the tank?

   A) $50 \leq r \leq 500$

   B) $50 < r < 500$

   C) $90 \leq r \leq 150$

   D) $90 < r < 150$

UNIT TWO

Algebra

IN THIS UNIT, YOU WILL LEARN HOW TO:

1. Apply the rules of exponents and roots
2. Simplify polynomial expressions
3. Interpret function notation
4. Solve quadratic equations
5. Solve systems of linear quadratic equations

CHAPTER 11

Exponents and Roots

CHAPTER OBJECTIVES

By the end of this chapter, you will be able to:

1. Apply the rules of positive and negative exponents to solving problems
2. Manipulate expressions containing roots

THE KAPLAN METHOD FOR MATH

Step 1: Read the question, identifying and organizing important information as you go

- What information am I given?
- Separate the question from the context.
- How are the answer choices written?
- Should you label or draw a diagram?

Step 2: Choose the best strategy to answer the question

- Look for patterns.
- Pick numbers or use straightforward math.

Step 3: Check that you answered the *right* question

- Review the question stem.
- Check units of measurement.
- Double-check your work.

EXPONENTS AND ROOTS

Properties of Exponents

Just as multiplication is a shorthand notation for addition ($x + x + x + x + x = 5x$), exponents are a shorthand notation for multiplication ($x \cdot x \cdot x \cdot x \cdot x = x^5$). In the expression x^5, x is the **base** and 5 is the **power**.

The expression y^7 is "y **raised** to the seventh power," which can also be represented as $y \cdot y \cdot y \cdot y \cdot y \cdot y \cdot y$.

Exponent Rules

When multiplying the same bases raised to powers, add the exponents.

$$a^b \times a^c = a^{b+c}$$
$$4^2 \times 4^3 = 4^{2+3} = 4^5$$
$$(4 \times 4)(4 \times 4 \times 4) = (4 \times 4 \times 4 \times 4 \times 4) = 4^5$$

This rule helps explain **fractional exponents.**

$$a^{\frac{b}{c}} = \sqrt[c]{a^b}$$
$$a^{\frac{1}{2}} \times a^{\frac{1}{2}} = a^{\frac{1}{2}+\frac{1}{2}} = a^1 = \sqrt{a} \times \sqrt{a} \Rightarrow a^{\frac{1}{2}} = \sqrt[2]{a^1}$$
$$4^{\frac{3}{2}} = \sqrt[2]{4^3} = \sqrt{64} = 8$$
$$4^{\frac{1}{2}} \times 4^{\frac{1}{2}} \times 4^{\frac{1}{2}} = \sqrt{4} \times \sqrt{4} \times \sqrt{4} = 2 \times 2 \times 2 = 8$$

When dividing the same bases raised to powers, subtract the exponents.

$$\frac{a^b}{a^c} = a^{b-c}$$
$$\frac{4^3}{4^2} = 4^{3-2} = 4^1$$
$$\frac{4 \times 4 \times 4}{4 \times 4} = 4$$

This rule helps explain **negative exponents.**

$$a^{-b} = \frac{1}{a^b}$$
$$\frac{4^2}{4^5} = 4^{2-5} = 4^{-3}$$
$$\frac{4 \times 4}{4 \times 4 \times 4 \times 4 \times 4} = \frac{1}{4^3} = 4^{-3}$$

The exponent subtraction rule also helps explain why any nonzero number raised to the zero power is 1.

$$\frac{a^b}{a^b} = a^{b-b} = a^0 = 1$$

$$\frac{4^2}{4^2} = 4^{2-2} = 4^0 = 1$$

When multiplying or dividing different bases raised to the same power, perform the multiplication or division and raise the result to the power.

$$a^c \times b^c = (ab)^c$$

$$2^2 \times 3^2 = (2 \times 2)(3 \times 3) = (2 \times 3)(2 \times 3) = (2 \times 3)^2 = 6^2 = 36$$

$$\frac{a^c}{b^c} = \left(\frac{a}{b}\right)^c$$

$$\frac{6^3}{3^3} = \frac{6}{3} \times \frac{6}{3} \times \frac{6}{3} = \left(\frac{6}{3}\right)^3 = 2^3 = 8$$

When a base is raised to a power, and that entire quantity is raised to another power, multiply the exponents.

$$(a^b)^c = a^{b \times c}$$

$$(2^3)^2 = (2 \times 2 \times 2)(2 \times 2 \times 2) = 2^6 = 64$$

✔ Helpful Hint

If you are unsure about an exponent rule, expand the expression and follow the rules for multiplication and division.

Properties of Roots

The **square root** of a number is the **nonnegative** number whose square equals the number under the square root symbol (also known as the radical sign).

$\sqrt{16} = 4$ because $4^2 = 16$

If $a^2 = 81$, then $a = 9$ or $a = -9$

$\sqrt{81} = 9$ only

The **cube root** of a number is the **negative** or **nonnegative** number whose cube equals the number under the cube root symbol.

$\sqrt[3]{27} = 3$ because $3^3 = 27$

$\sqrt[3]{-27} = -3$ because $(-3)^3 = -27$

Factor and simplify to solve complicated root questions.

$$\frac{\sqrt{a^2b}}{\sqrt{ab^2}} = \sqrt{\frac{a^2b}{ab^2}} = \sqrt{\frac{a}{b}}$$

$$\frac{\sqrt{75}}{\sqrt{12}} = \sqrt{\frac{75}{12}} = \sqrt{\frac{25 \times 3}{4 \times 3}} = \sqrt{\frac{25}{4}} \times \sqrt{\frac{3}{3}} = \frac{5}{2} \times 1 = \frac{5}{2}$$

✔ Helpful Hint

Always factor and simplify complicated root questions as your first step.

Try It Out! **Work through the following multiple-choice question.**

The expression $\sqrt{\frac{72}{108}}$ is equivalent to which of the following?

A) $\frac{1}{3}$

B) $\sqrt{\frac{1}{3}}$

C) $\frac{2}{3}$

D) $\sqrt{\frac{2}{3}}$

Step 1: Factor the numbers under the square root symbol.

$$\sqrt{\frac{8\times 9}{4\times 27}}=\sqrt{\frac{2^3\times 3^2}{2^2\times 3^3}}$$

Step 2: Simplify.

$$\sqrt{\frac{2^3\times 3^2}{2^2\times 3^3}}=\sqrt{\frac{2\times 2\times 2\times 3\times 3}{2\times 2\times 3\times 3\times 3}}=\sqrt{\frac{2}{3}}$$

This worked solution would resemble the following:

The expression $\sqrt{\frac{72}{108}}$ is equivalent to which of the following?

A) $\frac{1}{3}$

B) $\sqrt{\frac{1}{3}}$

C) $\frac{2}{3}$

D) $\sqrt{\frac{2}{3}}$

Straightforward math:

$$\sqrt{\frac{8\times 9}{4\times 27}}=\sqrt{\frac{2^3\times 3^2}{2^2\times 3^3}}=\sqrt{\frac{2}{3}}$$

Use your calculator to check your answer:

$$\sqrt{\frac{72}{108}}=\sqrt{0.667}=\sqrt{\frac{2}{3}}\ \checkmark$$

Use the Kaplan Method to answer the following questions. Use the hints provided as needed.

1. If $p^3 \times p^n = p^7$, n is equal to what value?

A) $\frac{7}{3}$

B) 4

C) 7

D) 10

hint *Follow the rule for adding exponents when the same base is raised to different powers.*

2. For all nonzero values of x, $\frac{(2x^2)^{-2}(20x^5)}{\sqrt{25x^4}} = ?$

A) $\frac{x}{5}$

B) $4x^7$

C) $\frac{1}{x^2}$

D) $\frac{1}{x}$

hint *Pay close attention to the exponents' signs. Factor and simplify the denominator.*

3. Which of the following is equivalent to $\frac{4\sqrt{2} \times 5\sqrt{6} - 13\sqrt{3}}{3}$?

A) $\frac{7\sqrt{3}}{3}$

B) $\frac{10\sqrt{3}}{3}$

C) $9\sqrt{3}$

D) 27

hint *When adding or subtracting, treat the radical sign like a variable:* $2x + 3x + 2y - 5y = 5x - 3y$ *and* $2\sqrt{7} + 3\sqrt{7} + 2\sqrt{3} - 5\sqrt{3} = 5\sqrt{7} - 3\sqrt{3}$.

Use the Kaplan Method to answer the following questions on your own.

1. What does $3x^3 \cdot 5x^2y^4 \cdot 2x^{-7}y^2 \cdot 2^{-2}y^3$ equal?

   A) $6x^{12}y^9$

   B) $\frac{6y^9}{x^2}$

   C) $\frac{15y^9}{2x^2}$

   D) $\frac{15y^9}{x^2}$

2. If x is a real number such that $x^3 = 64$, then

   $\frac{x^2}{\sqrt{x}} = ?$

   A) 2

   B) 4

   C) 8

   D) 16

3. Which real number satisfies $(3^n)(27) = 9^4$?

   A) 3

   B) 5

   C) 7

   D) 9

Use the Kaplan Method to answer the following questions for homework.

1. If $t^5 = \frac{t^3}{t^x}$, x is equal to what value?

   A) −2

   B) −1

   C) 2

   D) 8

2. What is the value of $\left(12^{\frac{3}{2}}\right)^{\frac{1}{3}}$?

   A) $\frac{1}{4\sqrt{3}}$

   B) $\frac{1}{2\sqrt{3}}$

   C) $2\sqrt{3}$

   D) $4\sqrt{3}$

3. If $2\sqrt{7} = y + 3$, what is the value of $(y + 3)^2$?

   A) 28

   B) 31

   C) 98

   D) 196

The following questions are similar to what you would encounter on a college admissions test such as the SAT or ACT. Apply the Kaplan Method and your knowledge of exponents and roots to answer the following questions.

1. Which expression is equivalent to $\dfrac{(6xy^2z^4)(3x^{-1}z^3)^{-2}}{(xy^5z^{-4})}$?

   A) $\dfrac{2x^4z^{-6}}{3y^3}$

   B) $\dfrac{2x^4z^2}{3y^3}$

   C) $\dfrac{2x^4z^{-6}}{y^3}$

   D) $\dfrac{2x^2z^2}{3y^3}$

2. Which expression is equivalent to $(x^{\frac{1}{3}})(\sqrt{x})$?

   A) $x^{\frac{1}{6}}$
   B) $x^{\frac{1}{5}}$
   C) $x^{\frac{5}{6}}$
   D) $x^{\frac{6}{5}}$

CHAPTER 12

Polynomial Operations

CHAPTER OBJECTIVES

By the end of this chapter, you will be able to:

1. Add and subtract polynomials by combining like terms
2. Multiply polynomials
3. Perform polynomial long division

THE KAPLAN METHOD FOR MATH

Step 1: Read the question, identifying and organizing important information as you go

- What information am I given?
- Separate the question from the context.
- How are the answer choices written?
- Should you label or draw a diagram?

Step 2: Choose the best strategy to answer the question

- Look for patterns.
- Pick numbers or use straightforward math.

Step 3: Check that you answered the *right* question

- Review the question stem.
- Check units of measurement.
- Double-check your work.

12

POLYNOMIAL

A **polynomial** is an expression consisting of variables, nonnegative whole number exponents, and constants. A **term** in a polynomial can be a constant, a variable, the product of a constant and one or more variables, or the product of a variable and one or more variables. The different terms in a polynomial are separated by the "+" and "–" operators. All terms may be multiplied, but only **like terms** can be added or subtracted.

Terms	Operation	Result
$3, x, x, y$	$3 \cdot x \cdot x \cdot y$	$3x^2y$
$3, x, x, y$	$3 + x + x + y$	$3 + 2x + y$

Polynomials can be named based on the **number** of terms in the polynomial. Polynomials also can be named based on **degree**. To find the degree of a polynomial, find the sum of the values of the exponents on each term. The term with the greatest sum names the polynomial. In the polynomial $x^3y^2 + x^4 + 2$, the exponents on the first term add to 5, on the second term to 4, and on the third term to 0 (think of the constant 2 as $2x^0$). As a result, this is a **fifth-degree** polynomial.

Terms	Name	Example	Degree
1	monomial	$5x^3y^2z$	$0 + 3 + 2 + 1 = $ 6th degree
2	binomial	$5x^3y^2 + z$	$0 + 3 + 2 = $ 5th degree
3	trinomial	$5x^3 + y^2 - z$	$0 + 3 = $ 3rd degree

Adding and Subtracting Polynomials

Polynomial expressions can sometimes be simplified by adding and subtracting terms that have the same variables raised to the same power, which is called **combining like terms.** In chapter 4, you combined like terms as a first step to solving linear equations. The same rules apply to polynomials, though the terms might look a little more complicated. To determine if two terms are like terms, match each variable and its exponent in one term to each variable and its exponent in the other term.

Try It Out! **Apply the same approach to answer the following question.**

If $D = 15x^2y + 10$ and $E = 7x^2y - 3$, $D - E$ is equal to which of the following expressions?

A) $8x^4y^2 + 7$

B) $8x^2y + 13$

C) $22x^2y + 7$

D) $22x^4y^2 + 13$

Step 1: Substitute the given expressions for D and E.

$$D - E = 15x^2y + 10 - (7x^2y - 3)$$

✔ Helpful Hint

When subtracting polynomials, be very careful to distribute the negative sign.

Step 2: Distribute the negative to each of the terms inside the parentheses.

$$D - E = 15x^2y + 10 - 7x^2y + 3$$

Step 3: Simplify by combining like terms.

$$D - E = 15x^2y - 7x^2y + 10 + 3 = 8x^2y + 13$$

Choice (B) is correct.

Multiplying Polynomials

Multiplying polynomials is just like multiplying integers:

$5 \cdot 5 = 5^2$ and $x \cdot x = x^2$

$5(y + 5) = 5y + 25$ and $x(y + 5) = xy + 5x$

When multiplying polynomials with two or more terms, pay close attention to distribution and combining like terms. To multiply the polynomials $(2x^2 - 4)(3x^3 - x^2 + 5)$, distribute the first term in the first polynomial over each term in the second polynomial, and then repeat the process with the second term:

$2x^2(3x^3 - x + 5) - 4(3x^3 - x^2 + 5)$

$2x^2(3x^3) + 2x^2(-x) + 2x^2(5) - 4(3x^3) - 4(-x^2) - 4(5)$

$6x^5 - 2x^3 + 10x^2 - 12x^3 + 4x^2 - 20$

$6x^5 - 2x^3 - 12x^3 + 10x^2 + 4x^2 - 20$

$6x^5 - 14x^3 + 14x^2 - 20$

A second-degree polynomial is called a quadratic. Quadratics can be created by multiplying two first-degree binomials together. To properly multiply two binomials, you need to apply the FOIL method. FOIL stands for First, Outer, Inner, Last.

First Outer Inner Last

$(x + 3)(x + 2) = (x)(x) + (x)(2) + (3)(x) + (3)(2)$

$(x + 3)(x + 2) = x^2 + 2x + 3x + 6$

$2x$ and $3x$ are **like terms**, because they are both multiples of the variable x. Because they are like terms, you can combine them by adding their coefficients, creating a single term, $5x$.

$(x + 3)(x + 2) = x^2 + 5x + 6$

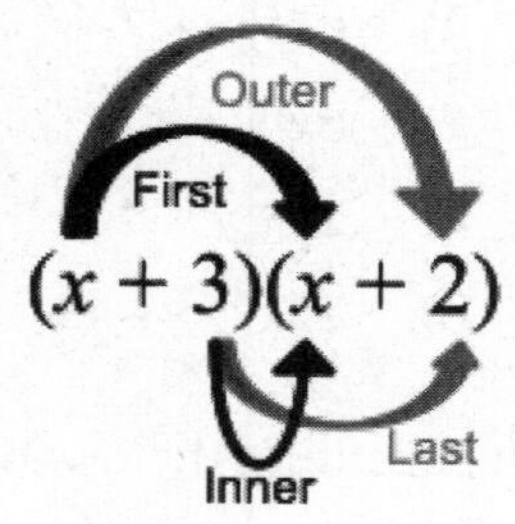

Dividing Polynomials

Adding, subtracting, and multiplying polynomials are all straightforward processes. Dividing polynomials can be a bit more complicated and time-consuming when it requires polynomial long division. Polynomial long division uses the same process as regular long division, only instead of numbers, you will divide polynomials.

Try It Out! **Work through the following multiple-choice question.**

Which of the following is equal to $\frac{z^3 - 12z + 16}{z + 4}$?

A) $z^2 - 4z - 4$

B) $z^2 + 4z - 4$

C) $z^2 - 4z + 4$

D) $z^2 + 4z + 4$

Step 1: Organize the terms as long division.

$$z + 4\overline{\big)\, z^3 + 0z^2 - 12z + 16}$$

hint *Adding the placeholder $0z^2$ helps keep track of your place.*

Step 2: Divide the first term under the division sign (the dividend) by the first term (z) of the divisor ($z + 4$). Multiply the quotient (z^2) by the whole divisor ($z + 4$) and subtract.

$$
\begin{array}{r|l}
 & z^2 \\
\hline
z+4 & z^3 + 0z^2 - 12z + 16 \\
 & \underline{-(z^3 + 4z^2)} \\
 & \quad -4z^2
\end{array}
$$

Step 3: Bring down the 3rd term in the dividend ($-12z$). Divide the resulting term ($-4z^2 - 12z$) by the first term (z) of the divisor ($z + 4$). Multiply the quotient ($-4z$) by the whole divisor ($z + 4$) and subtract.

$$
\begin{array}{r|l}
 & z^2 - 4z \\
\hline
z+4 & z^3 + 0z^2 - 12z + 16 \\
 & \underline{-(z^3 + 4z^2)} \downarrow \\
 & \quad -4z^2 - 12z \\
 & \quad \underline{-(-4z^2 - 16z)} \\
 & \qquad\quad +4z
\end{array}
$$

Step 4: Bring down the 4th term in the dividend (16). Divide the resulting term ($4z + 16$) by the first term (z) of the divisor ($z + 4$). Multiply the quotient ($+4$) by the whole divisor ($z + 4$) and subtract.

$$
\begin{array}{r|l}
 & z^2 - 4z + 4 \\
\hline
z+4 & z^3 + 0z^2 - 12z + 16 \\
 & \underline{-(z^3 + 4z^2)} \quad \downarrow \\
 & \quad -4z^2 - 12z \\
 & \quad \underline{-(-4z^2 - 16z)} \\
 & \qquad\quad +4z + 16 \\
 & \qquad\quad \underline{-(4z + 16)} \\
 & \qquad\qquad\quad 0
\end{array}
$$

Choice (C) is correct.

Use the Kaplan Method to answer the following questions. Use the hints provided as needed.

1. Simplify $(x + 3)(x - 1)$.

   A) $x^2 + 3x + 3$

   B) $x^2 + 2x - 3$

   C) $2x^2 + 3x + 1$

   D) $x^2 - 3x - 1$

hint *Be careful with the negative sign in the second binomial.*

2. Simplify $(7x^4 - 10x^3 + 3x^2 + 3x - 3) \div (x - 1)$.

   A) $(7x^2 + 3x - 3)$

   B) $(7x^2 + 3x + 3)$

   C) $(7x^3 + 3x^2 - 3)$

   D) $(7x^3 - 3x^2 + 3)$

hint *Use polynomial long division.*

3. Simplify $(x + 3)(x - 2) + (2x + 1)(x + 1)$.

   A) $3x^2 + 4x - 5$

   B) $x^2 + 7x + 1$

   C) $2x^2 + 4x + 7$

   D) $3x^2 + 2x - 8$

hint *Because this question has two binomial products, perform each FOIL operation separately and then combine like terms.*

Use the Kaplan Method to answer the following questions on your own.

1. Simplify $3x^2 + 7x + 9 - 2x - 4 - 4x^2$.
   A) $x^2 + 7x - 3$
   B) $-2x^2 + 4x + 5$
   C) $-x^2 + 5x + 5$
   D) $3x^2 + 2x - 2$
2. Simplify $(3 + x)(x + 4)$.
   A) $x^2 + 7x + 12$
   B) $x^2 + 12x + 7$
   C) $3x^2 + 4x + 3$
   D) $4x^2 + 7x + 12$
3. Simplify $(27x^3 + 9x^2 - 3x - 10) \div (3x - 2)$.
   A) $9x^2 + 3x + 5$
   B) $9x^2 + 3x + 7$
   C) $9x^2 + 9x + 5$
   D) $9x^2 + 9x + 7$

Use the Kaplan Method to answer the following questions for homework.

1. What is $x^2 - 49$ divided by $x - 7$?

   A) $x - 7$

   B) $x + 7$

   C) $x^2 - 7$

   D) $x^2 + 7$

2. What is $3x^3 - 6x^2 - 9x$ divided by $3x$?

   A) $x^2 - 2x - 3$

   B) $3x^3 - 6x - 3$

   C) $x^2 + 2x - 6$

   D) $2x^2 - 3x - 9$

3. Simplify $(x + 3)(x - 5) + (x + 1)(x + 2)$.

   A) $x^2 - x - 13$

   B) $2x^2 + x + 17$

   C) $2x^2 + x - 13$

   D) $3x^2 + x - 13$

The following questions are similar to what you would encounter on a college admissions test such as the SAT or ACT. Apply the Kaplan Method and your knowledge of polynomial operations to answer the following questions.

1. Which of the following polynomials yields $11x + 2$ when divided by $2x$?

   A) $2x^4 - 6x - 10$

   B) $14x - 6x^2$

   C) $4x + 22x^2$

   D) $10x - 2x^2 + 12x^3$

2. Simplify $(x + 3)(1 - x) + (2 + x)(x + 3) - x(x + 9)$.

   A) $9 - 6x - x^2$

   B) $x^2 - 12x + 3$

   C) $3 - x^2 - 6x$

   D) $-x^2 - 5x + 3$

13

CHAPTER 13

Understanding Linear Functions

CHAPTER OBJECTIVES

By the end of this chapter, you will be able to:

1. Interpret linear function notation algebraically
2. Interpret linear function notation graphically

THE KAPLAN METHOD FOR MATH

Step 1: Read the question, identifying and organizing important information as you go

- What information am I given?
- Separate the question from the context.
- How are the answer choices written?
- Should you label or draw a diagram?

Step 2: Choose the best strategy to answer the question

- Look for patterns.
- Pick numbers or use straightforward math.

Step 3: Check that you answered the *right* question

- Review the question stem.
- Check units of measurement.
- Double-check your work.

FUNCTIONS

A **function** operates like an instruction book that gives the rules on how to transform a group of **inputs** into a group of **outputs**. In a function, each input must produce one and only one corresponding output.

13

For example, if you and your friends are deciding whether or not to see a movie, the potential total ticket cost for your group can be represented by a function.

What are some possible inputs? ____

What are some possible outputs? ____

The following table summarizes a few possible inputs and the resulting outputs:

Number of people	Total ticket cost
0	0
1	8
2	16
3	24

The table shows that the output is always \$8 times the input. You can express this relationship in words such as: "the total ticket cost *is a function of* (depends on) the number of people attending" or algebraically as: $f(x) = 8x$ where x is the number of people and $f(x)$ is the total cost.

Domain: The possible inputs are called the **domain** of the function. Sometimes the question will define the domain: x is an integer. Other times, the real-world situation will define the domain. For example, in the function for the ticket cost where x equals the number of people attending, the domain cannot include negative numbers or non-integers.

Range: The **range** of a function includes all the possible outputs of the function, which depend on the domain, and is written as $f(x)$.

✔ Helpful Hint

Functions are often notated as $f(x)$ but can be notated in many other ways such as $g(x)$, $h(t)$, and $f(s)$, to name a few. Don't worry if a question uses something other than $f(x)$ to notate a function. Treat the function as you would any other.

13

SOLVING FUNCTION QUESTIONS

To solve a function question, apply the rules of the function to the input. In the movie-ticket example, the total ticket cost for a group of friends to see a movie can be modeled by the function $f(x) = 8x$. If 4 people attend the movie, you can substitute 4 for x and evaluate the expression $f(x) = 8x$. This is written as $f(4) = 8(4) = 32$.

What is the total ticket cost if 7 friends attend the movie?

Substitute the input into the function and evaluate: $f(\ ) = 8(\ ) =$ ________.

RATE OF CHANGE

The **rate of change** determines how much $f(x)$ changes per unit of x and is written as k.

Initial quantity: The **initial quantity** is the value of the output when the input is 0 and is written as $f(0)$. When graphed, the initial quantity equals the y-intercept. The standard format for a linear function is written as $f(x) = kx + f(0)$ and is a variation of the **equation of a line** written in the **slope-intercept form**, $y = mx + b$.

The following table compares elements of the two ways to represent a linear relationship:

Linear function $f(x) = kx + f(0)$	What it is	Slope-intercept $y = mx + b$
x	input or independent variable	x
$f(x)$	output or dependent variable	y
k	rate of change or slope	m
$f(0)$	initial quantity or y-intercept	b

Follow the prompts below to determine the parts of the function and derive its equation.

Luc and Javier are renting a 10-seater bus to take them and some friends to see a soccer playoff game. The nonrefundable rental fee for the bus and driver is \$40.00, and each ticket costs \$15.00.

A. Determine the input or independent variable

- What number can change and, as a result, change the output? ________________

B. Determine the rate of change for the function

- For each unit of input, how much will the output change? ________________

C. Determine the initial quantity

- How much will Luc and Javier pay even if the game is cancelled? ________________

D. What is the domain of the function?

- What is the maximum number of paying passengers on the bus? ________________
- What is the minimum number of paying passengers on the bus? ________________

E. Derive the equation for this function:

13

- Output = (rate of change)(input) + initial quantity
- $f(x) = k(x) + f(0)$ ________________________________

F. Determine the range of this function by plugging in the minimum and maximum inputs:

- $f(0)$ = minimum and $f(10)$ = maximum ________________________

✔ Helpful Hint

A function is are a form of equation. Follow the Order of Operations and the Cardinal Rule of Equations if you need to rearrange a function to solve for an unknown quantity.

USING FUNCTIONS TO SOLVE REAL-WORLD QUESTIONS

Functions, like equations, can be used to understand real-world situations. For example, Carli can choose between two different cell phone plans. One plan charges a monthly connection fee of \$30.00 per month and \$0.05 per minute of cell phone use. The other plan has no connection fee and charges \$0.20 per minute of cell phone use. Which plan will cost Carli less money based on the number of minutes she uses?

Use a table to derive the equation for each function:

Plan	Independent Variable	Rate of Change	Initial Quantity	Function
Fee	time t	\$0.05/min	\$30.00	$f(t) = 0.05t + 30$
No-fee	time t	\$0.20/min	\$0.00	$n(t) = 0.20t$

Determine the value of *t* when both plans cost the same amount:

A. The plans cost the same amount when the output of each function is the same

- When $f(t) = n(t)$
- In other words, when $0.20t = 0.05t + 30$

B. Solve for t in the equation: $0.20t = 0.05t + 30$

- Subtract $0.05t$ from both sides of the equation: $0.20t - 0.05t = 0.05t - 0.05t + 30 \Rightarrow 0.15t = 30$
- Divide both sides by 0.15: $\frac{0.15t}{0.15} = \frac{30}{0.15} \Rightarrow t = 200$

Define the domain of *t* for each function that produces the lowest monthly cost for Carli:

- The no-fee plan doesn't cost Carli anything if she doesn't use her phone and costs less than the fee plan if she uses less than 200 minutes:
  - If Carli never uses more than 200 minutes per month, she should choose the no-fee plan when the domain of t is defined as $0 \leq t \leq 200$.
- The fee plan costs Carli less if she uses more than 200 minutes:
  - If Carli always uses at least 200 minutes per month, she should choose the fee plan when the domain of t is defined as $t \geq 200$.

13

COMPOSITION FUNCTIONS

Sometimes the input of one function is the output of another function. This is referred to as a **composition function** and can be written as $f(g(x))$. You say that as "*f* of *g* of *x*." In a composition function question, you will be given the different functions and the value of the input of the inner function:

If $f(x) = 2x + 7$ and $g(x) = 3x - 2$, what is the value of $f(g(2))$?

- Plug the input $x = 2$ into the inner function: $g(2) = 3(2) - 2 \Rightarrow g(2) = 4$
- Substitute the output of the inner function for $g(2)$ in the nested function: $f(g(2)) = f(4)$
- Evaluate the outer function at $x = 4$: $f(4) = 2(4) + 7 = 15$

13

GRAPHING LINEAR FUNCTIONS

Linear functions can be graphed in the same way as linear equations. Representing the pairs of **inputs** and **outputs** of a function visually makes it easier to understand how the function behaves. Graphs can be especially useful when comparing different functions. Because the **input** is changed purposely, it is the *independent variable* and is plotted on the x-axis. The resultant **output** is called the *dependent variable* and is plotted on the y-axis.

Take another look at the earlier question about cell phone plans by representing each plan graphically:

Carli can choose between two different cell phone plans. One plan charges a monthly connection fee of \$30.00 per month and \$0.05 per minute of cell phone use. The other plan has no connection fee and charges \$0.20 per minute of cell phone use. Which plan will cost Carli less money based on the number of minutes she uses?

Set up an x–y table for each function.

Because the **output** (monthly cost) of the function **depends** on the number of minutes Carli uses her phone, plot the monthly cost on the y-axis.

$f(t) = 0.05t + 30$		$n(t) = 0.20t$	
x-axis	**y-axis**	**x-axis**	**y-axis**
t	$f(t)$	t	$n(t)$
0	30	0	0
200	40	200	40
400	50	400	80

Plot those points on a graph.

The intersection of the lines shows the number of minutes at which the no-fee plan becomes more expensive than the fee plan.

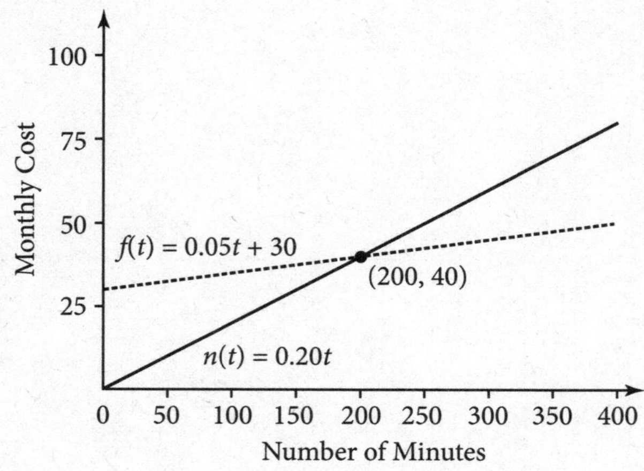

TRANSFORMATIONS OF FUNCTIONS

The graph of a function is **transformed** when a constant is added to or subtracted from either the input or the output.

- Take the function $f(x) = 2x$, which graphs as a straight line with a slope of 2 and a y-intercept of 0.
- When the constant 1 is added to the output, or the range, of the function, the new function becomes $f(x) = 2x + 1$, and the graph of the function moves up one unit making the y-intercept 1.
- When the constant 1 is subtracted from the output, or the range, of the function, the new function becomes $f(x) = 2x - 1$, and the graph of the function moves down one unit making the y-intercept –1.

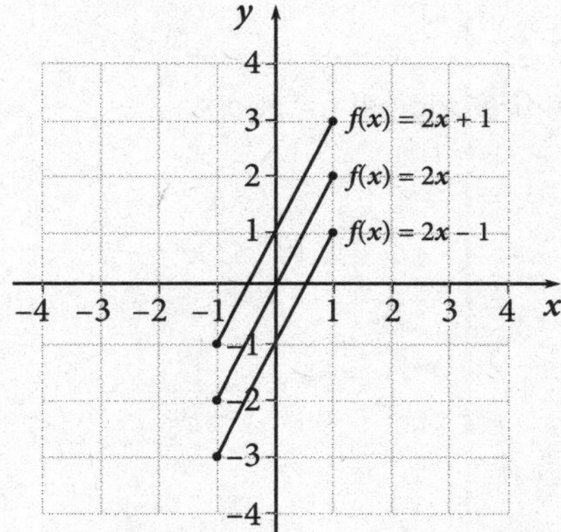

- When the constant 1 is added to the input, or the domain, of the function, the new function becomes $f(x) = 2(x + 1)$, and the graph of the function moves to the left one unit.
- When the constant 1 is subtracted from the input, or the domain, of the function, the new function becomes $f(x) = 2(x - 1)$, and the graph of the function moves to the right one unit.

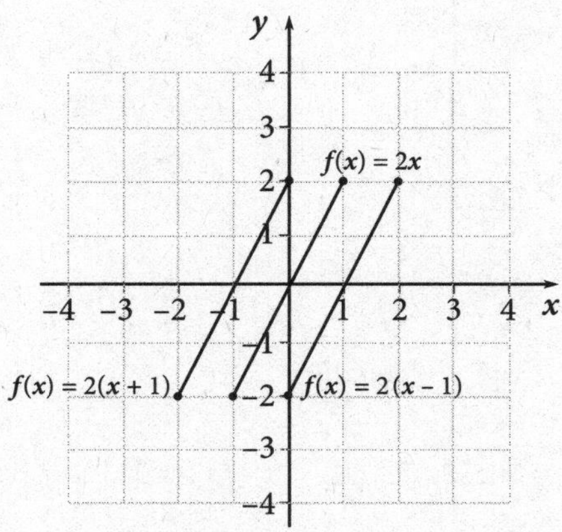

Try It Out! **Work through the following multiple-choice question.**

If $g(a) = 2a - 1$ and $h(a) = 3a + 5$, what is the value of $g(h(a))$ when $a = -7$?

A) −53

B) −40

C) −33

D) 31

Step 1: Evaluate the innermost function at $a = -7$

$h(-7) = 3(-7) + 5$
$h(-7) = -21 + 5 = -16$

Step 2: Substitute −16 for $h(a)$ in the original function

$g(h(a)) = g(-16)$

Step 3: Evaluate $g(a)$ at $a = -16$

$g(-16) = 2(-16) - 1$
$g(-16) = -32 - 1 = -33$

Use the Kaplan Method to answer the following questions. Use the hints provided as needed.

1. Anton teaches guitar lessons in a studio he rents for $450 per month. If he charges $15 for a 30-minute lesson, l, which function models Anton's monthly earnings, e?

   A) $e(l) = 450 - 15l$

   B) $e(l) = 450 + 15l$

   C) $e(l) = 15l - 450$

   D) $e(l) = 15l + 450$

hint *Remember that the initial quantity may be less than zero.*

2. If $j(a) = 2a + 1$ and $k(a) = 3a - 2$, what is the value of $j(k(3)) - k(j(4))$?

   A) −10

   B) −7

   C) 7

   D) 10

hint *Keep your work organized. Start with the innermost function each time.*

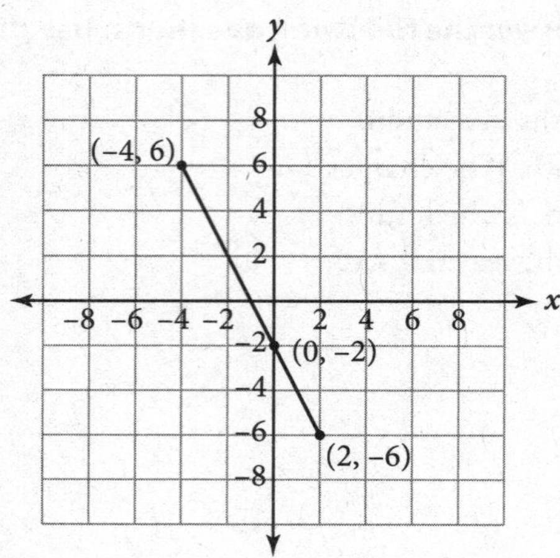

3. Part of the graph above shows the plot of the function $f(x) = -2x - 2$. Which graph shows the translation of this part of the function if 1 is added to the input?

A) 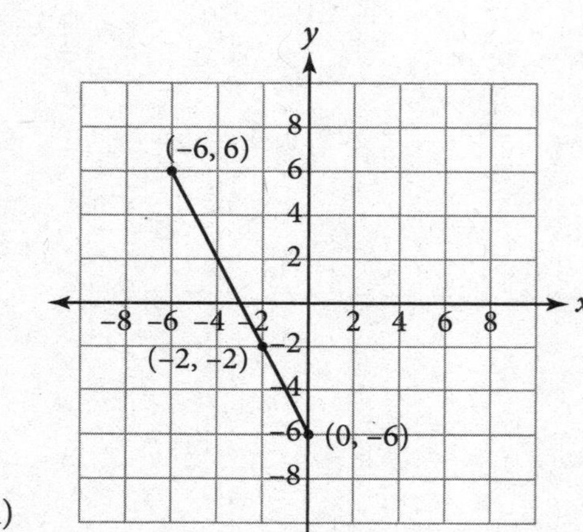

C) 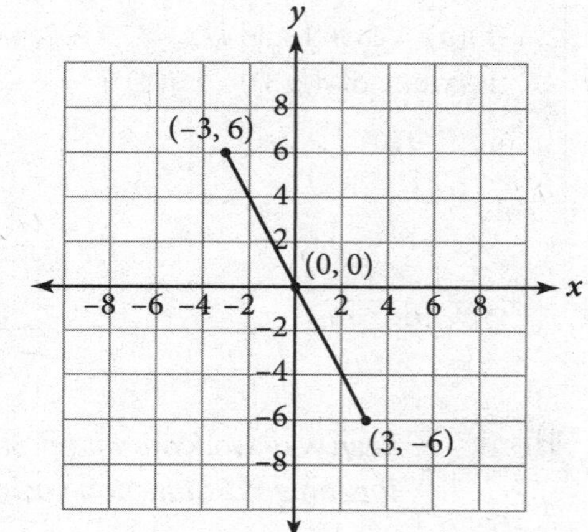

B) 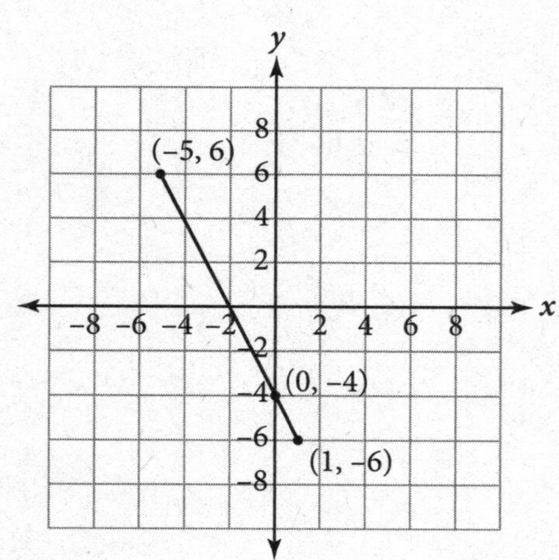

D) 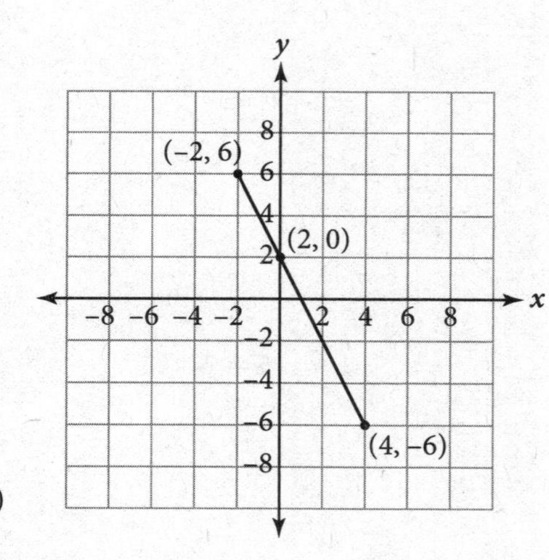

hint *Because you're given specific points on the graph, use the translations to move the points (by adjusting the coordinates of the points) instead of rewriting the equation of the function.*

13

Use the Kaplan Method to answer the following questions on your own.

1. Martina lives 500 miles from her college. If she averages 55 miles per hour on her drive to campus, which function approximates the distance that she has left to travel after driving for t hours?

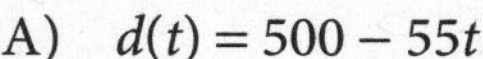

A) $d(t) = 500 - 55t$

B) $d(t) = 500 + 55t$

C) $d(t) = 55t - 500$

D) $d(t) = 55t + 500$

x	g(x)
−7	−14
−4	−11
2	−5
5	−2
8	1

x	h(x)
−2	−7
−1	−4
0	2
1	5
2	8

2. Several values for the functions $g(x)$ and $h(x)$ are shown in the tables. What is the value of $g(h(2))$?

A) −14

B) −5

C) 1

D) 8

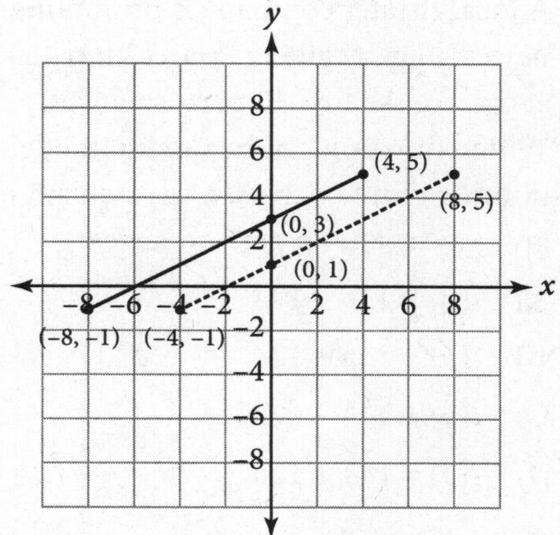

3. In the graph above, the dashed line represents part of the original function $f(x) = \frac{1}{2}x + 1$. Which of the following transformed functions would produce the solid line segment?

A) $f(x) = \frac{1}{2}(x - 4) + 1$

B) $f(x) = \frac{1}{2}(x + 4) + 1$

C) $f(x) = \frac{1}{2}(x - 4) + 3$

D) $f(x) = \frac{1}{2}(x + 4) + 3$

Use the Kaplan Method to answer the following questions for homework.

1. A local theater company is promoting its newest play by giving away 12 free tickets at each of the first 12 performances. Which function can be used to model the number of free tickets, t, that remain to be given away after p performances?

   A) $t(p) = 12p - 144$

   B) $t(p) = 12p + 144$

   C) $t(p) = 144 - 12p$

   D) $t(p) = 144 + 12p$

2. If $m(a) = 4a - 3$ and $n(a) = 2a + 3$, what is the value of $\frac{m(n(0))}{n(m(-2))}$?

   A) -19

   B) $-\frac{9}{19}$

   C) $\frac{9}{19}$

   D) 9

3. A company offers part-time salespeople two choices for their compensation. In Option A, the employee receives a base salary of $120 per week plus 5% commission on every sale. In Option B, the employee receives no base salary, but receives 15% commission on every sale. How much money in sales must an employee generate for Option B to be the better choice?

   A) 600

   B) 800

   C) 1,200

   D) 1,250

The following questions are similar to what you would encounter on a college admissions test like the SAT or ACT. Apply the Kaplan Method and your knowledge of linear functions to answer the following questions.

Questions 1–2 refer to the following information.

Arielle recently spent $510 to convert her sprinkler irrigation to a drip irrigation system that saves her approximately 1,700 gallons of water per week. Her local water company charges her a $35 per month service fee and 0.2 cents per gallon of water she uses.

1. Which function correctly models the monthly cost, c, in dollars that Arielle pays for the water, w, she uses?

   A) $c(w) = 0.0002w + 35$

   B) $c(w) = 0.002w + 35$

   C) $c(w) = 0.02w + 35$

   D) $c(w) = 0.2w + 35$

2. How many weeks will it take before Arielle's savings pay for her investment in the new irrigation equipment?

   A) 1.5

   B) 15

   C) 150

   D) 1,500

CHAPTER 14

Solving Quadratic Equations

14

CHAPTER OBJECTIVES

By the end of this chapter, you will be able to:

1. Apply reverse-FOIL to factor a quadratic equation
2. Apply the quadratic formula to solve quadratic equations

THE KAPLAN METHOD FOR MATH

Step 1: Read the question, identifying and organizing important information as you go

- What information am I given?
- Separate the question from the context.
- How are the answer choices written?
- Should you label or draw a diagram?

Step 2: Choose the best strategy to answer the question

- Look for patterns.
- Pick numbers or use straightforward math.

Step 3: Check that you answered the *right* question

- Review the question stem.
- Check units of measurement.
- Double-check your work.

QUADRATIC EQUATIONS

A quadratic equation is a polynomial with a squared variable (x^2) as the highest-order term. Quadratic equations are most commonly shown in the standard form, as seen here:

$$\boldsymbol{a}x^2 + \boldsymbol{b}x + \boldsymbol{c} = 0$$

In the standard form, ***a***, ***b***, and ***c*** are constants. Constants are nonvariable numbers (i.e., integers, decimals, or fractions); constants can be positive or negative numbers.

Always put the quadratic equation into standard form by rearranging it to equal zero.

14

A solution for a quadratic equation is a constant value for x that will make the equation equal to zero. All quadratic equations have two, one, or zero real solutions. These solutions are sometimes called roots, zeros, or x-intercepts.

Factoring Quadratic Equations

In chapter 12, you learned to multiply polynomials using the **FOIL method**. Think of a **quadratic equation** as the product of two **first-degree** binomials, and use the FOIL method **in reverse** to determine what those two binomial factors are.

Helpful Hint

This method is easiest to use when the *a* equals 1.

Follow the steps to reverse-FOIL, or factor, a quadratic equation.

$$x^2 - 5x + 6 = 0$$

Last

Use the sign of the ***c*** term to determine the signs between the terms of the factors. The ***c*** term is a nonvariable real number and is the product of the **Last** terms of the factors.

- If ***c*** is **positive**, the signs are the same: (__ + __)(__ + __) or (__ – __)(__ – __)
- If ***c*** is **negative**, the signs are different: (__ + __)(__ – __)

Factor the ***c*** term, making sure to include the negative factors.

- The factor pairs are: (1)(6); (2)(3); (–1)(–6); (–2)(–3)

Inner and Outer

Look for the factor pair that adds to the ***b*** term.

$b = -5$
$(1) + (6) = 7$
$(2) + (3) = 5$
$(-1) + (-6) = -7$
$(-2) + (-3) = -5$ ✓

Fill in the information you have:

- (__ – 2)(__ – 3)

First

Use the ***a*** term to determine the **First"** terms of the factors:

- Factor the constant ***a*** and take the square root of the squared variable.
- In the example, ***a*** is 1 and the first terms are x and x: $(x - 2)(x - 3)$

Check your work:

- Use FOIL to multiply: $(x - 2)(x - 3) = (x)(x) + (-3)(x) + (-2)(x) + (-2)(-3) = 0$
- Combine the like terms: $x^2 - 5x + 6 = (x - 2)(x - 3) = 0$ ✓

Solve

Use the Cardinal Rule of Equations to solve for the values of x that satisfy the equation:

- $(x - 2)(x - 3) = 0$
- Divide both sides of the equation by $(x - 2)$: $\cancel{(x-2)}(x - 3) \div \cancel{(x-2)} = 0 \div \cancel{(x-2)}$
- Isolate the variable: $x - 3 = 0 \rightarrow x - 3 + 3 = 0 + 3$
- Simplify: $x = 3$
- Repeat the steps: $(x - 2)\cancel{(x-3)} \div \cancel{(x-3)} = 0 \div \cancel{(x-3)} = x - 2 = 0 \rightarrow x = 2$
- The solutions for $x^2 - 5x + 6 = 0$ are $x = 3$ and $x = 2$

The Quadratic Formula

When the solutions to a quadratic equation are not integers, the **quadratic formula** may be the best way to solve the equation. If needed, rearrange the quadratic equation to set it equal to zero and substitute the values for ***a***, ***b***, and ***c*** from the standard form.

$$x = \frac{-b \pm \sqrt{b^2 - 4ac}}{2a}$$

Use the quadratic formula to solve: $2x^2 - 5x - 2 = 5$

- Rearrange the equation: $2x^2 - 5x - 2 - 5 = 5 - 5 \rightarrow 2x^2 - 5x - 7 = 0$
- Substitute: $\boldsymbol{a} = 2$, $\boldsymbol{b} = -5$, and $\boldsymbol{c} = -7$ into the quadratic formula.

$$x = \frac{-(-5) \pm \sqrt{(-5)^2 - 4(2)(-7)}}{2(2)}$$

$$x = \frac{5 \pm \sqrt{25 - (-56)}}{4}$$

$$x = \frac{5 \pm \sqrt{81}}{4}$$

$$x = \frac{5 \pm 9}{4}$$

- Simplify to find the two solutions.

$$x = \frac{5+9}{4} = \frac{14}{4} = 3.5$$

$$x = \frac{5-9}{4} = \frac{-4}{4} = -1$$

$x = 3.5$ and -1

Check your work:

- Use FOIL to multiply: $(x - 3.5)(x + 1) = (x)(x) + (1)(x) + (-3.5)(x) + (-3.5)(1) = 0$
- Combine the like terms: $x^2 - 2.5x - 3.5 = 0$
- Because $\boldsymbol{a} = 2$ in the original equation, multiply both sides by 2:

  $2(x^2 - 2.5x - 3.5) = 2(0) \rightarrow 2x^2 - 5x - 7 = 0$

Try It Out! **Apply the same approach to solve the following multiple-choice questions.**

1. Which of the following are solutions to the quadratic equation $x^2 + 7x = 18$?

   A) $x = 1$ and $x = -18$

   B) $x = -1$ and $x = 18$

   C) $x = 2$ and $x = -9$

   D) $x = -2$ and $x = 9$

✓ Helpful Hint

Because the answer choices are all integers, use the reverse-FOIL method to find the factors of the quadratic equation.

Rearrange the equation into the standard form and use the reverse-FOIL method to solve this quadratic equation:

Rearrange: $x^2 + 7x - 18 = 18 - 18 \rightarrow x^2 + 7x - 18 = 0$

Last: The ***c*** term is negative; the binomial factors have different signs in the middle:

- (__ + __)(__ – __)
- The integer factor pairs are: (1)(–18), (–1)(18), (2)(–9), (–2)(9), (3)(–6), (–3)(6)

Outer-Inner: In the equation, $\boldsymbol{b} = 7$:

- Identify the factor pair that adds to 7: (–2) + (9) = 7
- Fill in the information you have: (__ + 9)(__ – 2)

First: Factor the ***a*** term:

- $\boldsymbol{a} = 1$
- The ***a*** term equals $1x^2$ and factors to $(x)(x)$
- The factors are: $(x + 9)(x - 2)$

Solve: Use the Cardinal Rule of Equations to find the solutions for x:

- $(x + 9)\cancel{(x - 2)} \div \cancel{(x - 2)} = 0 \div \cancel{(x - 2)}$
- $x + 9 = 0 \rightarrow x = -9$
- $\cancel{(x + 9)}(x - 2) \div \cancel{(x + 9)} = 0 \div \cancel{(x + 9)}$
- $x - 2 = 0 \rightarrow$
- $x = 2$ and $x = -9$

Choice (C) is correct.

Check: Apply the FOIL method to the factors:

- $(x + 9)(x - 2) = (x)(x) + (-2)(x) + (9)(x) + (9)(-2) = 0$
- Simplify: $x^2 + 7x - 18 = 0$

2. Which are the real values of x that satisfy the equation $5x^2 - 4x - 2 = -7x$?

   A) -2 and $\frac{4}{5}$

   B) -1 and $\frac{2}{5}$

   C) $-\frac{2}{5}$ and 1

   D) No real solutions

14

Use the quadratic formula to solve: $5x^2 - 4x - 2 = -7x$

- Rearrange the equation: $5x^2 - 4x + 7x - 2 = -7x + 7x \rightarrow 5x^2 + 3x - 2 = 0$
- Substitute $\boldsymbol{a} = 5$, $\boldsymbol{b} = 3$, and $\boldsymbol{c} = -2$ into the quadratic formula.

$$x = \frac{-(3) \pm \sqrt{(3)^2 - 4(5)(-2)}}{2(5)}$$

$$x = \frac{-3 \pm \sqrt{9 - (-40)}}{10}$$

$$x = \frac{-3 \pm \sqrt{49}}{10}$$

$$x = \frac{-3 \pm 7}{10}$$

- Simplify to find the two solutions:

$$x = \frac{-3 + 7}{10} = \frac{4}{10} = \frac{2}{5}$$

$$x = \frac{-3 - 7}{10} = \frac{-10}{10} = -1$$

$$x = \frac{2}{5} \text{ and } -1$$

Choice (B) is correct.

Use the Kaplan Method to answer the following questions. Use the hints provided as needed.

1. Factor the following quadratic equation:
   $x^2 + 4x + 4 = 0$
   A) $(x + 1)^2$
   B) $(x + 2)^2$
   C) $(x + 3)^2$
   D) $(x + 4)^2$

hint *$(x + 1)^2$ can also be written as $(x + 1)(x + 1)$.*

2. What is the value of *z*?
   $x^2 + 6x + 8 = (x + 4)(x + z)$
   A) 2
   B) 4
   C) 6
   D) 8

hint *Factor the quadratic to find the value of z.*

3. What is one possible value of *x*?
   $2x^2 + 7x + 3 = 0$
   A) $\frac{1}{3}$
   B) $-\frac{1}{2}$
   C) 3
   D) -2

hint *Use the quadratic formula to find the possible values of x.*

Use the Kaplan Method to answer the following questions on your own.

1. If $3x^2 - 8x - 3 = 0$, what is one possible value of x?

   A) −3

   B) −1

   C) 3

   D) 9

2. Factor the following equation:
   $\frac{x^2 + 5x}{2} = -2$

   A) $(x + 4)(x - 2)$

   B) $(x + 2)(x + 2)$

   C) $(x + 4)(x + 1)$

   D) $(x - 2)(x - 4)$

3. What is the value of g?
   $(x + g)\ (x - 2) = x^2 + 7x - 18$

   A) 2

   B) −2

   C) 9

   D) −9

Use the Kaplan Method to answer the following questions for homework.

1. Solve for x: $x^2 + 4x = 6$.

   A) $x = 4 \pm \sqrt{10}$

   B) $x = \dfrac{2 \pm \sqrt{40}}{2}$

   C) $x = \dfrac{-8 \pm \sqrt{80}}{3}$

   D) $x = -2 \pm \sqrt{10}$

2. Factor $2x^2 + 5x + 2 = 0$.

   A) $(x + 2)(x + 1)$

   B) $(2x + 2)(x + 1)$

   C) $(x + 2)(2x - 1)$

   D) $(2x + 1)(x + 2)$

3. If $4x^2 + 4x + 1 = 0$, what is one possible value of x?

   A) 2

   B) $-\dfrac{1}{2}$

   C) $\dfrac{1}{2}$

   D) 4

The following questions are similar to what you would encounter on a college admissions test like the SAT or ACT. Use the Kaplan Method for Math and your knowledge of quadratic equations to answer the following questions.

1. Rewrite the following equation in factored form: $5x = 3 + 2x^2$

   A) $(2x - 3)(x + 1)$

   B) $(x + 3)(x + 1)$

   C) $(2x - 3)(1 - x)$

   D) $(x + 1)(3 - x)$

2. What is the value of $\frac{x^2 + 2x - 35}{x^2 + 10x + 21}$ when $x = -5$?

   A) -5

   B) -1

   C) 0

   D) 5

CHAPTER 15

Solving Systems of Linear-Quadratic Equations

15

CHAPTER OBJECTIVES

By the end of this chapter, you will be able to:

1. Graph a linear-quadratic system of equations
2. Solve a linear-quadratic system of equations algebraically

THE KAPLAN METHOD FOR MATH

Step 1: Read the question, identifying and organizing important information as you go

- What information am I given?
- Separate the question from the context.
- How are the answer choices written?
- Should you label or draw a diagram?

Step 2: Choose the best strategy to answer the question

- Look for patterns.
- Pick numbers or use straightforward math.

Step 3: Check that you answered the *right* question

- Review the question stem.
- Check units of measurement.
- Double-check your work.

GRAPHING SYSTEMS OF NONLINEAR EQUATIONS

Two or more equations that share at least one variable form a system of equations. To graphically solve, you must find all ordered pairs (x, y) that make *both* equations true.

- **If the equations intersect** at **two** points, there are **two solutions.**
- **If the equations intersect** at **one** point, there is **one solution.**
- **If the equations do not intersect**, there is **no solution.**

Try It Out! **Follow the steps in bold to solve the system of equations using graphing.**

$$y - x = -3$$
$$y + 3 = x^2 - 2x$$

Step 1: Rewrite the linear equation in $y = mx + b$ form and the quadratic equation in $y = ax^2 + bx + c$ form.

$y - x = -3$	$y + 3 = x^2 - 2x$
$+x \quad +x$	$-3 \qquad -3$
$y = x - 3$	$y = x^2 - 2x - 3$

Step 2A: Find the axis of symmetry and set up an x–y table for the quadratic equation.

$y = x^2 - 2x - 3$

Axis of symmetry formula: $x = \dfrac{-b}{2a}$

$a = 1, b = -2, c = -3$

$x = \dfrac{-(-2)}{2(1)} = \dfrac{2}{2} = 1$

Use $x = 1$ as the center value for your x–y table.

x	$x^2 - 2x - 3$	y	ordered pairs (x, y)
–1	$(-1)^2 - 2(-1) - 3$	0	(–1, 0)
0	$(0)^2 - 2(0) - 3$	–3	(0, –3)
1	$(1)^2 - 2(1) - 3$	–4	(1, –4)
2	$(2)^2 - 2(2) - 3$	–3	(2, –3)
3	$(3)^2 - 2(3) - 3$	0	(3, 0)

Step 2B: Set up an x–y table for the linear equation, using the same center value.

x	$x - 3$	y	ordered pairs (x, y)
–1	$(-1) - 3$	–4	(–1, –4)
0	$(0) - 3$	–3	(0, –3)
1	$(1) - 3$	–2	(1, –2)
2	$(2) - 3$	–1	(2, –1)
3	$(3) - 3$	0	(3, 0)

Step 3: Graph $y = x - 3$ and $y = x^2 - 2x - 3$ in the same coordinate plane.

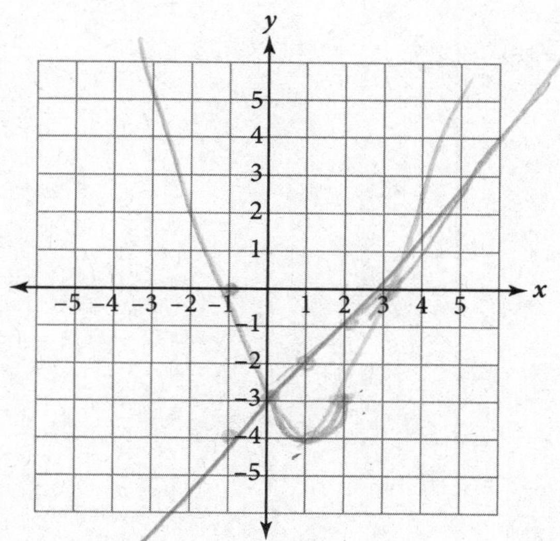

Will the line and the parabola intersect? Yes

If yes, what are are the points of intersection? (0,-3) and (3,0)

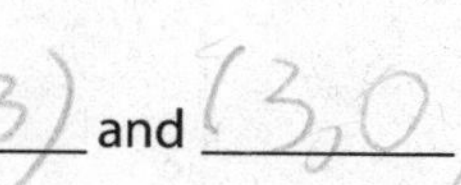

Step 4: Double-check the solution by substituting the values into each equation.

$y - x = -3$ $\qquad$ $y + 3 = x^2 - 2x$

Try It Out! **Follow the steps in bold to solve the system using graphing.**

$y+3=-\frac{1}{2}x$
$y+1=\frac{1}{2}x^2+x$

Step 1: Rewrite the linear equation in $y = mx + b$ form and the quadratic equation in $y = ax^2 + bx + c$ form.

$y+3=-\frac{1}{2}x$	$y+1=\frac{1}{2}x^2+x$
$-3 \qquad -3$	$-1 \qquad -1$
$y=-\frac{1}{2}x-3$	$y=\frac{1}{2}x^2+x-1$

15

Step 2A: Find the axis of symmetry and set up an x–y table for the quadratic equation.

$$y=\frac{1}{2}x^2+x-1$$

Axis of symmetry formula: $x=\frac{-b}{2a}$

$$a=\frac{1}{2},\ b=1,\ c=-1$$

$$x=\frac{-(1)}{2\left(\frac{1}{2}\right)}=\frac{-1}{1}=-1$$

Use $x = -1$ as the center value for your x–y table.

x	$\frac{1}{2}x^2 + x - 1$	y	**ordered pairs (x, y)**
−3	$\frac{1}{2}(-3)^2 + (-3) - 1$	$\frac{1}{2}$	$\left(-3, \frac{1}{2}\right)$
−2	$\frac{1}{2}(-2)^2 + (-2) - 1$	−1	(−2, −1)
−1	$\frac{1}{2}(-1)^2 + (-1) - 1$	$-1\frac{1}{2}$	$\left(-1, -1\frac{1}{2}\right)$
0	$\frac{1}{2}(0)^2 + (0) - 1$	−1	(0, −1)
1	$\frac{1}{2}(1)^2 + (1) - 1$	$\frac{1}{2}$	$\left(1, \frac{1}{2}\right)$

15

Step 2B: Set up an x–y table for the linear equation, using the same center value.

x	$-\frac{1}{2}x - 3$	y	**ordered pairs (x, y)**
−3	$-\frac{1}{2}(-3) - 3$	$-1\frac{1}{2}$	$\left(-3, -1\frac{1}{2}\right)$
−2	$-\frac{1}{2}(-2) - 3$	−2	(−2, −2)
−1	$-\frac{1}{2}(-1) - 3$	$-2\frac{1}{2}$	$\left(-1, -2\frac{1}{2}\right)$
0	$-\frac{1}{2}(0) - 3$	−3	(0, −3)
1	$-\frac{1}{2}(1) - 3$	$-3\frac{1}{2}$	$\left(1, -3\frac{1}{2}\right)$
2	$-\frac{1}{2}(2) - 3$	−4	(2, −4)
3	$-\frac{1}{2}(3) - 3$	$-4\frac{1}{2}$	$\left(3, -4\frac{1}{2}\right)$

Step 3: Graph $y = -\frac{1}{2}x - 3$ and $y = \frac{1}{2}x^2 + x - 1$ in the same coordinate plane.

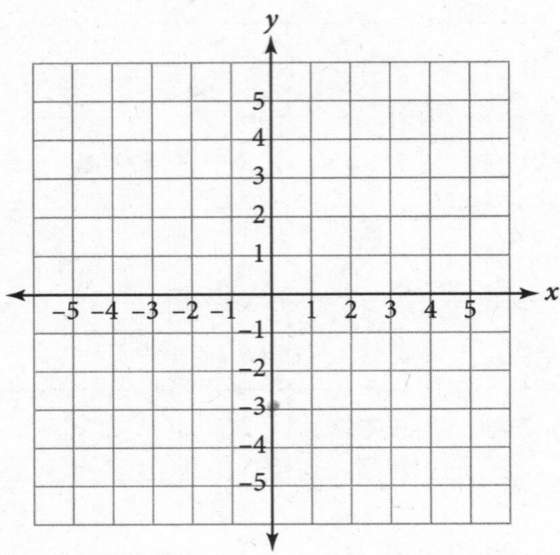

15

Will the line and the parabola intersect? __________

If yes, what are are the points of intersection? __________ and __________

SOLVING SYSTEMS OF LINEAR-QUADRATIC EQUATIONS ALGEBRAICALLY

Substitution is the most straightforward method for solving a system of nonlinear equations, and it can be applied in every situation. To use substitution, solve the linear equation for one variable, and then substitute that result into the quadratic equation.

Follow the steps to solve using substitution.

$$y - 2 = 2x$$
$$y = x^2 - x - 8$$

Step 1: Solve for y in the linear equation

$$y - 2 = 2x$$
$$+2 \quad +2$$
$$y = 2x + 2$$

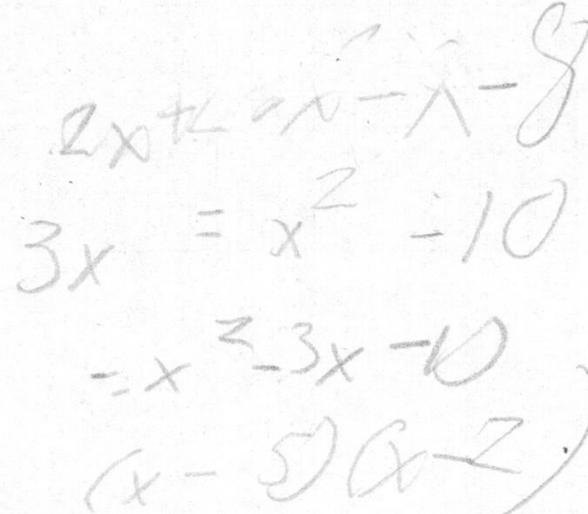

Step 2: Substitute the result into the quadratic equation and solve

$y = x^2 - x - 8$

$2x + 2 = x^2 - x - 8$

$\quad -2 \qquad\qquad -2$

$2x = x^2 - x - 10$

$-2x \qquad -2x$

$0 = x^2 - 3x - 10$

$0 = (x - 5)(x + 2)$

$x - 5 = 0 \qquad x + 2 = 0$

$+5 \;\; +5 \qquad -2 \;\; -2$

$x = 5 \qquad\qquad x = -2$

Step 3: Substitute the *x*-values into the linear equation and solve

$x = 5$	$x = -2$
$y - 2 = 2x$ $y - 2 = 2(5)$ $y - 2 = 10$ $+2 \quad +2$ $y = 12$	$y - 2 = 2x$ $y - 2 = 2(-2)$ $y - 2 = -4$ $+2 \quad +2$ $y = -2$

What are the points of intersection? __________ and __________

Step 4: Double-check the solution by substituting the values into each equation

$y + 2 = 2x \qquad\qquad y = x^2 - x - 8$

15

Use the Kaplan Method to answer the following questions. Use the hints provided as needed.

$$y + 5 = x$$
$$y = x^2 - 6x + 5$$

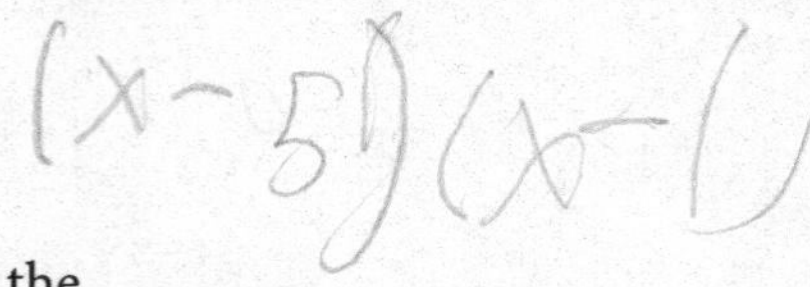

1. Which ordered pairs (x, y) represent the points of intersection for the system of equations above?

   A) (3, 2) and (−5, 0)

   B) (−2, 3) and (0, 5)

   C) (2, −3) and (−5, 0)

   D) (2, −3) and (5, 0)

hint *Solve for y in the linear equation, substitute the result into the quadratic equation, and solve. Then plug the x-values back into the linear equation to determine the y-values of the system.*

15

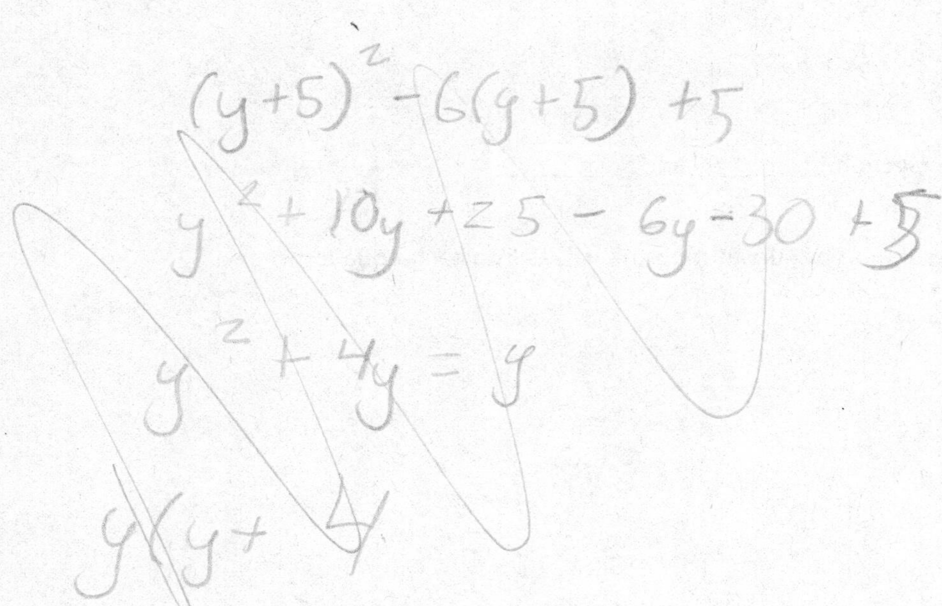

2. Solve the system by graphing:
   $y - x^2 = -4x + 8$ $\qquad$ $y = x + 2$

x		y	ordered pairs (x, y)

x		y	ordered pairs (x, y)

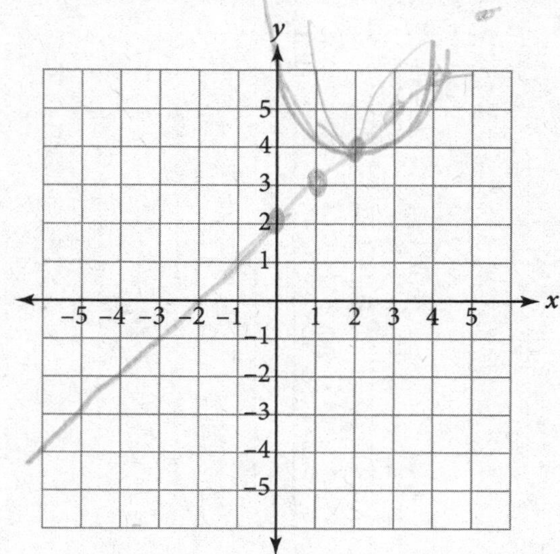

Will the line and the parabola intersect?

____

If yes, what are are the points of intersection?

________ and ________

hint *Double-check your work by plugging the points of intersection back into each equation.*

Use the Kaplan Method to answer the following questions on your own.

$$y - 6 = x$$
$$-x^2 = -y + 8x + 16$$

1. Which ordered pairs (x, y) represent the points of intersection for the system of equations above?

   A) $(-2, -4)$ and $(-5, 1)$

   B) $(-2, 4)$ and $(-5, 1)$

   C) $(-4, -2)$ and $(-5, 1)$

   D) $(4, -2)$ and $(1, -5)$

2. Solve the system by graphing:

   $y - 2x = x^2 + 4$ $\qquad$ $y - 1 = x$

x		y	ordered pairs (x, y)

x		y	ordered pairs (x, y)

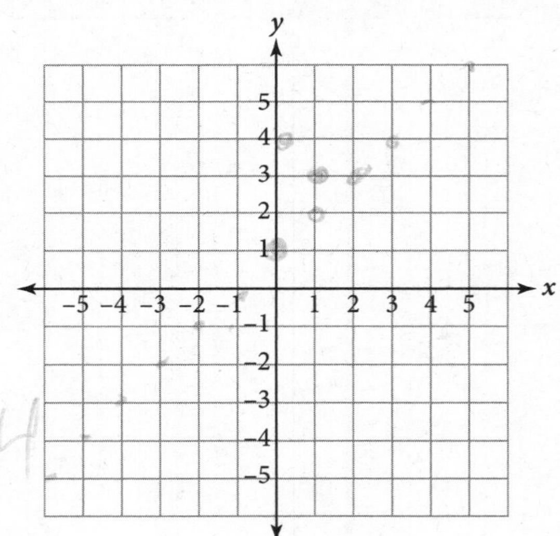

Will the line and the parabola intersect?

____

If yes, what are are the points of intersection?

__________ and __________

Use the Kaplan Method to answer the following questions for homework.

$$y = x + 3$$
$$y = x^2 + 9x + 18$$

1. Which ordered pairs (x, y) represent the points of intersection for the system of equations above?

   A) (−3, 0) and (−5, −2)

   B) (3, 0) and (5, 2)

   C) (0, −3) and (−2, −5)

   D) (0, 3) and (2, 5)

2. Solve the system by graphing:

   $y + 4x = x^2 + 6$ $\qquad$ $y - 2 = x$

x		y	ordered pairs (x, y)

x		y	ordered pairs (x, y)

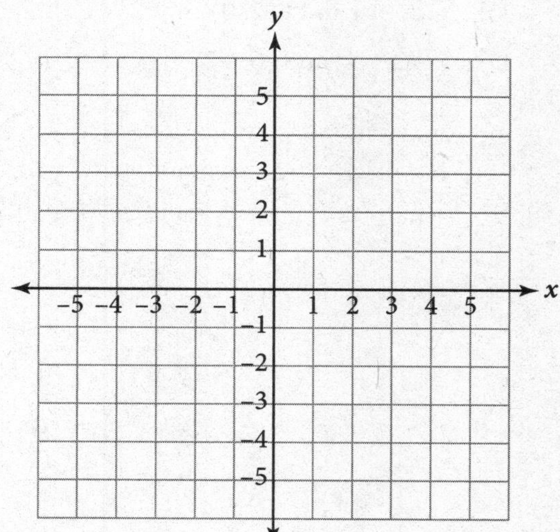

Will the line and the parabola intersect?

____

If yes, what are are the points of intersection?

__________ and __________

The following questions are similar to what you would encounter on a college admissions test such as the SAT or ACT. Apply your knowledge of systems of linear-quadratic equations to tackle the following questions.

$$-x = -y + 2$$
$$-2x^2 + y = 3 + x$$

1. The system of equations above has
   A) no solution.
   B) infinitely many solutions.
   C) one solution.
   D) two solutions.

$$y + 2x = 4$$
$$y + x^2 = -4x + 12$$

15

2. Which ordered pairs (x, y) represent the points of intersection for the system of equations above?
   A) (−4, 12) and (2, 0)
   B) (4, −12) and (0, 2)
   C) (12, −4) and (−2, 0)
   D) (−12, −4) and (0, −2)

UNIT THREE

Problem Solving & Data Analysis

IN THIS UNIT, YOU WILL LEARN HOW TO:

1. Write ratios and calculate unknown quantities using proportions
2. Calculate percents and their decimal and fractional equivalents
3. Calculate percent increase and percent decrease
4. Determine desired and possible outcomes using probability rules
5. Interpret data presented in a two-way table
6. Calculate mean, median, mode, and range
7. Interpret the slope and *y*-intercept of a scatter plot

CHAPTER 16

Ratios, Proportions, & Rates

CHAPTER OBJECTIVES

By the end of this chapter, you will be able to:

1. Write ratios relating two quantities to one another
2. Use ratios to set up a proportion equation
3. Use proportions to solve for an unknown quantity
4. Use rates to solve for unknown quantities

16

THE KAPLAN METHOD FOR MATH

Step 1: Read the question, identifying and organizing important information as you go

- What information am I given?
- Separate the question from the context.
- How are the answer choices written?
- Should you label or draw a diagram?

Step 2: Choose the best strategy to answer the question

- Look for patterns.
- Pick numbers or use straightforward math.

Step 3: Check that you answered the *right* question

- Review the question stem.
- Check units of measurement.
- Double-check your work.

RATIOS

A ratio shows the relationship between two quantities. Ratios can be represented three different ways. If there are 5 dimes for every 9 quarters in a cash register, the ratio of dimes to quarters can be written as 5 to 9, 5:9, and $\frac{5}{9}$. This is an example of a **part:part** ratio because the ratio compares the quantity of one part to the quantity of the other part: $\frac{\text{part 1}}{\text{part 2}}$.

Ratios can also be expressed as **part:whole**: $\frac{\text{part 1}}{\text{part 1} + \text{part 2}}$ or $\frac{\text{part 2}}{\text{part 1} + \text{part 2}}$.

Because the dimes and quarters are both **coins**, you can set up a part-to-whole ratio to relate each quantity to the total number of coins: $\frac{\text{5 dimes}}{\text{14 coins}}$ and $\frac{\text{9 quarters}}{\text{14 coins}}$.

SOLVING RATIO QUESTIONS

You can approach each ratio question in the same way:

Step 1: Identify what kind of ratio the question asks for—part-to-part or part-to-whole.

Step 2: Plug the information provided in the question stem into the ratio.

Try It Out! **Work through the following sample questions.**

1. In a local newspaper, there must be three current events articles for every one opinion editorial published. What is the ratio of current events articles to opinion editorials?

Step 1: Identify what kind of ratio the question asks for—part-to-part or whole-to-whole.

You are asked to compare articles to editorials.

It is a part-to-part ratio.

$$\frac{\text{part 1}}{\text{part 2}} = \frac{\text{the number of articles}}{\text{the number of editorials}}$$

Step 2: Plug the information provided in the question stem into the ratio.

3 parts (units) of articles **per** every 1 part (unit) of editorials

$\frac{\text{3 articles}}{\text{1 editorial}}$ or 3:1

2. An animal shelter takes care of 25 dogs and 15 cats. If the only pets at the shelter are dogs and cats, what is the ratio of dogs to pets?

Step 1: Identify what kind of ratio the question asks for—part-to-part or whole-to-whole.

This question asks you to compare dogs to pets.

It is a part-to-whole ratio.

$$\frac{\text{part 1}}{\text{part 1} + \text{part 2}} = \frac{\text{the number of dogs}}{\text{the number of dogs} + \text{cats}}$$

Step 2: Plug the information provided in the question stem into the ratio.

25 units of dogs **per** every 25 units of dogs + 15 units of cats

$$\frac{25 \text{ dogs}}{40 \text{ pets}}$$

Simplify the ratio:

$\frac{25}{40} = \frac{5}{8}$, or 5 dogs to 8 pets

Try It Out! **Work through the following multiple-choice question.**

At an independent video game company, there are 22 programmers and 4 storyboarders. What is the ratio of storyboarders to programmers?

A) $\frac{22}{4}$

B) $\frac{11}{1}$

C) $\frac{2}{11}$

D) $\frac{4}{26}$

Step 1: Identify what kind of ratio the question asks for—part-to-part or part-to-whole.

The question stem provides you with two quantities: The first quantity is 22 programmers and the second quantity is 4 storyboarders (programmers and storyboarders are job roles at a video game company). This is a part-to-part ratio.

Step 2: Plug the information provided in the question stem into the ratio.

16

$$\text{Ratio} = \frac{\text{storyboarders}}{\text{programmers}} = \frac{4}{22}$$

$$\text{Simplify: } \frac{4}{22} = \frac{2}{11}$$

This worked solution would resemble the following:

At an independent video game company, there are 22 programmers and 4 storyboarders. What is the ratio of storyboarders to programmers?

A) $\frac{22}{4}$

B) $\frac{11}{1}$

C) $\frac{2}{11}$

D) $\frac{4}{26}$

Straightforward math:

$$\text{Ratio} = \frac{\text{storyboarders}}{\text{programmers}} = \frac{4}{22} = \frac{2}{11}$$

PROPORTIONS

Proportions are two ratios set equal to one another. When two ratios are **proportional**, the two ratios are equal. In other words, if you carry out the division operation of each fraction, the results will be equal. Proportions are useful in a wide range of applications in mathematics, science, and everyday activities. The ratios in a proportion can be **part:part** or **part:whole**.

Part-to-Part Proportions

If you are cooking dinner, and your pasta recipe states that for every one tablespoon of butter, you should add three teaspoons of salt, the recipe has provided you a ratio of butter to salt.

$$\text{Ratio} = \frac{\text{1 tablespoon of butter}}{\text{3 teaspoons of salt}}$$

If you're making a large batch of pasta and you want to use five tablespoons of butter instead of just one, you can use proportions to find out how many teaspoons of salt you need to maintain the same ratio as in the recipe.

$$\frac{\text{1 tbsp butter}}{\text{3 tsp salt}} = \frac{\text{5 tbsp butter}}{x \text{ tsp salt}}$$

In the proportion, x represents the unknown quantity of salt you need to add to your five tablespoons of butter. By cross-multiplying, you can solve for x.

$$(x \text{ tsp salt}) \times (\text{1 tbsp butter}) = (\text{3 tsp salt}) \times (\text{5 tbsp butter})$$

16

Solving for x yields:

$$x = 15 \text{ tsp salt}$$

To check your answer, plug in 15 for x and see if your ratios are equal.

$$\frac{\text{1 tbsp butter}}{\text{3 tsp salt}} \simeq 0.33$$

$$\frac{\text{5 tbsp butter}}{\text{15 tsp salt}} \simeq 0.33 \checkmark$$

Part-to-Whole Proportions

To make the color you want to paint your room, you need to mix 3 parts white paint with 2 parts blue paint. How many pints of blue paint will you need to make 15 pints of this color?

Here you are given a **part-to-part** ratio: $\frac{3 \text{ parts white paint}}{2 \text{ parts blue paint}}$ and asked to solve a **part-to-whole** ratio.

The part to whole ratio you need is: $\frac{2 \text{ blue}}{5 \text{ paint}}$

Now determine the part-to-whole ratio you need to find: $\frac{x \text{ blue}}{15 \text{ paint}}$

Make a proportion by setting the two ratios equal to each other: $\frac{2}{5} = \frac{x \text{ blue}}{15 \text{ paint}}$

Cross-multiply and solve for the unknown quantity:

$$(2 \text{ blue}) \times (15 \text{ paint}) = (x \text{ blue}) \times (5 \text{ paint})$$

$$\frac{30(\text{blue} \times \text{paint})}{5 \text{ paint}} = x \text{ blue} \Rightarrow x = 6 \text{ blue}$$

16

SOLVING PROPORTIONS QUESTIONS

You can approach each proportions question in the same way:

Step 1: Identify the first ratio.

Step 2: Identify the second ratio with the missing quantity.

Step 3: Construct the proportionality equation.

Step 4: Cross-multiply and solve for the unknown quantity.

Try It Out! **Complete the following sample questions.**

1. At Johnny's pizzeria, the most popular order is the pepperoni sausage pie. For every one slice of pepperoni, two slices of sausage need to be added. If there are 10 pepperoni slices on a large pie, how many sausage slices are there?

   Step 1: Identify the first ratio. ____________________

   Step 2: Identify the second ratio with the missing quantity. ____________________

   Step 3: Construct the proportionality equation. ____________________

   Step 4: Cross-multiply and solve for the unknown quantity. ____________________

2. Roman makes his own toothpaste at home with a simple recipe: five parts coconut oil and two parts baking soda. If he wants to make a batch of toothpaste using 12.5 tablespoons of coconut oil, how much baking soda should he add to the mixture?

   Step 1: Identify the first ratio. ____________________

   Step 2: Identify the second ratio with the missing quantity. ____________________

   Step 3: Construct the proportionality equation. ____________________

   Step 4: Cross-multiply and solve for the unknown quantity. ____________________

16

RATES

A **rate** is a **ratio**. It shows how many units of one thing there are per each unit of something else. Like **percents** and **averages**, rates can be expressed as **three-part formulas**. A basic three-part formula is the "*dirt*" formula, which stands for *distance* = *rate* × *time* or $d = rt$. If you know any two parts of the three-part formula, you can find the third by isolating the unknown part.

$$d = rt$$

To solve for "rate," divide both sides by time: $\frac{d}{t} = \frac{rt}{t} \Rightarrow r = \frac{d}{t}$

To solve for "time," divide both sides by rate: $\frac{d}{r} = \frac{rt}{r} \Rightarrow t = \frac{d}{r}$

Even when questions are not about actual distances or times, rates are always expressed as ratios. Some common rates are miles per gallon and dollars per gallon. You can use the *dirt* formula to solve many rate questions.

Using Rates to Calculate Unknown Quantities

If you are planning a trip to visit colleges, you may want to estimate how many gallons of gasoline you will need for your drive. The known quantities are the rate: your car's mpg, say $32\frac{\text{miles}}{\text{gallon}}$, and

16 the total distance, say 512 miles. The unknown quantity is the number of gallons.

Set up the dirt formula, and plug in the quantities from the question:

$$d = rt \text{ or } 512 \text{ miles} = 32\frac{\text{miles}}{\text{gallon}} \times \text{gallons}$$

Divide both sides by the rate to solve for gallons:

$$\frac{512 \text{ miles}}{32\frac{\text{miles}}{\text{gallon}}} = 16 \text{ gallons}$$

After you determine how many gallons you need, you can estimate how much the gas will cost by applying the *dirt* formula. If the cost of gasoline is $3.25\ \frac{\$}{\text{gal}}$, how much will the gas cost?

Use the *dirt* formula as a model for your equation:

$$\$ = \frac{\$}{\text{gal}} \times \text{gal}$$

Plug in the known quantities and solve for \$:

$$\$ = 3.25\frac{\$}{\text{gal}} \times 16 \text{ gal} \Rightarrow \$ = 3.25 \times 16\ \frac{(\$) \times (\text{gal})}{(\text{gal})}$$

$$\$ = \$52$$

SOLVING RATES QUESTIONS

You can approach each rates question in the same way:

Step 1: Identify the rate(s)

Step 2: Determine what quantity the question is asking you to find

Step 3: Use the *dirt* formula to model your equation

Step 4: Solve for the unknown quantity

Follow the steps to practice solving rates questions.

1. A fighter jet is traveling at mach 3, which is roughly 1,000 meters per second. How far does the jet travel in 10 seconds?

   Step 1: Identify the rate(s) ____________________

   Step 2: Determine what quantity the question is asking you to find ____________________

   Step 3: Use the *dirt* formula to model your equation ____________________

   Step 4: Solve for the unknown quantity ____________________

2. A water pump fills a well with groundwater at a rate of 15 gallons per hour. How much time does it take the pump to fill the well with 45 gallons of water?

   Step 1: Identify the rate(s) ____________________

   Step 2: Determine what quantity the question is asking you to find ____________________

   Step 3: Use the *dirt* formula to model your equation ____________________

   Step 4: Solve for the unknown quantity ____________________

Use the Kaplan Method to answer the following questions. Use the hints provided as needed.

1. In a ninth grade English classroom, all the students are either 14 or 15 years old. There are nine 14-year-olds and 22 students total. What is the ratio of 14-year-old students to 15-year-olds students?

   A) 9:22

   B) 13:22

   C) 9:13

   D) 22:13

hint *First, find the number of 15-year-olds in the classroom.*

2. If you're driving at 30 kilometers per hour, how far will you have traveled in 90 minutes?

   A) 30 km

   B) 45 km

   C) 60 km

   D) 75 km

hint *Convert 90 minutes to hours before solving.*

3. To make aquamarine oil paint, an artist mixes 3 parts blue paint and 2 parts green paint. If the artist adds 7 parts green paint to his pallette, how many parts blue paint should he add?

   A) 9

   B) 10.5

   C) 11

   D) 11.5

hint *First, identify your two ratios and what the unknown quantity is, then solve.*

Use the Kaplan Method to answer the following questions on your own.

1. A team of bakers can make 34 loaves of rye bread every 3 hours. What is their rate of bread production in loaves per hour?

   A) $9\frac{1}{4}$

   B) $11\frac{1}{3}$

   C) $13\frac{2}{3}$

   D) $14\frac{3}{4}$

2. The ratio of native plant species to foreign plant species on a tropical island is 19:3. If there are 45 total foreign plant species on the island, how many native species are there?

   A) 57

   B) 135

   C) 285

   D) 855

3. On the starting 11 for a soccer team, nine of the players are right-footed and two are left-footed. What is the ratio of right-footed to left-footed players?

   A) $\frac{2}{9}$

   B) $\frac{2}{11}$

   C) $\frac{9}{11}$

   D) $\frac{9}{2}$

Use the Kaplan Method to answer the following questions for homework.

1. In the month of July, the ratio of cirrus to altocumulus clouds in the sky was 4:3. If there were 21 altocumulus clouds that month, how many cirrus clouds were there?

   A) 7

   B) 12

   C) 28

   D) 63

2. Jackie's motorcycle can travel as fast as 100 miles per hour. How far does she need to travel if she is planning to ride for two hours at half of the top speed?

   A) 50 miles

   B) 100 miles

   C) 150 miles

   D) 200 miles

3. At a comic convention, there are 17 cosplayers who have entered in the costume contest. If 6 of the cosplayers are male, what is the ratio of male to female cosplayers?

   A) 6:17

   B) 6:11

   C) 17:6

   D) 10:6

The following questions are similar to what you would encounter on a college admissions test like the SAT or ACT. Use the Kaplan Method for Math and your knowledge of ratios, proportions, and rates to answer the following questions.

1. During flight, a commercial airliner traveled at a speed of 510 knots. If the airliner traveled 1467.5 miles in 2.5 hours, what is the conversion factor between knots and mph?

   A) 1 knot:1.15 mph

   B) 1 knot:1.67 mph

   C) 1 knot:2.33 mph

   D) 1 knot:2.35 mph

2. If the radius of the following circle is 3.5, what is the ratio of the triangle's area to the area of the shaded region?

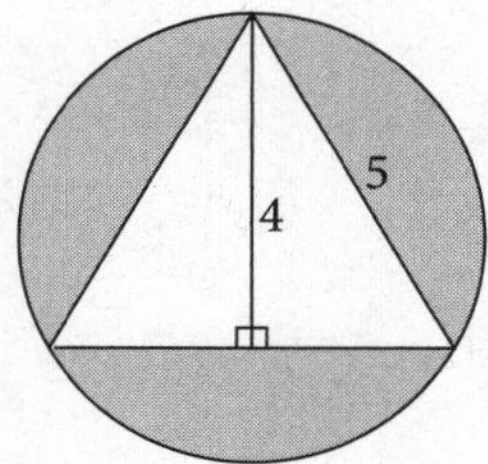

   A) 0.31

   B) 0.37

   C) 0.45

   D) 0.69

CHAPTER 17

Percents

CHAPTER OBJECTIVES

By the end of this chapter, you will be able to:

1. Calculate percents and their decimal and fractional equivalents
2. Calculate percent increase and percent decrease

THE KAPLAN METHOD FOR MATH

Step 1: Read the question, identifying and organizing important information as you go

- What information am I given?
- Separate the question from the context.
- How are the answer choices written?
- Should you label or draw a diagram?

Step 2: Choose the best strategy to answer the question

- Look for patterns.
- Pick numbers or use straightforward math.

Step 3: Check that you answered the *right* question

- Review the question stem.
- Check units of measurement.
- Double-check your work.

PERCENTS

Expressing ratios as percents allows you to combine and compare unlike fractions in a standard way. In chapter 2, you added and subtracted unlike fractions by using the **least common multiple** as the **lowest common denominator**. With percents, you will use a common denominator of 100 to combine and compare unlike fractions.

✔ Helpful Hint

Fractions are used to name parts of a whole object or part of a whole collection of objects and can be thought of as: $\frac{\text{part}}{\text{whole}}$.

Follow the prompts below to rewrite the fractions with a denominator of 100.

Compare $\frac{11}{20}$ and $\frac{13}{25}$.

By what number do you need to multiply 20 to make 100? ______________________

By what number do you need to multiply 25 to make 100? ______________________

$\frac{11}{20} =$

$\frac{13}{25} =$

Multiply $\frac{11}{20}$ by $\frac{5}{5}$ and $\frac{13}{25}$ by $\frac{4}{4}$ to find your new fractions. Write these fractions into the empty spaces above.

17

Now you can easily compare the two fractions: $\frac{11}{20} = \frac{55}{100}$ and $\frac{13}{25} = \frac{52}{100}$. Therefore, $\frac{11}{20} > \frac{13}{25}$.

Decimal equivalents: Each of the fractions above can be written as its **decimal equivalent** simply by dividing its original numerator by its original denominator. $\frac{11}{20} = 0.55$ and $\frac{13}{25} = 0.52$.

Use your calculator to find the decimal equivalents of the following fractions:

$\frac{5}{8} =$

$\frac{3}{5} =$

$\frac{27}{80} =$

Converting to decimal equivalents allows you to more easily combine and compare unlike fractions.

$$\frac{5}{8}+\frac{3}{5}+\frac{27}{80}=0.625+0.600+0.3375=1.5625$$

THREE-PART FORMULA

Converting ratios to percents provides a method to compare different values in a standard way. Like **rates** and **ratios**, **percents** are determined using a **three-part formula**.

Percent Formula:

$$\text{Percent}=\frac{\text{part}}{\text{whole}}\times 100\%$$

Because the percent formula is a three-part formula, you can rearrange it to solve for any one of the three parts.

To find the whole:

Multiply both sides of the equation by the whole and divide both sides by the percent.

$$\frac{\text{whole}\times\text{percent}}{\text{percent}}=\frac{\text{whole}\times\frac{\text{part}}{\text{whole}}}{\text{percent}}\times 100\% \Rightarrow \text{whole}=\frac{\text{part}}{\text{percent}}\times 100\%$$

To find the part:

Multiply both sides of the equation by the whole and divide both sides by the 100%.

$$\frac{\text{whole}\times\text{percent}}{100\%}=\frac{\text{whole}\times\frac{\text{part}}{\text{whole}}}{100\%}\times 100\% \Rightarrow \text{part}=\frac{\text{whole}\times\text{percent}}{100\%}$$

17

✔ Helpful Hint

Think of the percent formula as the decimal equivalent of the original fraction times a form of 1 $\left(\text{mathematically, therefore, } 100\% = 100\left(\frac{1}{100}\right)\right)$.

Follow the steps to practice converting fractions to percents.

Convert $\frac{13}{20}$ to its percent equivalent.

Set up your **percent formula** and plug in the numbers:

$$\text{Percent}=\frac{13}{20}\times 100\%$$

Convert the fraction to its **decimal equivalent**.

Percent = $0.65 \times 100\%$

Distribute the 100.

Percent = 65%

Apply the same approach to solve the following multiple-choice question.

Last season, Maddy was up to bat 65 times. If she reached base safely 20% of the time, how many times did she get on base last season?

A) 11

B) 12

C) 13

D) 14

Step 1: Determine what information you are given and what you need to find.

You are given:

The total at bats for Maddy: 65 (the whole)

Her on-base percentage: 20% (the percent)

You need to find:

17

The number of times she got on base: *b* (the part)

Step 2: Use the arrangement of the percent formula that solves for the part.

$$\text{Part} = \frac{\text{Whole} \times \text{Percent}}{100\%}$$

$$b = \frac{65 \times 20\%}{100\%} = 65 \times 20\left(\frac{1}{100}\right) \div 100\left(\frac{1}{100}\right) = 65 \times 0.20 = 13$$

This worked solution would resemble the following:

Last season, Maddy was up to bat 65 times. If she reached base safely 20% of the time, how many times did she get on base last season?

A) 11
B) 12
C) 13
D) 14

Use Straightforward math:

$$\frac{65 \times 20\%}{100\%} = 65 \times 20\left(\frac{1}{100}\right) \div 100\left(\frac{1}{100}\right) = 65 \times 0.20 = 13$$

Double-check:

$$\frac{13}{65} \times 100\% = 0.20 \times 100\% = 20\% \checkmark$$

PERCENT INCREASE AND DECREASE

Calculating **percent change** allows you to compare the effect of some change on a situation. The formula for **percent change** is:

$$\text{Percent change} = \frac{\text{Actual change}}{\text{Original amount}} \times 100\%$$

Notice that now the part, or numerator, is the difference between the new amount and the beginning, or original, amount. The whole, or denominator, is the amount you started with.

Follow the prompts below to find the actual change and determine whether percent increase or decrease exists.

On opening night, 76 people attended the school play. On the second night, the attendance was 101 people. To the nearest hundredth, what was the percent increase or decrease in attendance between the two nights?

What is the actual change? ______________________________

New amount – *Original amount* = 101 − 76

Is there a percent increase or decrease? ______________________________

101 − 76 = 25

17

What is the percent increase or decrease? ______________________

$$\text{Percent Change} = \frac{101 - 76}{76} \times 100\% = 32.89\%$$

Apply the same approach to solve the following multiple-choice question.

Tonya worked for two hours and made 84 flashcards for her French test. If she was able to make 48 flashcards in the first hour, what was the percent increase or decrease in the number of cards she produced in the second hour (round your answer to the nearest whole percent)?

A) 14% decrease

B) 25% decrease

C) 14% increase

D) 25% increase

Step 1: Determine what information you are given and what you need to find.

You are given:

Number produced in the first hour: 48 (original amount)

Number produced in the second hour: 36 (84 – 48 = 36, Total original = New amount)

You need to find:

The percent change in the second hour compared to the first hour

Step 2: Use the percent change formula to determine the percent increase or decrease.

$$\text{Percent change} = \frac{\text{Actual change}}{\text{Original amount}} \times 100\%$$

$$\text{Percent change} = \frac{\text{New amount} - \text{Original amount}}{\text{Original amount}} \times 100\%$$

$$\text{Percent change} = \frac{36 - 48}{48} \times 100\% \Rightarrow \text{Percent change} = \frac{-12}{48} \times 100\% = -25\%$$

This worked solution would resemble the following:

Tonya worked for two hours and made 84 flashcards for her French test. If she was able to make 48 flashcards in the first hour, what was the percent increase or decrease in the number of cards she produced in the second hour (round your answer to the nearest whole percent)?

A) 14% decrease

B) 25% decrease

C) 14% increase

D) 25% increase

Straightforward math:

$$\% \text{ change} = \frac{(84 - 48) - 48}{48} \times 100\% = \frac{-12}{48} \times 100\% = -0.25 \times 100\% = -25\%$$

Use the Kaplan Method to answer the following questions. Use the hints provided as needed.

1. When Kylee averages 55 mph while driving to and from college, she can travel 32 miles per gallon of gas. When she averages 65 mph on the same trip, she can travel 24 miles per gallon of gas. What is the percent change in the miles per gallon when she increases her speed from 55 mph to 65 mph? (Round to the nearest whole percent.)

   A) 25% decrease

   B) 33% increase

   C) 15% increase

   D) 18% increase

hint *Carefully determine the original amount and the actual change asked for in the question.*

2. At a local high school, there are 450 seniors. Of those seniors, 30% are enrolled in at least one AP class, and 20% of that group takes two or more AP classes. What percentage of the entire senior class takes two or more AP classes?

   A) 4%

   B) 5%

   C) 6%

   D) 7%

hint *Use the* part $= \frac{\text{whole} \times \text{percent}}{100\%}$ *formula to get started on this question.*

3. An Internet service provider charges $48 per month and plans to increase its rate by 12.5%. What will its new monthly rate be?

   A) $6.00

   B) $42.00

   C) $54.00

   D) $60.50

hint *To find the new amount, add the amount of the increase to the original amount.*

17

Use the Kaplan Method to answer the following questions on your own.

1. During the school year, Darya practices the piano for 15 hours per week. If she increases her practice time by 40% over her summer vacation, how many additional hours per week will Darya practice?

   A) 5

   B) 6

   C) 20

   D) 21

2. A jacket on sale for 25% off its original price sells for $66. What is the original price of the jacket?

   A) $16.50

   B) $22.00

   C) $82.50

   D) $88.00

3. The minute hand on a clock completes one full revolution every 60 minutes. What percent of a full revolution does the minute hand complete in 18 minutes?

   A) 18%

   B) 25%

   C) 30%

   D) 33%

Use the Kaplan Method to answer the following questions for homework.

1. After receiving a 10% raise, Hunter makes \$15.95 an hour. How much was Hunter's hourly wage before his raise?

   A) \$14.36

   B) \$14.50

   C) \$17.40

   D) \$17.55

2. On the first day of class, 25 students are enrolled. After three more boys join the class, 50% of the class consists of boys. What percent of the original class did girls comprise?

   A) 50%

   B) 52%

   C) 54%

   D) 56%

3. A baseball team has played 32 games of its 72 game season and has won 50% of the games it has played so far. How many additional games must it win in order to finish the season winning 75% of all the games it played?

   A) 16

   B) 24

   C) 32

   D) 38

The following questions are similar to what you would encounter on a college admissions test like the SAT or ACT. Use the Kaplan Method for Math and your knowledge of percents to answer the following questions.

1. Mylan drives for 10 hours and travels 480 miles. By what percent must he increase his speed if he wants to make the return journey in 8 hours?

   A) 12%

   B) 15%

   C) 20%

   D) 25%

2. The number of tomatoes that Jonelle harvested from her garden in its second year is 20% lower than it was in its first year. By what percent of the second year's harvest must the third year's harvest increase in order to match the first year's?

   A) 20%

   B) 25%

   C) 30%

   D) 35%

CHAPTER 18

Probability

CHAPTER OBJECTIVES

By the end of this chapter, you will be able to:

1. Determine desired and possible outcomes using probability rules
2. Express probabilities as fractions, decimals, and percents

THE KAPLAN METHOD FOR MATH

Step 1: Read the question, identifying and organizing important information as you go

- What information am I given?
- Separate the question from the context.
- How are the answer choices written?
- Should you label or draw a diagram?

Step 2: Choose the best strategy to answer the question

- Look for patterns.
- Pick numbers or use straightforward math.

Step 3: Check that you answered the *right* question

- Review the question stem.
- Check units of measurement.
- Double-check your work.

PROBABILITY

Probability is the measure of the likelihood that an event will happen. It is expressed as a ratio that compares the **number of desired outcomes** to the **total number of possible outcomes**:

$$\text{Probability} = \frac{\text{Number of desired outcomes}}{\text{Number of total possible outcomes}}$$

If you use a coin toss to determine if you or your friend gets to choose a movie to watch, the total number of possible outcomes is two: heads and tails. The desired outcome is one because you want the coin to land on the side that will give you the power to choose the movie. Plugging those numbers into the formula, the probability of you choosing the movie is $\frac{1}{2}$:

$$\text{Probability} = \frac{\text{Number of desired outcomes}}{\text{Number of total possible outcomes}} = \frac{1}{2}$$

EXPRESSING PROBABILITY

Probability can be written as a fraction, decimal, or percent. To convert a fraction to a decimal, divide the numerator by the denominator. Using the coin-flip example, $\frac{1}{2} = 1 \div 2 = 0.5$. To convert a decimal to a percentage, you multiply the decimal by 100%:

$$0.5 \times 100\% = 50\%$$

✔ Helpful Hint

When you multiply a number by 100, all you need to do is move the decimal to the right two places because there are two zeros in 100.

To convert from a percentage to a decimal, divide the percentage by 100%:

$$\frac{50\%}{100\%} = 0.5$$

18 **Fill in the following table by converting among fractions, decimals, and percentages.**

Fraction	Decimal	Percentage
$\frac{1}{4}$	0.25	
$\frac{1}{2}$		50%
	0.20	20%
	0.75	
		12.5%

PROBABILITY: INDEPENDENT EVENTS

Two events are **independent** if they do not affect each others' number of desired and total outcomes. To find the probability that two independent events will occur, multiply their individual probabilities:

Probability of two independent events = probability of 1st event × probability of 2nd event

If the probability that it will rain on Monday is 30% and the probability that it will rain on Tuesday is 40%, what is the probability that it will rain on both days?

Probability that it will rain on both days = $0.30 \times 0.40 = 0.12$

The probability that it will rain on both Monday and Tuesday is 12%, given that $0.12 \times 100\% = 12\%$.

THE PROBABILITY THAT AN EVENT *WILL NOT* HAPPEN

You can find the probability that something will not occur using the following formula:

1 – probability that the event will occur

If you are standing in a group with 19 other students and a teacher chooses one person at random to help with a demonstration, what is the probability that the teacher will not choose you?

Probability that the teacher will not choose you = $1 - \frac{1}{20} = \frac{19}{20}$

Because you are 1 of 20 students the teacher can choose, the probability that you *will* be chosen is $\frac{1}{20}$. When you subtract that probability from 1, you can determine that there is a 95% chance you *will not* be chosen, given that $\frac{19}{20} \times 100\% = 95\%$.

SOLVING PROBABILITY QUESTIONS

You can approach each probability question in the same way:

- Determine which formula you need:
  - Probability = $\frac{\text{Number of desired outcomes}}{\text{Number of total possible outcomes}}$
  - Probability of two independent events = probability of 1st event × probability of 2nd event
  - Probability that an event will NOT happen = 1 – probability it will happen
- Plug the relevant information in the question stem into the correct formula
- Calculate and simplify

PREPARE

Follow the steps to practice determining the correct formula, plugging in the relevant information, and calculating.

1. Randomly selecting students from her class, a teacher is making a team of four students for a trivia contest. There are 14 students with brown eyes, 3 students with blue eyes, 2 students with hazel eyes, and 1 student with green eyes. What is the probability that the first student placed on the team has blue eyes?

   Step 1: Determine which formula you need ____________________

   Step 2: Plug in the relevant information ____________________

   Step 3: Calculate and simplify ____________________

2. In a standard deck of cards, there are 13 diamonds, 13 hearts, 13 spades, and 13 clubs. If you choose one card at random, what is the probability that the card you choose will not be a diamond card?

   Step 1: Determine which formula you need ____________________

   Step 2: Plug in the relevant information ____________________

   Step 3: Calculate and simplify ____________________

3. There are three types of juice available in the cafeteria: cran-apple, cran-grape, and orange. If you randomly choose a bottle of juice on Thursday and Friday, what is the probability that you will choose a bottle of orange juice on both days?

   Step 1: Determine which formula you need ____________________

   Step 2: Plug in the relevant information ____________________

   Step 3: Calculate and simplify ____________________

18

Apply the same approach to solve the following multiple-choice question.

There are 30 total gumballs in a candy machine: 22 lemon-flavored and 8 strawberry-flavored gumballs. The chance of getting any one particular gumball is random. What is the probability you will get a strawberry-flavored gumball on your first try?

A) $\frac{11}{15}$

B) $\frac{4}{15}$

C) $\frac{22}{30}$

D) $\frac{4}{11}$

Step 1: Determine which formula you need ____________________

Step 2: Plug in the relevant information ____________________

Step 3: Calculate and simplify ____________________

This worked solution would resemble the following:

There are 30 total gumballs in a candy machine: 22 lemon-flavored and 8 strawberry-flavored gumballs. The chance of getting any one particular gumball is random. What is the probability you will get a strawberry-flavored gumball on your first try?

A) $\frac{11}{15}$

B) $\frac{4}{15}$

C) $\frac{22}{30}$

D) $\frac{4}{11}$

Straightforward math:

$$\text{Probability} = \frac{\text{Number of desired outcomes}}{\text{Number of total possible outcomes}} = \frac{8}{30} = \frac{8 \div 2}{30 \div 2} = \frac{4}{15}$$

18

Use the Kaplan Method to answer the following questions. Use the hints provided as needed.

1. What is the probability that two coin flips will both land heads up?

   A) $\frac{1}{4}$

   B) $\frac{1}{2}$

   C) $\frac{3}{4}$

   D) 1

hint *You have two independent events, so multiply the two probabilities together.*

2. In a small county on the West Coast, there are 842 female and 918 male citizens. What is the probability that a randomly selected citizen is male?

   A) 49%

   B) 51%

   C) 52%

   D) 54%

hint *Be careful with the calculation—your answer should be rounded to the nearest ones place.*

3. Of all the 226 films released in 1950, 14 films were musicals. If one 1950 film is chosen at random, what is the probability that it is not a musical?

   A) 0.007

   B) 0.062

   C) 0.116

   D) 0.938

hint *Subtract the probability of choosing a musical from 1 to determine the probability that a musical will not be chosen. Round your answer to the thousandths place.*

Use the Kaplan Method to answer the following questions on your own.

1. You have 10 pennies, 3 nickels, and 8 dimes in your pocket. What is the probability that you will randomly select a nickel?

   A) $\frac{1}{7}$

   B) $\frac{4}{17}$

   C) $\frac{3}{8}$

   D) $\frac{8}{21}$

2. The probability that a blue balloon will be given out at the fair is 0.4. What is the percentage probability that a blue balloon will NOT be given out?

   A) 40%

   B) 50%

   C) 60%

   D) 70%

3. Of 144 sheep in a farmer's flock, 96 are brown. What is the probability that a brown sheep will be randomly selected for shearing?

   A) 0.25

   B) 0.33

   C) 0.50

   D) 0.67

Use the Kaplan Method to answer the following questions for homework.

1. According to a scientific study, campers at Green Rock Park have a 3% chance of encountering a bear. If you stay at Green Rock Park for two days, what is the probability that you will encounter a bear both days?

   A) 0.0009

   B) 0.0003

   C) 0.01

   D) 0.3

2. 14 children and 29 adults are browsing a farmer's market. Each person attending the market gets one raffle ticket. What is the chance that a child will win the market's raffle prize? (One person is randomly selected.)

   A) 20%

   B) 33%

   C) 45%

   D) 67%

3. Max is playing checkers with his brother, Chase. Max controls the 12 red pieces, and his brother controls the 12 black pieces. Five minutes into the game, Max is in the lead. Max has captured 8 of Chase's black pieces, and Chase has not captured any of Max's red pieces. If Max and Chase's 3-year-old sister Sloane randomly takes one of the pieces off the board, what is the probability that the piece she selects will be black?

   A) 16.67%

   B) 25%

   C) 33.33%

   D) 75%

The following questions are similar to what you would encounter on a college admissions test like the SAT or ACT. Use the Kaplan Method for Math and your knowledge of probability to answer the following questions.

1. A large aquarium contains 39 guppies and 26 clownfish. How much greater is the probability that a guppy will be caught by a net than the probability that a clownfish will be caught (assume random selection)?

   A) The probabilities are equal.

   B) The probability of catching a guppy is 1.5 times the probability of catching a clownfish.

   C) The probability of catching a guppy is one-half the probability of catching a clownfish.

   D) The probability of catching a guppy is 3 times the probability of catching a clownfish.

2. A market research firm is interested in determining how likely consumers are to buy a product after watching an Internet advertisement. They determine that out of 500 people who viewed the advertisement, 75 of them went to the store within one week and purchased the product. According to the study, what is the probability that someone who views the ad will not purchase the product?

   A) 15%

   B) 30%

   C) 70%

   D) 85%

CHAPTER 19

Two-Way Tables

CHAPTER OBJECTIVES

By the end of this chapter, you will be able to:

1. Interpret a two-way table
2. Answer questions using the data provided in a two-way table

THE KAPLAN METHOD FOR MATH

Step 1: Read the question, identifying and organizing important information as you go

- What information am I given?
- Separate the question from the context.
- How are the answer choices written?
- Should you label or draw a diagram?

Step 2: Choose the best strategy to answer the question

- Look for patterns.
- Pick numbers or use straightforward math.

Step 3: Check that you answered the *right* question

- Review the question stem.
- Check units of measurement.
- Double-check your work.

TWO-WAY TABLES

A two-way table is a table that contains information about two variables. Two-way tables feature rows and columns, with one variable listed as the column headings and the second variable listed as the row headings. The data is contained in the cells of the table.

	Column Heading 1	Column Heading 2	Column Heading 3
Row Heading 1	Data Cell	Data Cell	Data Cell
Row Heading 2	Data Cell	Data Cell	Data Cell

To analyze a two-way table, first look at the row headings and determine what data sets are being compared. Then look at the column headings to see what categories are being compared.

✓ Helpful Hint

Questions about two-way tables are often grouped together as question sets.

Try It Out! **Answer the questions that accompany this graph to practice analyzing two-way tables.**

Hours of Daylight				
Latitude North	**Vernal Equinox**	**Summer Solstice**	**Autumnal Equinox**	**Winter Solstice**
0° N	12	12	12	12
20° N	12	13.2	12	10.8
40° N	12	14.8	12	9.2
60° N	12	18.5	12	5.5
80° N	12	24	12	0
90° N	24	24	0	0

First: Look at the row headings.

- What data sets are being compared? ______________________________

Second: Look at the column headings.

19

- What categories within the data sets are being compared? ______________________________

Additional analysis:

- Look at a single row and see how it changes across different categories.
  - 40° N changes from 12 hours to 14.8 hours to 12 hours to 9.2 hours at different times.
- Look at a single column and see how it differs depending upon the group.
  - During the summer solstice, the hours increase as the latitude increases.

✔ Helpful Hint

Two-way table questions ask you to find data in the table or determine ratios, percentages, or probabilities. The type of data in the table will determine the type of question you are asked.

Try It Out! **Follow the steps to practice answering questions about two-way tables.**

According to the information in the table, what is the range between the greatest and least number of daylight hours for latitudes within the Northern Temperate Zone (23.5° N to 66.5° N)?

A) 5.6

B) 12

C) 13

D) 24

Step 1: Determine what information you need to find in the table.

The question defines the rows containing the pertinent information:

Only 40° N and 60° N lie within the specified latitudes.

You need to find:

The latitude with the most and least hours of daylight in the relevant latitudes

Step 2: Use that information to set up an expression and answer the question.

40° N has 14.8 hours at the summer solstice and 9.2 hours at the winter solstice.

60° N has 18.5 hours at the summer solstice and 5.5 hours at the winter solstice.

$14.8 - 9.2 = 5.6$

$18.5 - 5.5 = 13$

This worked solution would resemble the following:

Hours of Daylight				
Latitude North	**Vernal Equinox**	**Summer Solstice**	**Autumnal Equinox**	**Winter Solstice**
0° N	12	12	12	12
20° N	12	13.2	12	10.8
40° N	12	(14.8)	12	(9.2)
60° N	12	(18.5)	12	(5.5)
80° N	12	24	12	0
90° N	24	24	0	0

According to the information in the table, what is the range between the greatest and least number of daylight hours for latitudes within the Northern Temperate Zone (23.5° N to 66.5° N)?

A) 5.6
B) 12
C) 13
D) 24

Check using straightforward math:

$(18.5 - 5.5) > (14.8 - 9.2) \Rightarrow 13 > 5.6$

19

Use the Kaplan Method to answer the following questions. Use the hints provided as needed.

Questions 1–3 refer to the following table.

Net U.S. Electrical Energy Generation by Source (Thousand Megawatt Hours)						
	Hydrocarbons	**Nuclear**	**Hydroelectric**	**Renewable**	**Other**	**Total**
2005	2,909,522	781,986	263,763	87,329	12,821	4,055,421
2006	2,871,118	787,219	282,688	96,525	12,974	4,050,524
2007	2,978,785	806,425	240,614	105,238	12,231	4,143,293
2008	2,915,024	806,208	248,543	126,101	11,804	4,107,680
2009	2,715,819	798,855	268,818	144,279	11,928	3,939,699
2010	2,872,048	806,968	254,702	167,173	12,855	4,113,746
2011	2,777,301	790,204	312,934	193,981	14,154	4,088,574
2012	2,763,127	769,331	271,290	218,333	13,787	4,035,868
2013	2,733,115	789,016	263,884	253,508	13,588	4,053,111
2014	2,738,114	797,067	252,540	281,060	12,576	4,081,357
AVERAGE	2,827,397	793,328	265,978	167,353	12,872	4,066,927

1. Which of the sources of electrical energy experienced the greatest change in net generation over the 10-year period displayed in the table?

   A) Hydrocarbons

   B) Nuclear

   C) Hydroelectric

   D) Renewables

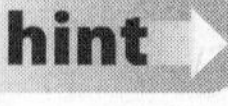

Subtract the last year from the first year for each of the sources in the answer choices.

2. In 2010, what percent of the net U.S. electrical energy was produced by nuclear power?

   A) 19.06%

   B) 19.33%

   C) 19.62%

   D) 20.28%

Use the percent $= \frac{\text{part}}{\text{whole}} \times 100\%$ *formula to get started on this question.*

3. What is the difference between the percent of the net U.S. electrical energy produced by renewable sources in 2014 and 2005?

   A) 2.22%

   B) 4.73%

   C) 47.3%

   D) 222%

hint *Find the percent for each year, and then subtract.*

19

Use the Kaplan Method to answer the following questions on your own.

Questions 1–3 refer to the following table.

Water Usage			
Year	**Population**	**Per Capita Urban Consumption (gallons per day)**	**Total Urban Consumption (gallons per day)**
1960	932,000	239	222,748,000
1980	1,674,000	304	508,896,000
1990	2,200,000	302	664,400,000
1995	2,372,000	288	683,136,000
2000	2,593,000	293	759,749,000
2005	2,877,000	249	716,373,000

1. During which time period did the population of the region grow the fastest?

   A) 1980–1990

   B) 1990–1995

   C) 1995–2000

   D) 2000–2005

2. By what percent did the population change between 1995 and 2000?

   A) 7.8%

   B) 8.4%

   C) 9.3%

   D) 10.5%

3. By what percent did the total water consumption change between 1995 and 2000?

   A) 11.2%

   B) 10.1%

   C) 2.8%

   D) 1.7%

Use the Kaplan Method to answer the following questions for homework.

Questions 1–3 refer to the following table.

U.S. Tax Receipts by Source (in millions of dollars)				
Fiscal Year	**1970**	**1980**	**1990**	**2000**
Individual Income Taxes	90,412	244,069	466,884	1,004,462
Corporate Income Taxes	32,829	64,600	93,507	207,289
Social Insurance Taxes	44,362	157,803	380,047	652,852
Excise Taxes	15,705	24,329	35,345	68,865
Other	9,499	26,311	56,174	91,723
Total Receipts	192,807	517,112	1,031,958	2,025,191

1. In which year was the percent of individual income tax receipts the least as a percent of total receipts?

   A) 1970

   B) 1980

   C) 1990

   D) 2000

2. If the ratio of corporate income taxes to individual income taxes in 2000 had remained the same as in 1970, what would the corporate income tax receipts (in millions of dollars) have been in 2000?

   A) 172,562

   B) 364,725

   C) 368,133

   D) 726,359

3. Which of the tax receipt sources had the greatest percent change between 1970 and 2000?

   A) Individual income taxes

   B) Corporate income taxes

   C) Social insurance taxes

   D) Excise taxes

The following questions are similar to what you would encounter on a college admissions test such as the SAT or ACT. Apply the Kaplan Method and your knowledge of two-way tables to answer the following questions.

Questions 1–2 refer to the following table.

Recommended Daily Amount of Dry Puppy Food (in cups)				
Weight (lb)	**6 to 11 Weeks**	**3 to 4 Months**	**5 to 7 Months**	**8 to 12 Months**
3	1.25 to 1.5	0.75 to 1.0	0.5 to 0.75	0.25 to 0.5
5	1.25 to 1.5	1.25 to 1.5	0.75 to 1.0	0.25 to 0.5
10	2.25 to 2.5	2.0 to 2.25	1.25 to 1.5	0.5 to 0.75
15	3.0 to 3.25	2.75 to 3.0	1.75 to 2.0	0.75 to 1.0
20	3.5 to 3.75	3.25 to 3.5	2.0 to 2.25	1.0 to 1.25

1. Miranda has two puppies. One is 3 months old and weighs 5 lb. The other is 9 months old and weighs 15 lb. Which of the following inequalities accurately expresses the number of cups, *c*, Miranda will feed her dogs each day?

   A) $1.5 \leq c \leq 2.25$

   B) $1.75 \leq c \leq 2.0$

   C) $2.0 \leq c \leq 2.5$

   D) $2.25 \leq c \leq 2.75$

2. Danielle feeds her 5-month-old puppy dry dog food that weighs 4 ounces per cup. If her dog weighs 20 lb, about how many days will a 5-pound bag of puppy food last? (There are 8 ounces in 1 cup.)

   A) 6 days

   B) 9 days

   C) 12 days

   D) 15 days

CHAPTER 20

Data Analysis

CHAPTER OBJECTIVES

By the end of this chapter, you will be able to:

1. Calculate the mean, median, mode, and range of a data set
2. Answer questions about statistical measures

THE KAPLAN METHOD FOR MATH

Step 1: Read the question, identifying and organizing important information as you go

- What information am I given?
- Separate the question from the context.
- How are the answer choices written?
- Should you label or draw a diagram?

Step 2: Choose the best strategy to answer the question

- Look for patterns.
- Pick numbers or use straightforward math.

Step 3: Check that you answered the *right* question

- Review the question stem.
- Check units of measurement.
- Double-check your work.

DATA SET

A **data set** is a collection, or list, of data points. Graphs—such as scatterplots, bar graphs, and line graphs—are plotted using one or more data sets.

If a researcher wanted to find out how many social media sites adults from ages 25 to 40 use, she could conduct a survey. The following data set is an example of the results the researcher could have collected from 10 individuals:

2, 1, 3, 0, 0, 4, 1, 4, 1, 5

Each number in the set is called a "data point" or "term." Many data sets are not arranged in ascending order, so reordering them is an important first step. The 10 responses in order are:

0, 0, 1, 1, 1, 2, 3, 4, 4, 5

MEAN

The **mean** of a data set is the average of its terms. In the social media website survey, there are 10 terms because 10 adults were surveyed, which provided 10 data points. To calculate the mean, add the terms and then divide by the number of terms:

$$\text{Mean} = \frac{\text{Sum of the terms}}{\text{Number of terms}} = \frac{0+0+1+1+1+2+3+4+4+5}{10} = 2.1$$

On average, an adult in the surveyed group belongs to 2.1 social media websites. A mean might not always make sense when written this way, but it's still mathematically correct. There is no such thing as one-tenth of a social media website, but you can say that on average, an adult in the surveyed group belongs to about 2 social media websites.

MEDIAN

The **median** is the middle value in the list of numbers when the numbers are arranged in ascending order. When a data set has an odd number of terms, finding the middle term is easy. When a data set has an even number of terms, you take the average of the two middle numbers.

In the social media website survey, the two middle-most numbers (the fifth and sixth terms) are 1 and 2, so you take the average of those numbers:

$$\text{Average of fifth and sixth terms} = \frac{1+2}{2} = 1.5$$

20

MODE

The **mode** of a data set is the number that appears most often. If each number in a data set appears an equal number of times, there is no mode, such as in the data set 6, 6, 7, 7, 10, 10. Some data sets have more than one mode, such as the data set 15, 15, 16, 17, 17, 18. In the social media website survey, the mode is 1 because the number 1 appears three times, which is the most often among the numbers 0, 1, 2, 3, 4, and 5.

RANGE

The **range** of a data set is the difference between the highest and lowest values of the data set. In the social media website survey, the highest value is 5 and the lowest is 0.

Range = highest value – lowest value = 5 – 0 = 5

✔ Helpful Hint

In addition to helping you evaluate the median and mode, putting a data set in ascending order makes it easier for you to identify the highest and lowest values.

SOLVING DATA ANALYSIS QUESTIONS

You can approach each data analysis question in the same way:

Step 1: Arrange the data set in ascending order

Step 2: Calculate the data analysis measurement(s) required by the question

Try It Out! **Complete the following sample questions.**

1. Below are the results of a survey on how many houseplants 10 families keep in their homes:

   7, 4, 2, 1, 0, 3, 3, 3, 2, 8

   What is the mean, median, mode, and range of the data set?

Step 1: Arrange the data set in ascending order ______________________________

Step 2: Calculate the data analysis measurement(s) required by the question

____

____

____

____

2. Rinny is trying to improve her favorite online video game win-loss percentage. She plays three 10-minute games per evening in between homework assignments. Each evening for 15 days, she writes down in her journal how many times she wins per evening. The results include:

   1, 2, 3, 3, 3, 2, 1, 0, 0, 1, 3, 1, 1, 1, 2

   What are the mean, median, mode, and range of the data set?

Step 1: Arrange the data set in ascending order. ______________________________

Step 2: Calculate the data analysis measurement(s) required by the question.

____

____

____

____

Try It Out! **Work through the following multiple-choice question.**

What is the median of a data set with an even number of terms and whose two middle terms are 9 and 14 when arranged in ascending order?

A) 11.5
B) 12
C) 12.5
D) 14

Step 1: Arrange the data set in ascending order.

You're not given a full data set. Instead, you're told that the data set has an even number of terms and the middle-most two numbers are 9 and 14. You could imagine the data set might look something like this:

__, __, __, __, 9, 14, __, __, __, __

Step 2: Calculate the data analysis measurement(s) required by the question.

Use straightforward math to average the two middle terms to find the median.

$$\text{Median} = \frac{9 + 14}{2} = 11.5$$

This worked solution would resemble the following:

What is the median of a data set with an even number of terms and whose two middle terms are 9 and 14 when arranged in ascending order?

A) 11.5
B) 12
C) 12.5
D) 14

Straightforward math:

$$\text{Median} = \frac{9 + 14}{2} = 11.5$$

Use the Kaplan Method to answer the following questions. Use the hints provided as needed.

Questions 1–3 refer to the following information.

A college conducted a survey among 13 full-time and part-time college students. They were asked, "In how many courses do you plan to enroll for your next semester?" Their answers included: 4, 3, 4, 4, 4, 5, 5, 5, 4, 1, 3, 4, 6.

1. What is the mean of the data set?

   A) 3.33

   B) 4.00

   C) 4.67

   D) 5.50

hint *The mean of the data set is the same as the average. Divide the sum of the terms by the number of the terms.*

2. What is the mode of the data set?

   A) 3

   B) 4

   C) 5

   D) There is no mode.

hint *Arranging the data set in ascending order will help you to pick out the number that appears the most.*

3. If a 14th student is surveyed and the student is enrolled in 7 classes the first semester, what would be the range of the new data?

   A) 4

   B) 5

   C) 6

   D) 7

hint *Add the new data point to your current list and then subtract the lowest value from the highest value.*

Use the Kaplan Method to answer the following questions on your own.

Questions 1–3 refer to the following information.

A shipping company tracked how many miles a cargo truck driver traveled each day during a nine-day westward trip: 522, 495, 508, 488, 432, 565, 542, 426, 513.

1. How many miles per day did the truck driver travel on average?

   A) 472

   B) 499

   C) 504

   D) 517

2. What is the median of the data set?

   A) 495

   B) 504

   C) 508

   D) 513

3. What is the range of the data set?

   A) 139

   B) 426

   C) 565

   D) 991

Use the Kaplan Method to answer the following questions for homework.

1. If the mean of a data set is 23.5 and there are seven terms in the data set, what is the sum of the terms?

   A) 114.5

   B) 132.3

   C) 164.5

   D) 192.4

2. The range of a data set is 942 and the highest-valued term is 1,439. What is the lowest-valued term?

   A) 497

   B) 838

   C) 1,541

   D) 2,381

3. If a data set's terms sum to 153 and there are 17 terms in the set, what is the mean of the data set?

   A) 8

   B) 9

   C) 10

   D) 11

The following questions are similar to what you would encounter on a college admissions test like the SAT or ACT. Use the Kaplan Method for Math and your knowledge of data analysis to answer the following questions.

1. The mean, median, and mode of a particular data set are all equal. Based on this information, which of the following data sets could it be?

   A) 1, 1, 1, 1, 1, 1

   B) 1, 3, 3, 3, 5

   C) 1, 2, 3, 4, 5

   D) 2, 2, 2, 4, 4, 4

2. A data set has eight terms and a mode of 19. All of the terms have the same value as the mode except for one term, which has a value of 2. What is the mean of the data set?

   A) 13.74

   B) 14.91

   C) 15.42

   D) 16.88

CHAPTER 21

Scatterplots

CHAPTER OBJECTIVES

By the end of this chapter, you will be able to:

1. Recognize scatterplot charts as visual representations of data from two variables
2. Estimate the shape of a best-fit line: linear or nonlinear
3. Examine the best-fit line to interpret the data and variables

THE KAPLAN METHOD FOR MATH

Step 1: Read the question, identifying and organizing important information as you go

- What information am I given?
- Separate the question from the context.
- How are the answer choices written?
- Should you label or draw a diagram?

Step 2: Choose the best strategy to answer the question

- Look for patterns.
- Pick numbers or use straightforward math.

Step 3: Check that you answered the *right* question

- Review the question stem.
- Check units of measurement.
- Double-check your work.

SCATTERPLOTS

Scatterplots are the data points from two variables plotted on an *xy*-coordinate plane. You can take data from any two variables and create a scatterplot.

x-value	1	3	4	5	7	8
y-value	5	7	8	6	9	11

Each data point consists of one *x*-value and its matching *y*-value. There are six (*x*, *y*) data points in the table above. If you plot them on an *xy*-coordinate plane, the result will look like the chart below:

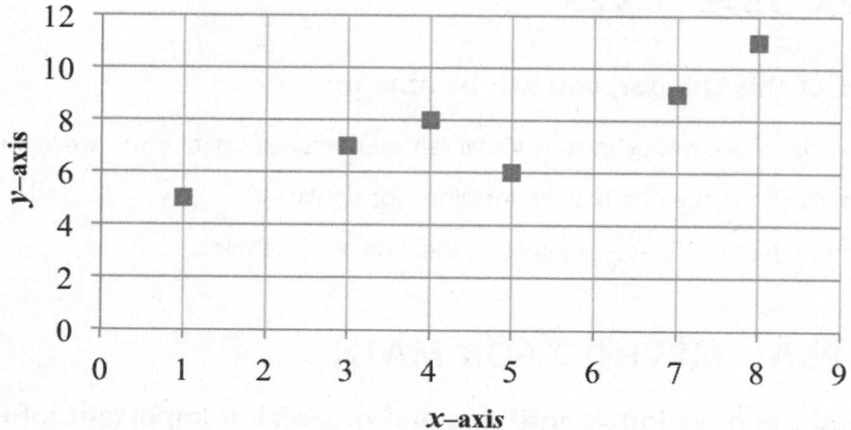

Because the values of *y* increase as the values of *x* increase (moving right along the *x*-axis), there is a **positive relationship** between the two variables.

> A **positive relationship** between two variables is one in which *y increases* as *x increases* and *y decreases* as *x decreases*. In a positive relationship, the variables **move in the same direction.**
>
> **If x ↑, y ↑** *and* **If x ↓, y ↓**

> An **inverse relationship** between two variables is one in which *y decreases* as *x increases* and *y increases* as *x decreases*. In an inverse relationship, the variables **move in opposite directions.**
>
> **If x ↑, y ↓** *and* **If x ↓, y ↑**

A **best-fit line**, also known as a line of best fit, is a line that a computer program places within a scatterplot to show the relationship between the variables. A positive relationship will be demonstrated by a line with an increasing (positive) slope, while a negative relationship will be demonstrated by a line with a decreasing (negative) slope. Each data point is some distance from the line. With a best-fit line, the sum of all the distances between the line and the data points is lowest. It fits the data better than any other line that could be drawn on the scatterplot.

Best-fit lines don't have to be drawn by computer programs with 100 percent accuracy. You can draw a best-fit line estimate and still get a good idea about the trends between the two variables.

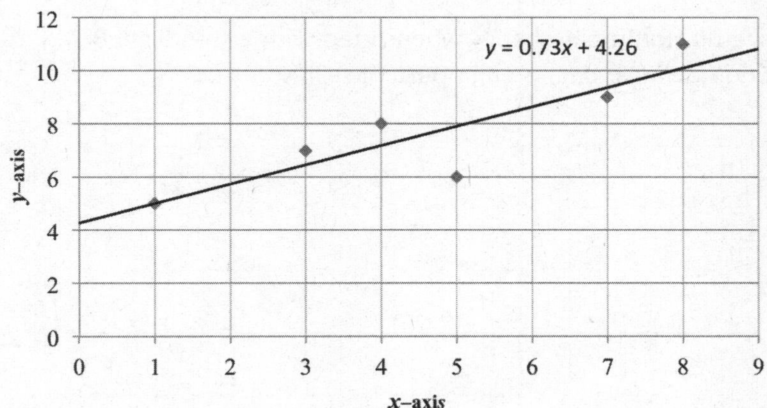

The best-fit line on the scatterplot above shows a positive relationship between the *x* and *y* variables. The slope of the line is increasing/positive.

Note that the data points don't all fit exactly on the line. Data points like the one at (5, 6) are relatively far away from the line and lower the effectiveness of the best-fit line to approximate the relationship between *x* and *y*. A data point that is very far away from a trendline ("trendline" is another term for best-fit line) is called an **outlier**. If a line looks linear except for an outlier (often somewhere in the middle), you can ignore the outlier when sketching your estimated trendline.

It is also important to note that the **interval** between *x*-values displayed on the graph is 1, while the interval between *y*-values is 2. Graphs will vary in terms of how their axes are set up. Keep track of how much each tick mark on an axis represents when you're visually estimating the slope of a line.

The equation of the best-fit line is provided on the chart. It is written in $\boldsymbol{y = mx + b}$ format. Based on the linear equation:

A. What is the slope of the line? ____________________

B. For every one unit increase in *x*, how much does *y* increase? ____________________

C. What is the *y*-intercept of the line? ____________________

D. What is the *x*-intercept of the line? ____________________

hint *The x-intercept can't be seen on the graph. It is located in the second quadrant (the part of the coordinate plane where x is negative and y is positive). To solve for the x-intercept, plug 0 into y and solve for x.*

LINEAR VS. NONLINEAR BEST-FIT LINES

The trendline you just examined shows a **linear** relationship between *x* and *y*.

Data can also take on **nonlinear** shapes when fitted with a trendline. Being able to distinguish between linear and nonlinear data is an important skill.

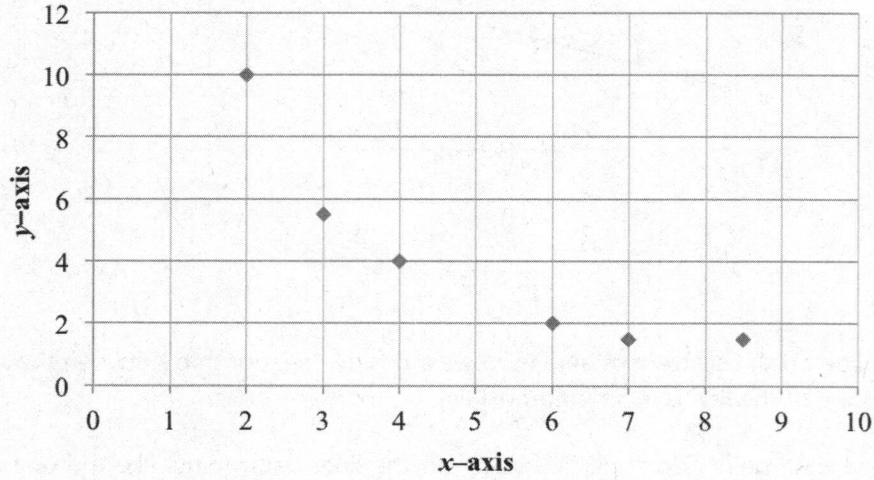

A linear equation will not be the best-fit option for the data set above. Notice how as *x* increases, the *y*-values decrease rapidly and then flatten out. A relationship involving a steadily changing slope is called an **exponential** relationship. Because *y* decreases as *x* increases (they move in opposite directions), it is a **negative exponential** relationship. The most important thing to recognize in the graph above is that a linear equation would not demonstrate the correct relationship between *x* and *y*. A nonlinear exponential best-fit line, as shown below, is optimal.

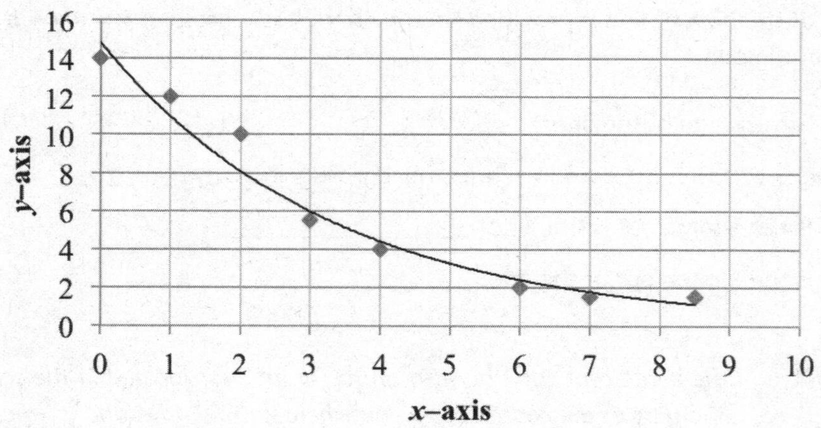

SOLVING SCATTERPLOT QUESTIONS

Try It Out! **Complete the following sample question.**

1. An environmental research team measured the number of sea urchins in a fixed 1,500 square-foot area on the southwest coast at different tide levels. Below is a scatterplot showing the data they collected. What is the relationship between tide level and sea urchin population? Is it linear or nonlinear? Positively or negatively related? At what tide level is the sea urchin population measurement farthest from the best-fit line?

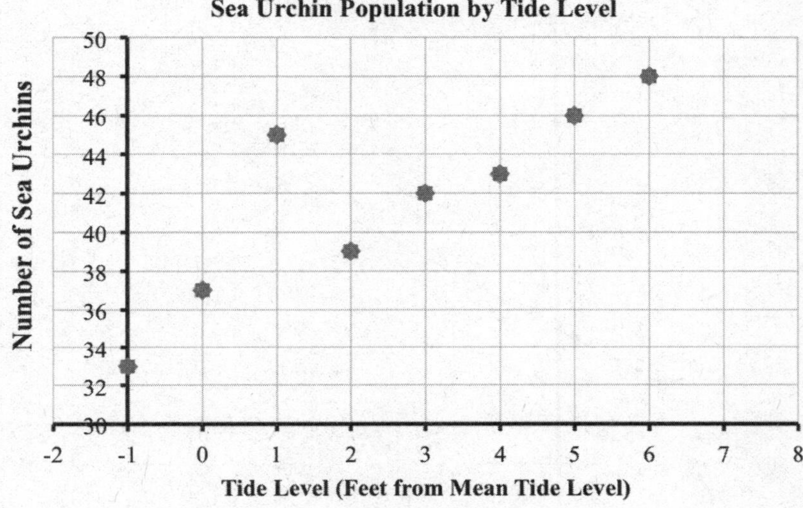

Step 1: Identify what the *x*- and *y*-values represent: *x*-values ________________

y-values ________________

Step 2: On the *x*-axis, what is the interval between each *x*-value? ________________

On the *y*-axis, what is the interval between each *y*-value? ________________

Step 3*a*: If a trendline is provided, determine if its slope is positive or negative: ________________

linear or nonlinear: ________________

Step 3*b*: If a trendline is not provided, does the data look linear or nonlinear? ________________

Draw an estimated trendline. Ignore far outliers.

Is its slope positive or negative? ________________

Step 4: Using the scatterplot and trendline, answer any questions about the data.

1. Are tide level and sea urchin population positively or negatively related? ____________
   As the tide gets higher, what happens to the sea urchin population? ____________
2. At what tide level is the sea urchin population measurement farthest from the trendline?
   ____

Step 5: Review your answer.

Try It Out! **Work through the following multiple-choice question.**

Based on the scatterplot below, how much does the value of *y* change for each unit increase of *x*?

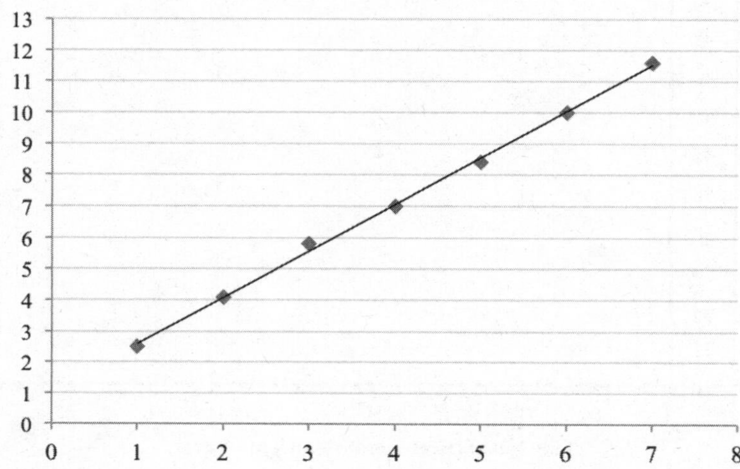

A) − 2.5

B) − 1.5

C) + 1.5

D) + 2.5

Step 1: Identify what the *x*- and *y*-values represent.
The figure shows a basic *x*–*y* plot with no axis labels. Based on the question stem, the *x*- and *y*-values don't represent any real-world quantities.

Step 2: On the *x*-axis, what is the interval between each *x*-value? ______
On the *x*-axis, what is the interval between each *y*-value? ______

Step 3*a*: If a trendline is provided, determine if its slope is positive or negative: ______
linear or nonlinear: ______

Step 4: Using the scatterplot and trendline, answer any questions about the data. For every one unit increase in *x* (moving to the right one tick on the *x*-axis), the value of *y* increases by about 1.5. Answer Choice (C) matches this measurement.

Step 5: Review your answer. The question is essentially asking for the slope of the trendline. Your analysis in Step 4 accurately determined the slope visually.

This worked solution would resemble the following:

Based on the scatterplot below, how much does the value of *y* change for each unit increase of *x*?

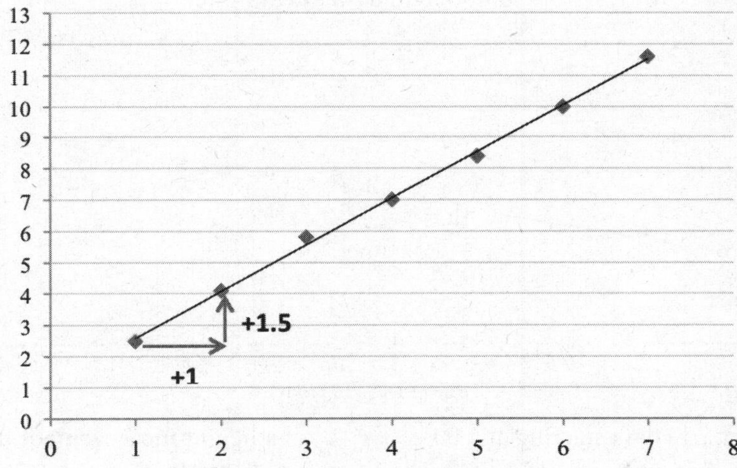

A) − 2.0

B) − 1.5

C) + 1.5

D) + 2.0

As *x* increases by one unit, *y* increases by about 1.5 units. Choice (C) is correct.

Use the Kaplan Method to answer the following questions. Use the hints provided as needed.

The following multiple-choice questions are based on the figure below.

The zebra pitch, a small carnivorous jungle plant, grows in height during the day to catch insect prey and recedes at night to avoid rodent predators.

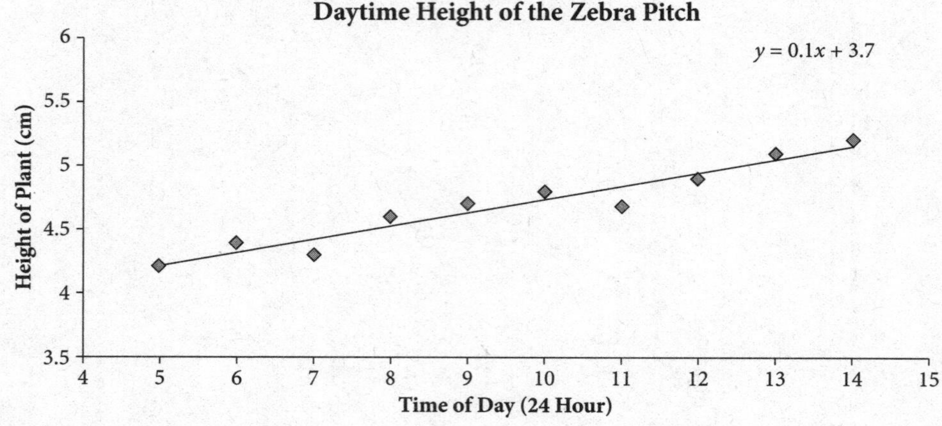

1. Based on the chart's data starting at 5:00, how much taller does the plant grow each hour?

   A) 0.01 cm

   B) 0.1 cm

   C) 1 cm

   D) 10 cm

hint *Using the slope of the best-fit line is easier than visually estimating the changes in y and x.*

2. If a height measurement had been taken at 15:00, what would the approximate height of the plant be? Based on the chart, the height of the plant at 14:00 is 5.2 cm.

   A) 5.2 cm

   B) 5.3 cm

   C) 5.4 cm

   D) 5.5 cm

hint *Use the trendline's slope to add the change in height per hour to 5.2 cm.*

Use the Kaplan Method to answer the following questions on your own.

The following multiple-choice questions are based on the figure below.

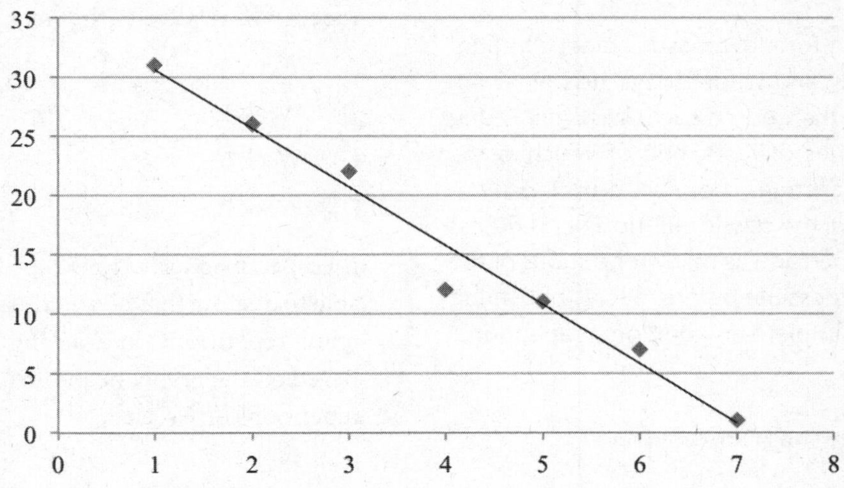

1. What is the approximate slope of the trendline?

   A) −5

   B) −2.5

   C) +2.5

   D) +5

2. If you extended the trendline to the left, what would the approximate y-value be at $x = -2$?

   A) 30

   B) 35

   C) 40

   D) 45

3. What is the estimated y-intercept of the trendline?

   A) (0, 30)

   B) (7, 0)

   C) (0, 35)

   D) (35, 7)

Use the Kaplan Method to answer the following questions for homework.

The following multiple-choice questions are based on the information below.

Fritz is training for a gymnastics meet. On Sundays, Mondays, and Wednesdays, he trains with his coach. At the end of each week on Friday, he does a series of tests, one of which is the muscle-up challenge. The muscle-up is a gymnastic variant of the classic pull-up. For his fitness test, he must perform as many repetitions of the muscle-up as possible before failure (becoming too tired to complete an additional repetition).

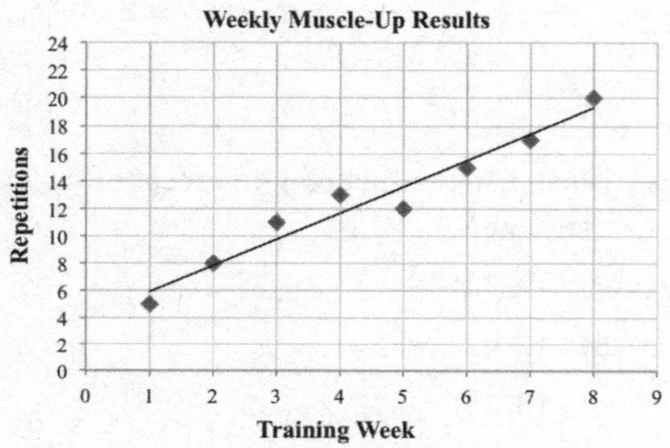

1. Based on the trendline's slope, how many muscle-up repetitions did Fritz gain each week on average?

   A) 1

   B) 2

   C) 4

   D) 6

2. Of the choices below, during which training week did Fritz see the largest gain in repetitions relative to the week before it?

   A) Week 4

   B) Week 5

   C) Week 6

   D) Week 7

3. If Fritz trained for 12 weeks total, it's reasonable to assume that he could perform how many repetitions on Training Week 12? Based on the graph, he performed 20 repetitions on Week 8.

   A) 22

   B) 25

   C) 28

   D) 33

The following questions are similar to what you would encounter on a college admissions test such as the SAT or ACT. Apply the Kaplan Method and your knowledge of scatterplots to answer the following questions.

1. Which type of trendline would best approximate the relationship between x and y in the plot below?

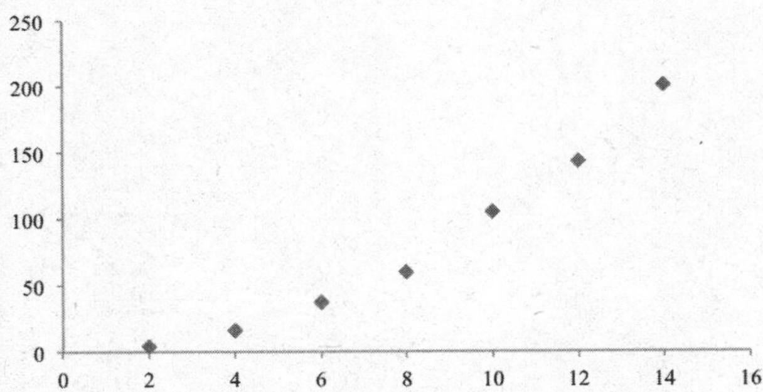

A) Linear

B) Exponential

C) Parabolic

D) Logarithmic

2. A scatterplot contains the following data points: (1, 1), (7, 6), (9, 9), (3, 4), (5, 5). If the points are placed on a scatterplot and a linear trendline is drawn, which of the following choices is closest to the line's slope?

A) −0.5

B) 0.5

C) 0.7

D) 1.0

UNIT FOUR

Geometry

IN THIS UNIT, YOU WILL LEARN HOW TO:

1. Find the measures of complementary and supplementary angles
2. Find the measures of angles formed by parallel lines intersected by a transversal
3. Find the measures of angles within a triangle
4. Find the measures of angles within a circle
5. Apply the Pythagorean theorem
6. Apply ratios involving special right triangles
7. Calculate the area of a triangle
8. Calculate the area and circumference of a circle
9. Calculate the length of a circle's arc
10. Calculate the area of a circle's sector
11. Write the equation of a circle given two points on a coordinate plane
12. Calculate the volume of pyramids, cones, and spheres

CHAPTER 22

Angles

CHAPTER OBJECTIVES

By the end of this chapter, you will be able to:

1. Find the measures of complementary and supplementary angles
2. Find the measures of angles formed by parallel lines intersected by a transversal
3. Find the measures of angles within a triangle
4. Find the measures of angles within a circle

THE KAPLAN METHOD FOR MATH

Step 1: Read the question, identifying and organizing important information as you go

- What information am I given?
- Separate the question from the context.
- How are the answer choices written?
- Should you label or draw a diagram?

Step 2: Choose the best strategy to answer the question

- Look for patterns.
- Pick numbers or use straightforward math.

Step 3: Check that you answered the *right* question

- Review the question stem.
- Check units of measurement.
- Double-check your work.

22

LINES AND ANGLES

Angle Type	Angle Measurement	Example
Acute	Less than 90° $0° < Acute < 90°$	
Right	90°	
Obtuse	Greater than 90° $90° < Obtuse < 180°$	
Straight	180°	
Complementary	Add to 90° $a° + b° = 90°$	$a°$ $b°$
Supplementary	Add to 180° $c° + d° = 180°$	$c°$ $d°$

✔ Helpful Hint

Two angles do not need to be next to each other to be complementary or supplementary.

Intersecting lines: When two lines **intersect**, the **adjacent** angles (next to each other) are supplementary and add to 180°. The **vertical** angles (across from each other) are equal.

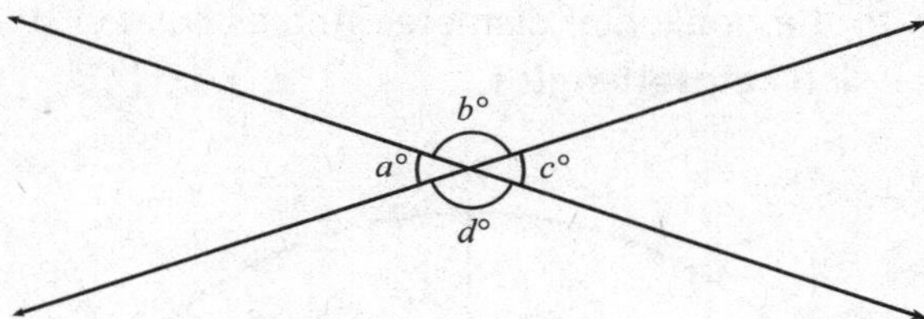

A. The vertical angles are ______________________________.

B. The supplementary angles are ______________________________.

Parallel lines: Parallel lines have equal slopes and never intersect. The symbol for parallel lines is ǀ.

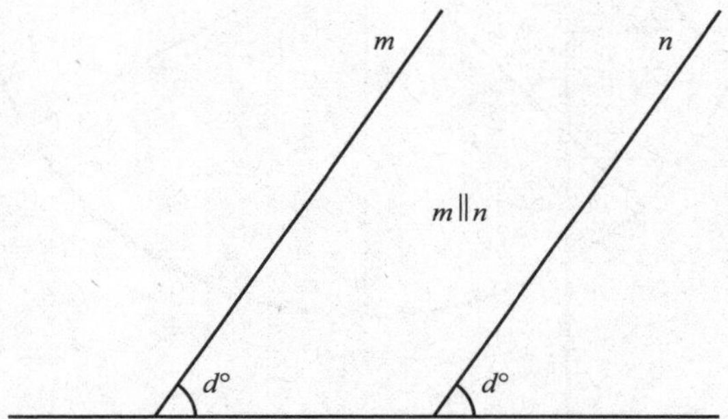

Transversals: A transversal is a line that intersects two parallel lines. When parallel lines are intersected by a transversal, all of the acute angles are equal, and all of the obtuse angles are equal.

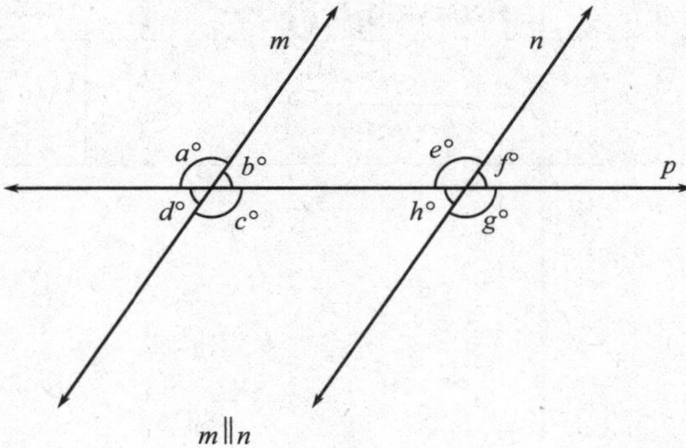

22

Angles in circles: A circle consists of points in a plane that are equidistant from a given point called the **center** or **origin**. There are 360° in a circle. Moving counterclockwise from the origin creates a **positive** angle in regard to the horizontal diameter. Moving clockwise from the origin creates a **negative** angle in regard to the horizontal diameter. Angles created by lines from the center of the circle to the edge are called **central angles**.

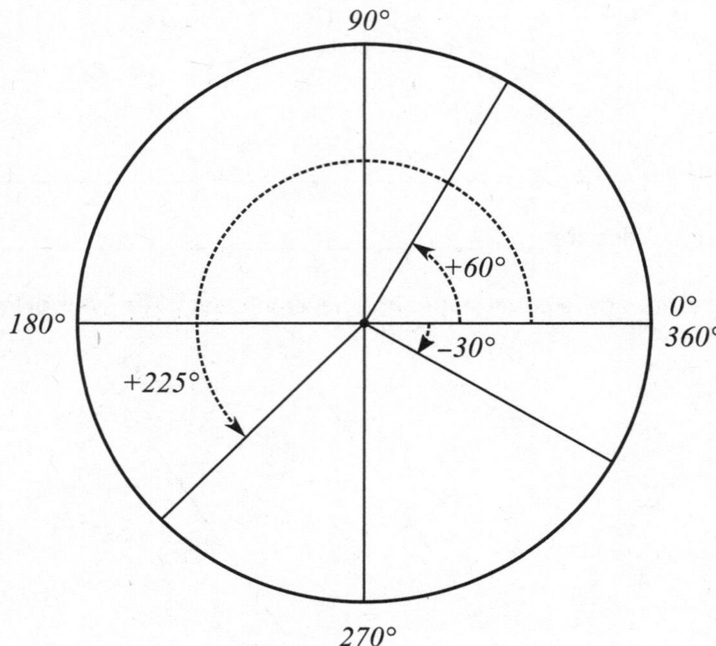

Central angle ratios: The ratio of the central angle to 360° equals the ratio of the **arc length** to the **circumference** and the ratio of the **area of the sector** to the **area of the circle**.

Central Angle Ratio		Arc Length Ratio		Area of the Sector Ratio
$\frac{\text{central angle}}{360°}$	=	$\frac{\text{arc length}}{\text{circumference}}$	=	$\frac{\text{area of the sector}}{\text{area of the circle}}$

Try It Out! **Complete the following sample question.**

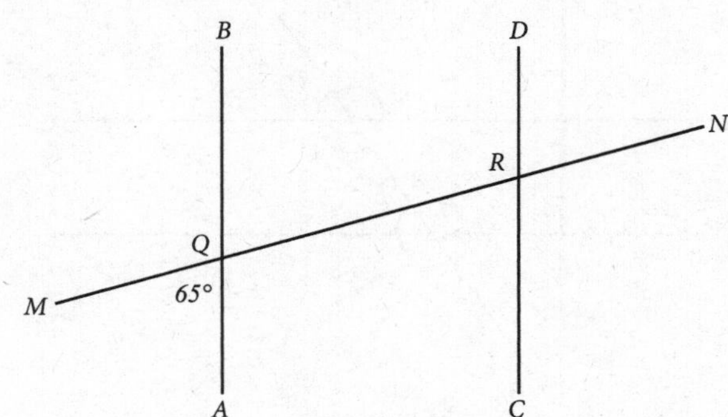

In the figure above, $\overline{AB}$ is parallel to $\overline{CD}$, and $\overline{MN}$ intersects $\overline{AB}$ at Q and $\overline{CD}$ at R. If the measure of $\angle AQM = 65°$, what is the sum of $\angle MQB + \angle CRN$?

Mark up the diagram with the missing angle measures:

A. All of the acute angles are ____________.

B. All of the obtuse angles are ____________.

Determine the measure of the angles you need:

C. $\angle MQB =$ ____________

D. $\angle CRN =$ ____________

E. What is the sum of the angles MQB and CRN? ____________

22

Try It Out! **Work through the following multiple-choice question.**

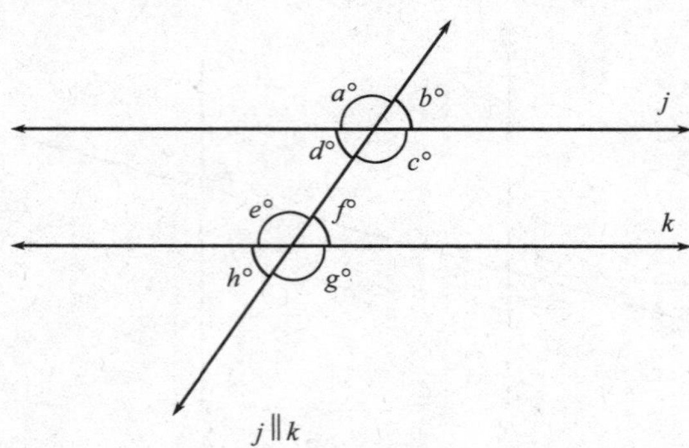

If $a° = 7f°$, what is the measure of $h°$?

A) 22.5

B) 45.0

C) 157.5

D) 180.0

Step 1: Determine if angles *a* and *f* are vertical or supplementary:

Angle *a* is obtuse and equal to angle *e*;

Angle *f* is acute and equal to angle *b*;

The angles are supplementary and add to 180°.

Step 2: Translate the information into math:

$$a + f = 180$$

Step 3: Substitute 7*f* for *a* in the expression and solve for *f*:

$$7f + f = 180 \Rightarrow 8f = 180 \Rightarrow f = 22.5$$

Step 4: What is the question? What is the value of *h*?

Angles *f* and *h* are both acute and equal.

$$h = 22.5$$

Use the Kaplan Method to answer the following questions. Use the hints provided as needed.

1. In the figure below, angles a and d are complementary and angle c is equal to $2d$. What is the sum of angles b and c?

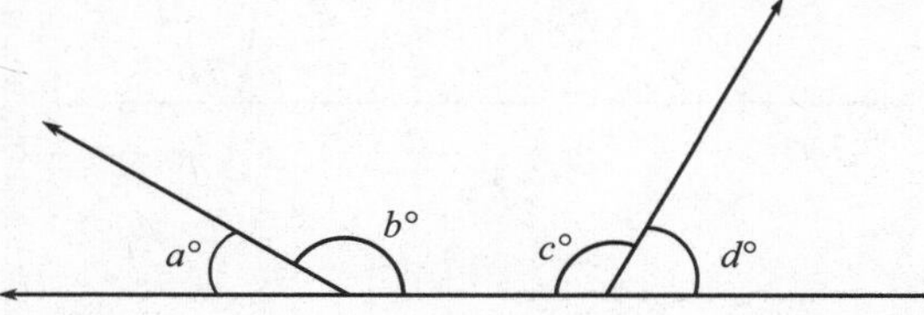

A) 90

B) 180

C) 270

D) 360

hint *Complementary angles add to 90°, and supplementary angles add to 180°.*

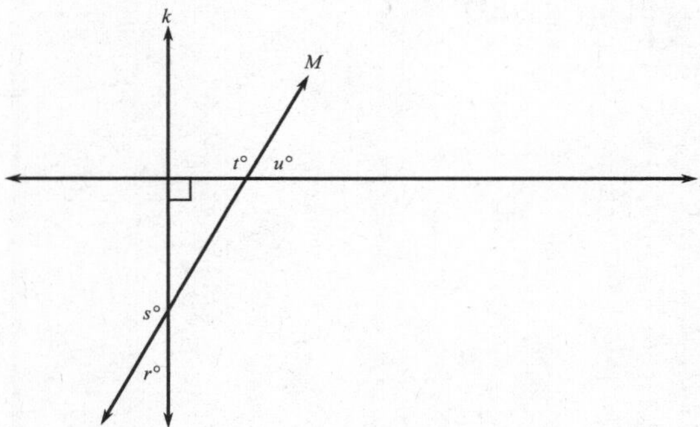

2. In the figure above, $t = 4r$ and $r = \frac{u}{2}$. What is the value of s?

A) 30

B) 60

C) 120

D) 150

hint *Keep your work organized. Rewrite the second equation to get rid of the fraction:* $2 \times r = 2 \times \frac{u}{2} \Rightarrow u = 2r$.

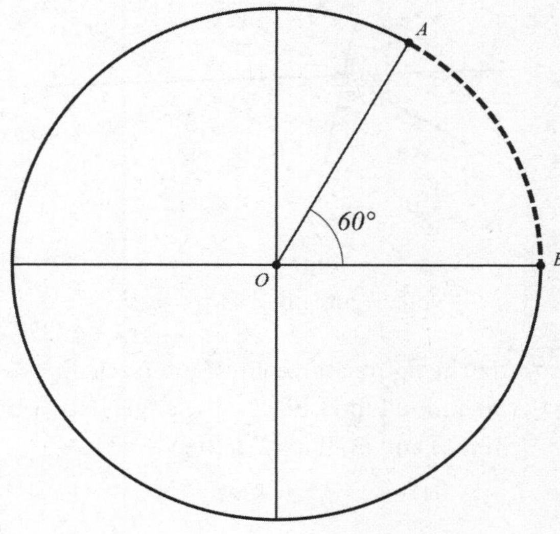

3. The circle above has a circumference of 12 inches. What is the length, in inches, of the arc that has a central angle of 60°?

A) 1

B) 2

C) 3

D) 4

hint *Set the ratios equal to each other and cross-multiply to solve for the unknown.*

Use the Kaplan Method to answer the following questions on your own.

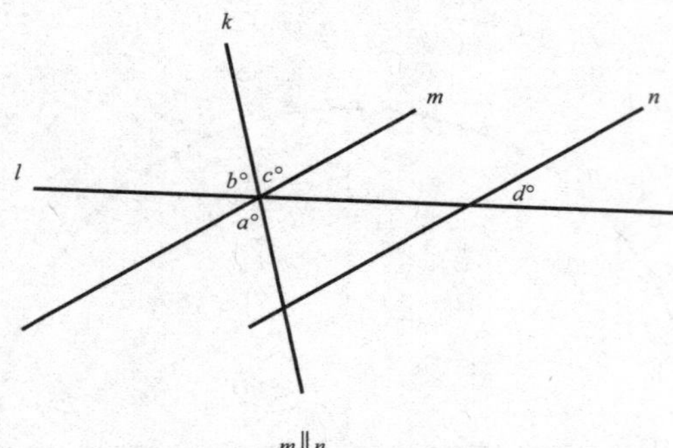

Note: Figure not drawn to scale.

1. In the figure above, line l intersects lines m and n. Line k bisects the angle between lines l and m. If $a = 72$, then $d =$?

   A) 36

   B) 72

   C) 108

   D) 144

2. Two friends are sharing a circular pizza that is divided into equal slices that have a central angle of 30°. How many slices will each friend get? (Assume that each person gets an equal number of slices.)

   A) 6

   B) 8

   C) 10

   D) 12

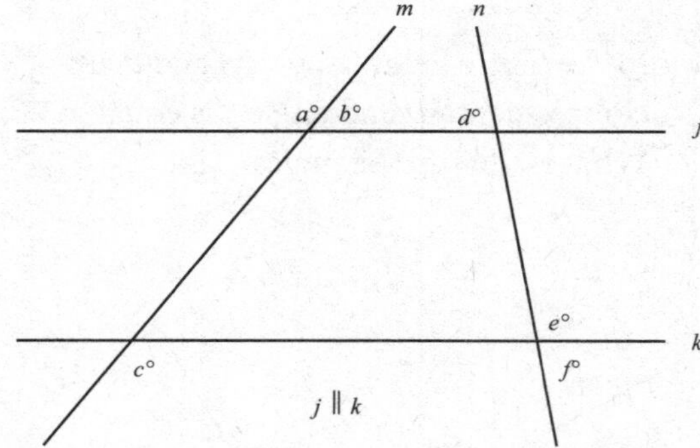

3. In the figure above, two parallel lines are intersected by two nonparallel line segments to create 16 angles. Which of the following pairs of angles is NOT sufficient for determining all 16 angle measures?

   A) a and d

   B) b and e

   C) c and d

   D) d and f

Use the Kaplan Method to answer the following questions for homework.

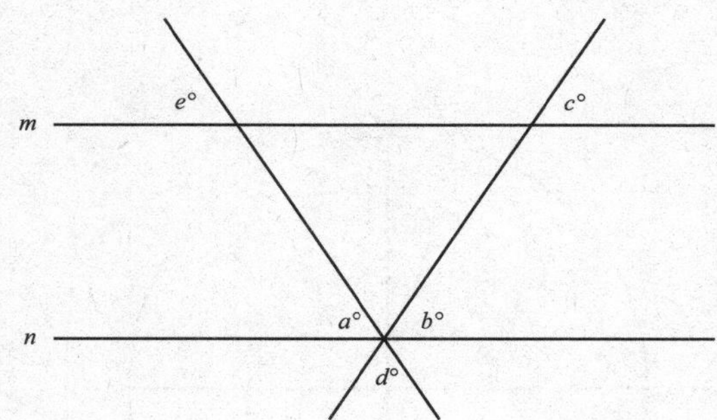

1. If line m is parallel to line n, which of the following must equal 180°?

   A) $c+d+e$

   B) $b+c+d$

   C) $a+d+e$

   D) $a+b+c$

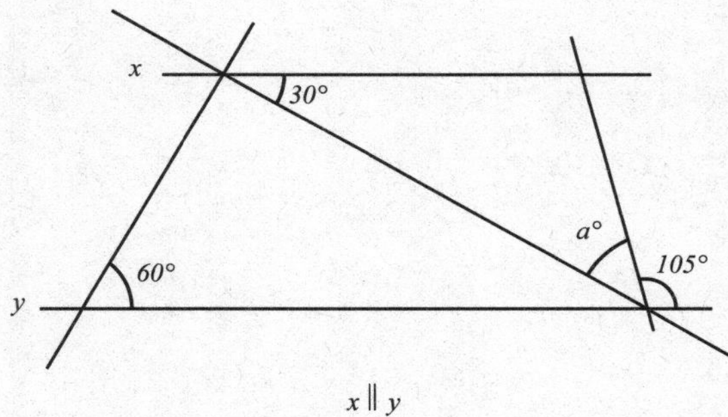

2. In the figure above, lines x and y are parallel, and the angle measures are as marked. What is the measure of angle a?

   A) 35

   B) 40

   C) 45

   D) 50

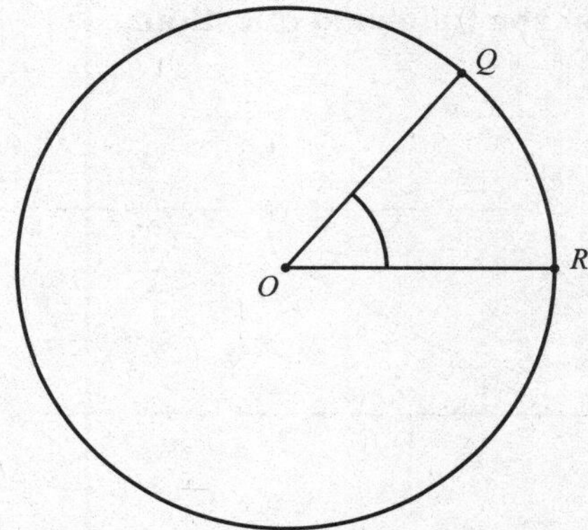

3. The circle above is centered at O and has a perimeter of 2π inches. What is the length, in inches, of the arc QR that has a central angle of 60°?

   A) $\frac{\pi}{5}$

   B) $\frac{\pi}{4}$

   C) $\frac{\pi}{3}$

   D) $\frac{\pi}{2}$

22

The following questions are similar to what you would encounter on a college admissions test such as the SAT or ACT. Apply the Kaplan Method and your knowledge of angles to answer the following questions.

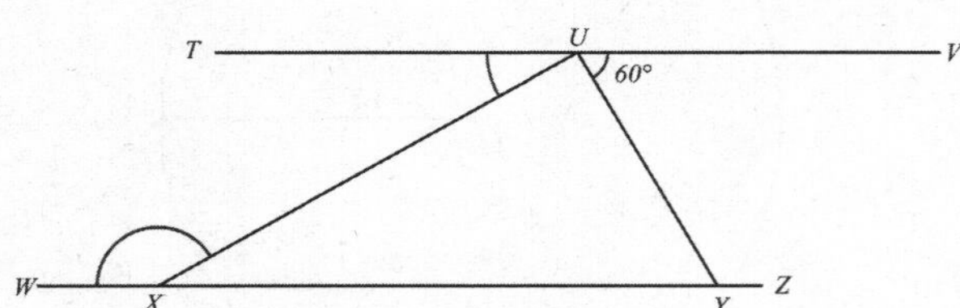

1. In the figure above, U is on $\overline{TV}$, X and Y are on $\overline{WZ}$, $\overline{TV}$ is parallel to $\overline{WZ}$, and $\angle XUT$ and $\angle VUY$ are complementary. What is the measure of $\angle WXU$?

   A) 75°

   B) 105°

   C) 120°

   D) 150°

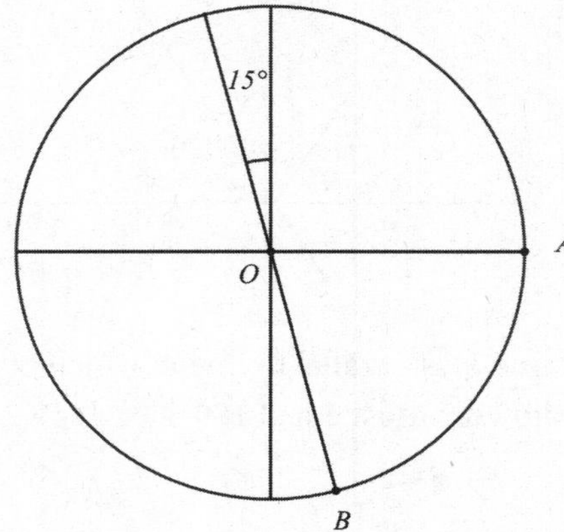

2. The circle above, centered at O, has a circumference of 96 inches. What is the length, in inches, of arc AB?

   A) 15

   B) 20

   C) 25

   D) 30

CHAPTER 23

Triangles

CHAPTER OBJECTIVES

By the end of this chapter, you will be able to:

1. Find the measures of angles within a triangle
2. Apply the Pythagorean theorem
3. Apply ratios involving special right triangles

THE KAPLAN METHOD FOR MATH

Step 1: Read the question, identifying and organizing important information as you go

- What information am I given?
- Separate the question from the context.
- How are the answer choices written?
- Should you label or draw a diagram?

Step 2: Choose the best strategy to answer the question

- Look for patterns.
- Pick numbers or use straightforward math.

Step 3: Check that you answered the *right* question

- Review the question stem.
- Check units of measurement.
- Double-check your work.

23

TRIANGLES

Triangles are formed from lines and angles. When two intersecting lines both intersect a third line, a triangle is formed.

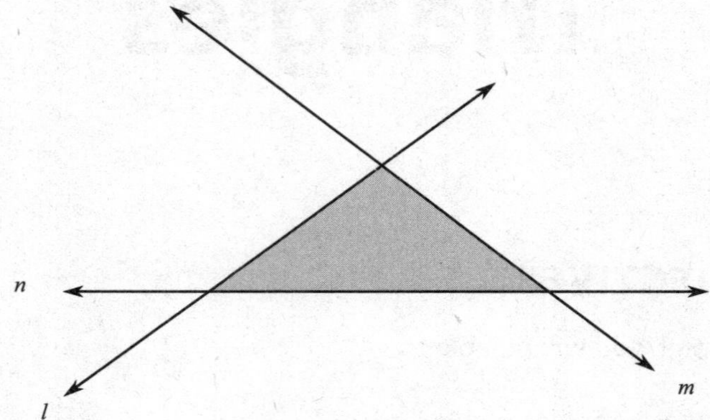

Triangle Rules

Every triangle follows the rules listed below, no matter what kind of triangle it is. When you are familiar with these rules, you can save time solving triangle questions. Use the diagram below to help you visualize the rules.

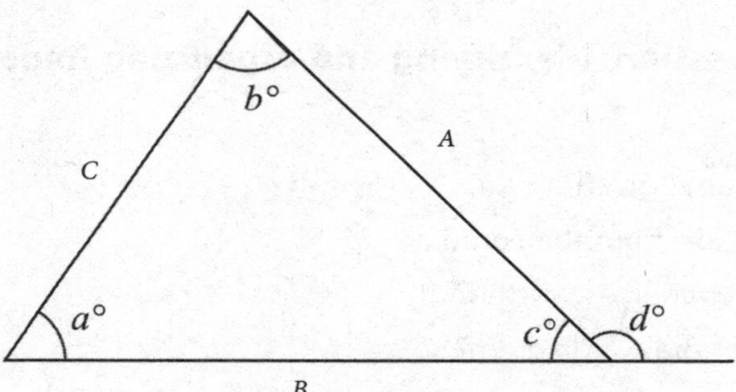

- The sum of the interior angles (*a*, *b*, and *c*) of a triangle is 180°.
    - $a+b+c=180$
- The exterior angle (in the diagram *d*) is supplementary with the adjacent interior angle (*c*) and equals the sum of the other two interior angles (*a* and *b*).
    - $c+d=180=a+b+c \Rightarrow d=180-c=a+b$
- A side opposite a greater angle is longer than a side opposite a smaller angle.
    - If $a=45$, $b=65$, and $c=70$, then $A<B<C$
- Similar triangles have equal angles and proportional sides.
- Triangle Inequality Theorem: The sum of any two side lengths must be greater that the third side length, and the positive difference of any two side lengths must be less than the third side length. $|A-B|<C<A+B$

PYTHAGOREAN THEOREM

If you know the lengths of any two sides of a **right triangle**, you can determine the unknown side by using the **Pythagorean theorem**, written as $a^2 + b^2 = c^2$, where a and b are the shorter sides, or **legs**, of the triangle and c is the longest side, or **hypotenuse**, of the triangle. The hypotenuse is always opposite the right angle, 90°, which is the greatest angle in a right triangle.

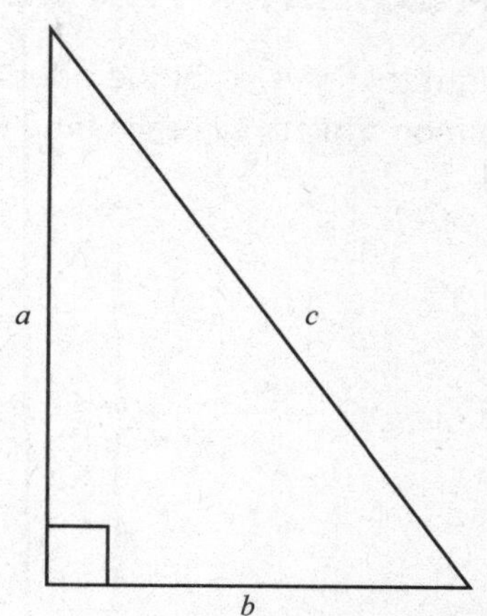

Try It Out! **Complete the following sample question.**

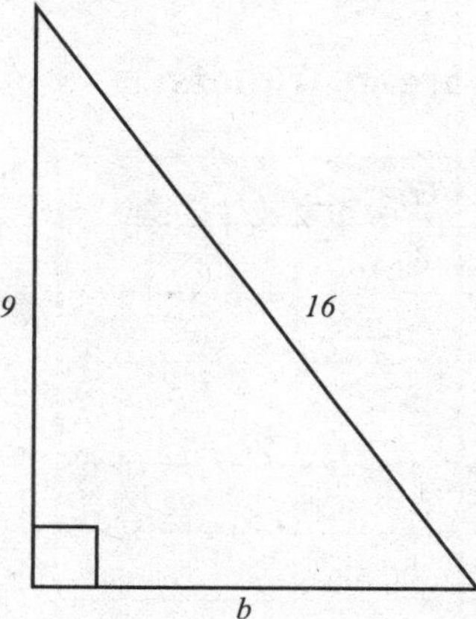

In the right triangle above, what is the length of side b?

Step 1: Setup the Pythagorean theorem and substitute the values given in the question:

$$a^2 + b^2 = c^2 \Rightarrow 9^2 + b^2 = 16^2 \Rightarrow 81 + b^2 = 256$$

Step 2: Subtract 81 from both sides of the equation to isolate b^2:

$$b^2 = 256 - 81 = 175$$

Step 3: Take the square root of both sides of the equation to solve for b:

$$\sqrt{b^2} = \sqrt{175}$$

Step 4: Simplify the radicals:

$$b = \sqrt{25 \times 7} = 5\sqrt{7}$$

✓ Helpful Hint

Leave your answer in radical form. Convert to the decimal form only if you need to.

PYTHAGOREAN TRIPLETS

In some right triangles, all of the sides are integers. These are called Pythagorean triplets. Learning some common triplets can save time when answering many triangle questions.

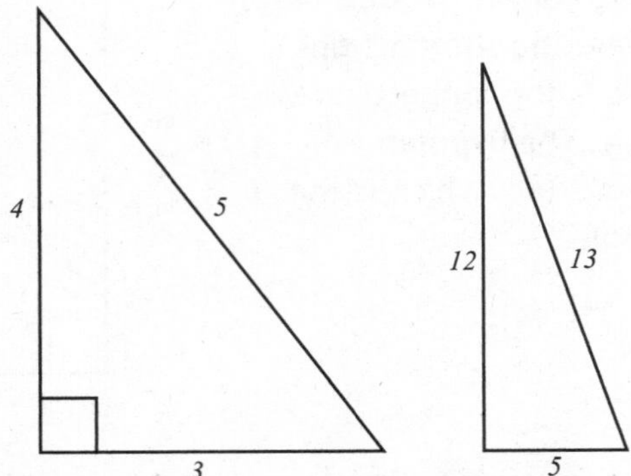

Multiples of Common Pythagorean Triplets

Multiple	Triangle
1	3:4:5
2	6:8:10
3	9:12:15
Multiple	**Triangle**
1	5:12:13
2	10:24:26

✔ Helpful Hint

Always look for common Pythagorean triplets and their multiples before taking the time to evaluate the Pythagorean theorem.

Try It Out! **Complete the following sample question.**

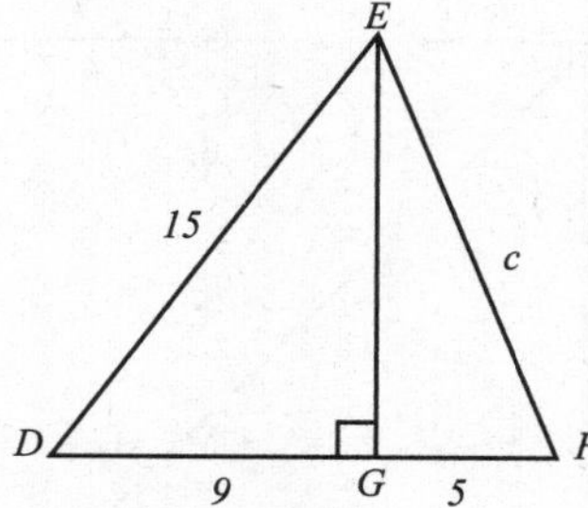

In the triangle above, what is the length of side c?

Step 1: Look for Pythagorean triplets:

The triangle ΔDEG is a multiple of the 3:4:5 triangle.

Step 2: Determine the unknown side of the triangle:

Because $DE = 15$ and $15 = 3 \times 5$, $EG = 3 \times 4 = 12$

Step 3: Look for the second triplet to solve for c:

The triangle ΔEFG has sides in the ratio of 5:12:c; therefore, $c = 13$.

Special right triangles are defined by their angle measures. In these triangles, you only need to know one side to calculate the other two. Also, if you see a right triangle with sides in the ratios of these triangles, you can determine the angle measures.

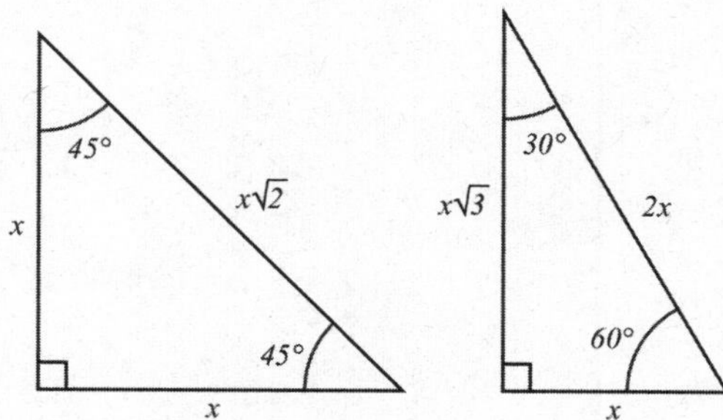

45-45-90 triangles have sides in the ratio of $x:x:x\sqrt{2}$.

30-60-90 triangles have sides in the ratio of $x:x\sqrt{3}:2x$.

23

Try It Out! **Complete the following sample question.**

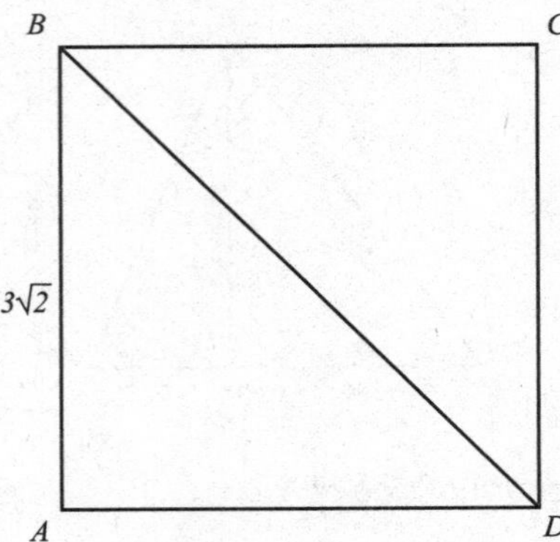

In the figure above, ABCD is a square with a side length of $3\sqrt{2}$*, and* $\overline{BD}$ *is a diagonal of the square. What is the length of* $\overline{BD}$*?*

Step 1: Determine what kind of right triangle this is.

Because a square has four equal sides and angle measures of 90°, the triangle formed by the diagonal is a 45-45-90 triangle.

Step 2: Use the ratio of sides to set up an expression to solve for $\overline{BD}$.

$\overline{BD} = x(\sqrt{2})$, where x is the side length of the square.

Step 3: Substitute the side length for x and evaluate your expression.

$\overline{BD} = 3\sqrt{2} \times \sqrt{2} = 3 \times \sqrt{4} = 3 \times 2 = 6$

Try It Out! **Work through the following mulitple-choice question.**

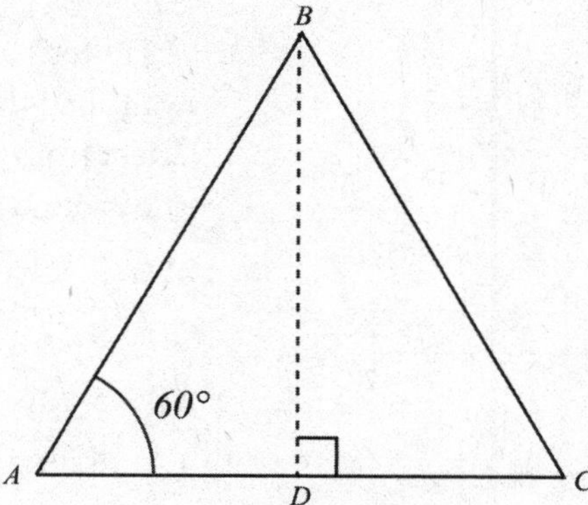

In the figure above, ΔABC is an equilateral triangle with side lengths of 8 inches. What is the length of $\overline{BD}$?

A) $4\sqrt{2}$

B) $4\sqrt{3}$

C) $8\sqrt{2}$

D) $8\sqrt{3}$

Step 1: Look for a special right triangle in the larger triangle:

ΔABD is a 30-60-90 triangle.

The sides are in the ratio of $x : x\sqrt{3} : 2x$.

Step 2: Use the ratio of sides and the information in the question to set up an expression to solve for $\overline{AD}$:

$2\overline{AD} = 8 \Rightarrow \overline{AD} = 4$

Step 3: Use the ratio of sides to set up an expression to solve for $\overline{BD}$:

$\overline{BD} = \overline{AD} \times \sqrt{3} \Rightarrow \overline{BD} = 4\sqrt{3}$

Use the Kaplan Method to answer the following questions. Use the hints provided as needed.

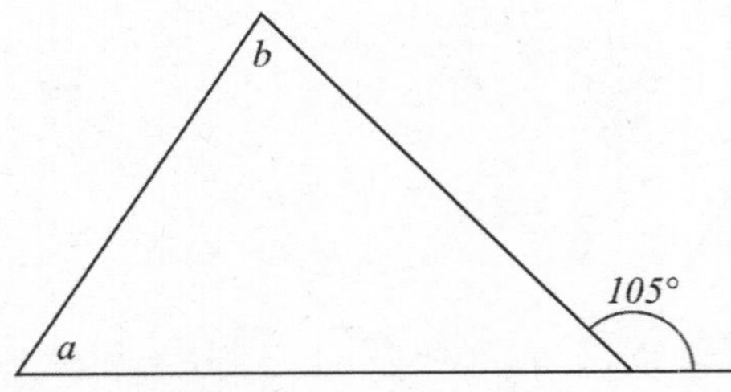

1. In the figure above, what is b in terms of a?

   A) $a - 105$

   B) $a - 75$

   C) $75 - a$

   D) $105 - a$

hint *The exterior angle is supplementary to the adjacent interior angle and equal to the the sum of the other two angles.*

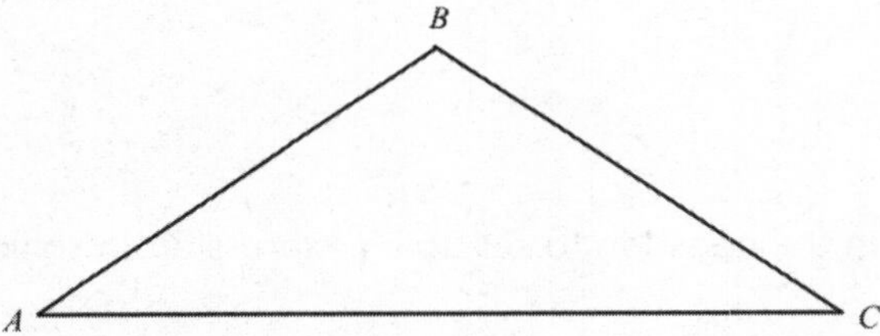

2. In isosceles triangle ABC, $\overline{AB} = \overline{BC}$. If angle $CAB = 30°$, what is the measure of angle ABC?

   A) 30

   B) 60

   C) 90

   D) 120

hint *In an isosceles triangle, the angles opposite equal sides are equal.*

3. A ladder 10 feet long is placed against a wall such that the base of the ladder is 5 feet from the wall. How many feet above the ground is the top of the ladder?

   A) 5

   B) $5\sqrt{2}$

   C) $5\sqrt{3}$

   D) $5\sqrt{5}$

hint *If you are not provided with a diagram, always make your own sketch.*

Use the Kaplan Method as you answer the following questions on your own.

1. If ΔEFG is a right triangle with sides of k, 16, and 20, what is the value of k?

   A) 4

   B) 5

   C) 6

   D) 12

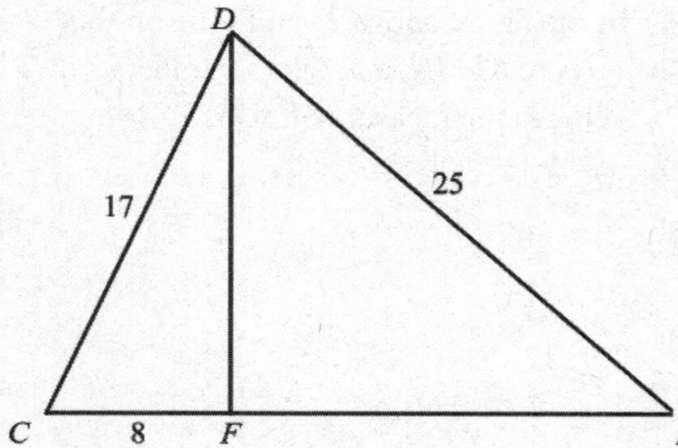

2. The triangle above has side lengths as marked, and ΔDEF is a right triangle. What is the length of $\overline{FE}$?

   A) $8\sqrt{3}$

   B) 15

   C) $\frac{25\sqrt{2}}{2}$

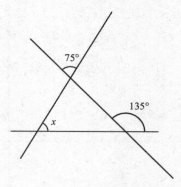

   D) 20

3. In the figure above, what is the measure of angle x?

   A) 30

   B) 45

   C) 60

   D) 75

Use the Kaplan Method to answer the following questions on your own.

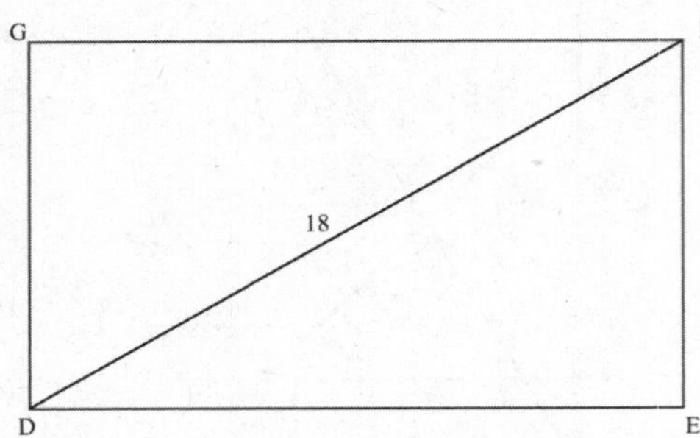

1. In rectangle $DEFG$, $\overline{DG}$ is half the length of $\overline{DF}$. What is the area of the rectangle?

   A) 81

   B) $81\sqrt{2}$

   C) $81\sqrt{3}$

   D) 162

2. If a 3-foot-tall post casts a shadow that is 17 feet long, how tall is the post that casts a shadow 51 feet long?

   A) 7

   B) 9

   C) 11

   D) 13

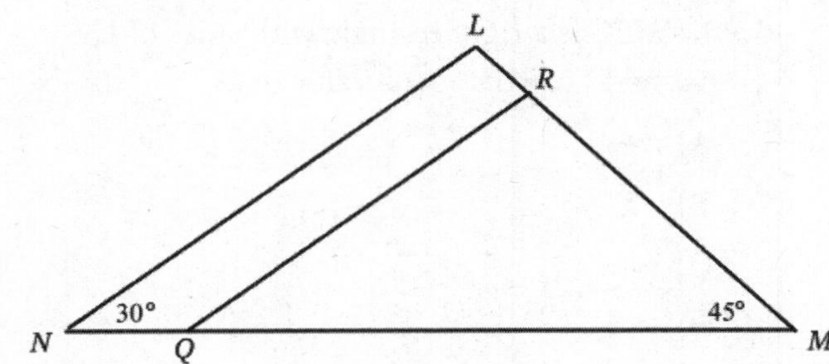

3. In the figure above, Q and R lie on the sides of ΔLMN, and $\overline{QR}$ is parallel to $\overline{LN}$. What is the measure of ΔQRM?

   A) 105

   B) 110

   C) 115

   D) 120

The following questions are similar to what you would encounter on a college admissions test such as the SAT or ACT. Apply the Kaplan Method and your knowledge of geometry to answer the following questions.

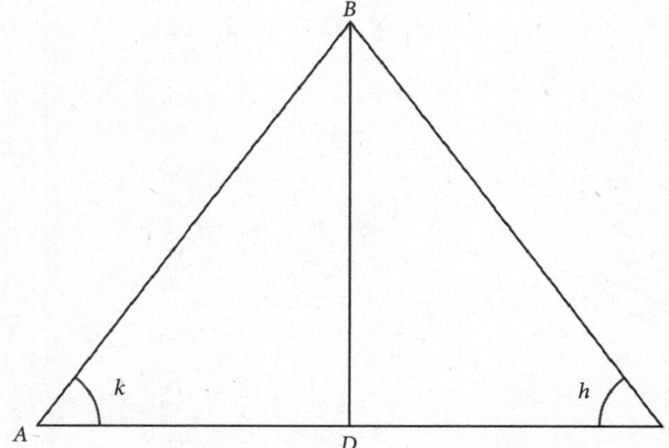

Note: Figure not drawn to scale.

1. In the figure above, the area of triangle ΔABC is 12 square inches, angles h and k are equal, and $\overline{BD}$ is perpendicular to $\overline{AC}$ and bisects ΔABC. If side AC is 6 inches, what is the length of side BC?

   A) 4

   B) 5

   C) 6

   D) 10

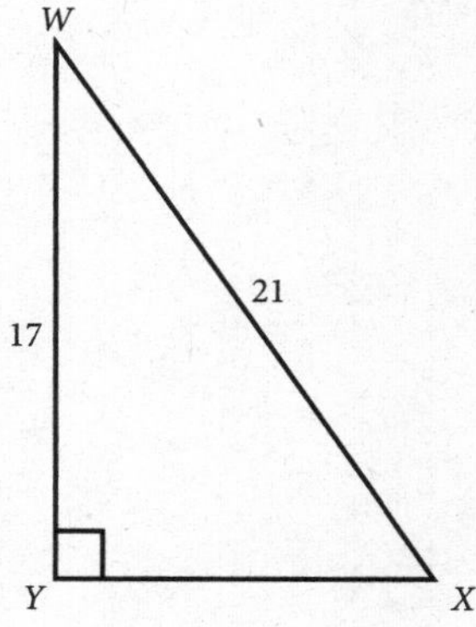

2. In the right triangle above, how long is side YX?

   A) $2\sqrt{38}$

   B) $5\sqrt{146}$

   C) 152

   D) 730

CHAPTER 24

Area & Volume

24

CHAPTER OBJECTIVES

By the end of this chapter, you will be able to:

1. Calculate the area of a triangle
2. Calculate the area and circumference of a circle
3. Calculate the length of a circle's arc
4. Calculate the area of a circle's sector
5. Write the equation of a circle given two points on a coordinate plane
6. Calculate the volume of pyramids, cones, and spheres

THE KAPLAN METHOD FOR MATH

Step 1: Read the question, identifying and organizing important information as you go

- What information am I given?
- Separate the question from the context.
- How are the answer choices written?
- Should you label or draw a diagram?

Step 2: Choose the best strategy to answer the question

- Look for patterns.
- Pick numbers or use straightforward math.

Step 3: Check that you answered the *right* question

- Review the question stem.
- Check units of measurement.
- Double-check your work.

24

TRIANGLES

Area of a triangle = $\frac{1}{2} \times$ base $\times$ height

The base and height of a triangle will look a little different depending on if the triangle is **right** (has a 90° angle), **obtuse** (has an angle greater than 90°), or **acute** (all three angles are less than 90°).

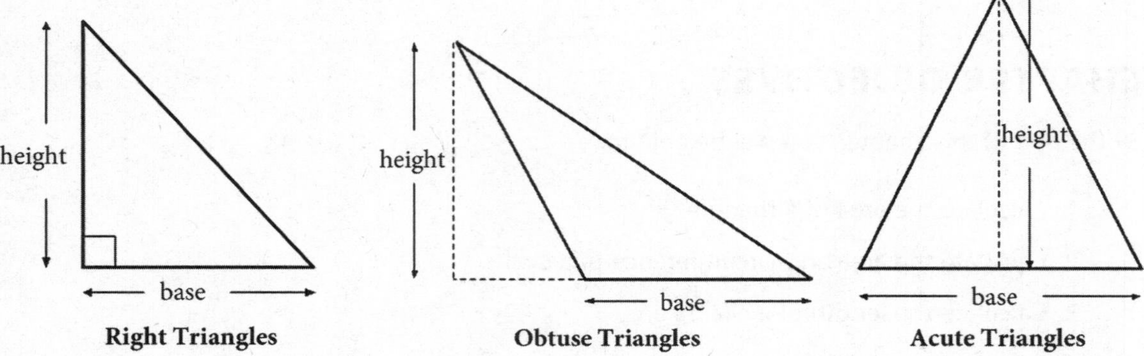

CIRCLES

Area of a circle $= \pi r^2$

Circumference of a circle $= 2\pi r$

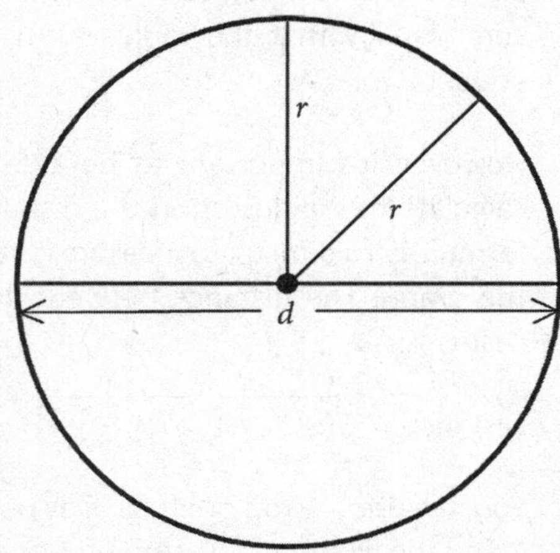

The **radius** of a circle is the distance from the center of the circle to any point on the circle. The radius is denoted by the variable *r*. The center of a circle is also called the circle's **origin**.

The area of a circle is π multiplied by the radius squared. Pi (π) is a mathematical constant whose value is approximately 3.14. Pi is the ratio between any circle's circumference and its diameter.

A circle's **diameter** is any straight line segment that passes through the center of the circle and whose endpoints are on the circle.

Diameter $= d = 2r$

Think of the circumference of a circle as the distance all the way around it. Imagine you drew a large perfect circle in the sand. If you walked around the circle, starting from the top, the circumference would be the distance you'd walk until you came back to the top of the circle.

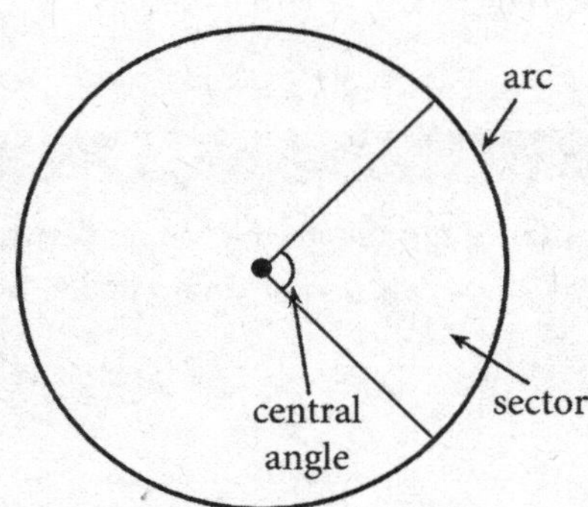

When two radii cut out the shape of a slice, the slice is called a **sector**. Think of a sector like a pie slice. The angle contained by the radii is called the **central angle** (also called the interior angle).

The portion of the circumference bound by the central angle is called an **arc**. You can use a special proportion involving a central angle to find the length of its arc and the area of its sector.

$$\frac{\textit{central angle}}{360^\circ} = \frac{\textit{arc length}}{\textit{circumference}} = \frac{\textit{sector area}}{\textit{circle area}}$$

The ratio between a central angle and 360° (all the way around the circle) is proportional to the ratio between an arc length and circumference as well as the ratio between a sector area and the circle's total area. The three ratios are equal because they are fractions of corresponding parts of the circle divided by the entire circle.

CALCULATING THE EQUATION OF A CIRCLE

The general equation for a circle is: $(x - h)^2 + (y - k)^2 = r^2$

The point (h, k) is the circle's center when plotted on an *xy*-coordinate plane, and r is the radius.

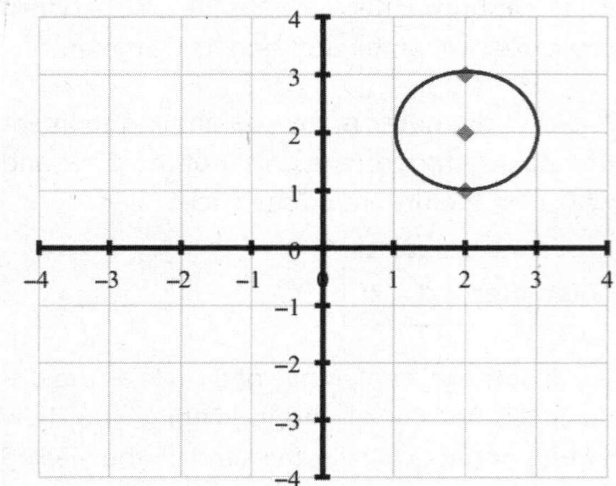

On the coordinate plane to the left, **the circle's center is at (2, 2)**. You can measure visually that the radius must be equal to 1.

However, it's important to be able to calculate the radius using the distance formula if it's difficult to measure it from the graph. The distance between two points is:

$$\text{Distance} = \sqrt{(x_2 - x_1)^2 + (y_2 - y_1)^2}$$

You can use the top point (2, 3) as point 1 and the center (2, 2) as point 2 to calculate the radius:

$$\text{Radius} = \sqrt{(2-2)^2 + (2-3)^2}$$

$$\text{Radius} = \sqrt{0^2 + (-1)^2} = 1$$

✔ Helpful Hint

You could also have calculated the radius by applying the distance formula to the top and bottom points on the circle. The result would be the diameter of the circle, which you would divide by 2 to get the radius.

You now have the center of the circle, (2, 2), and the radius, 1. You have everything you need to construct the circle's equation. Remember to square the radius.

$$(x - h)^2 + (y - k)^2 = r^2$$
$$(x - 2)^2 + (y - 2)^2 = 1$$

If you were **not** given that the center of the circle is at (2, 2), but you were only provided the top and bottom points, you could still find the equation of the circle.

First, you would need to find the circle's center using the midpoint formula.

The two points you have lie on a diameter of the circle. Therefore, the midpoint between them must be the circle's center. Your top point is (2, 3) and your bottom point is (2, 1).

Midpoint $= \left(\frac{(x_1 + x_2)}{2}, \frac{(y_1 + y_2)}{2}\right) = \left(\frac{(2+2)}{2}, \frac{(3+1)}{2}\right) = \left(\frac{4}{2}, \frac{4}{2}\right) = (2, 2) =$ center of circle

You would now find the radius using the distance formula as you did above. With the center (h, k) and the radius, you are ready to construct the circle's equation:

$$(x - h)^2 + (y - k)^2 = r^2$$

$$(x - 2)^2 + (y - 2)^2 = 1$$

VOLUME OF THREE-DIMENSIONAL SHAPES

Volume of a Sphere

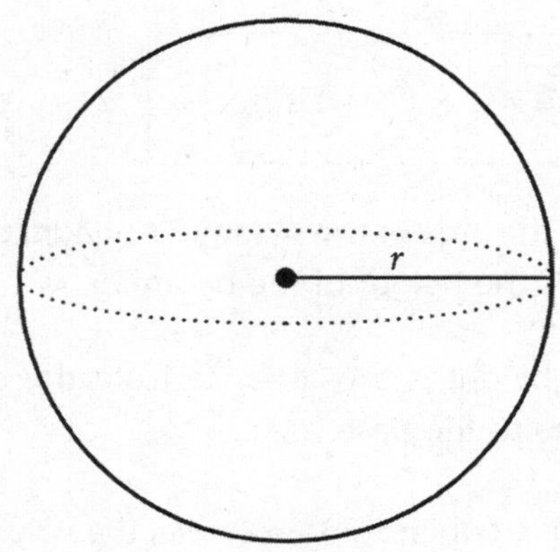

The formula for the volume of a sphere:

$$\text{Volume} = \frac{4}{3} \times \pi \times r^3$$

The r is the radius of the sphere.

A sphere's radius is the distance from the center of the sphere to any point on the sphere.

Note that the **center cross section** of the sphere (the dashed line) is a circle whose radius is also the radius of the sphere. This circle is also called an **equator**.

Volume of a Right Cone

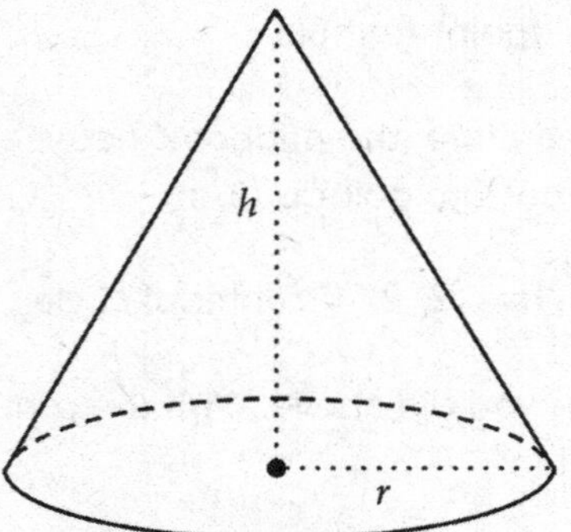

The formula for the volume of a right cone:

$$\text{Volume} = \frac{1}{3} \times (\pi r^2) \times h$$

The (πr^2) is the area of the cone's circular base, and h is the height of the cone.

A cone's height is the distance from the apex (also known as the peak) straight down to the base.

Note that the height, the radius, and the right side of the cone form a right triangle.

Volume of a Right Pyramid

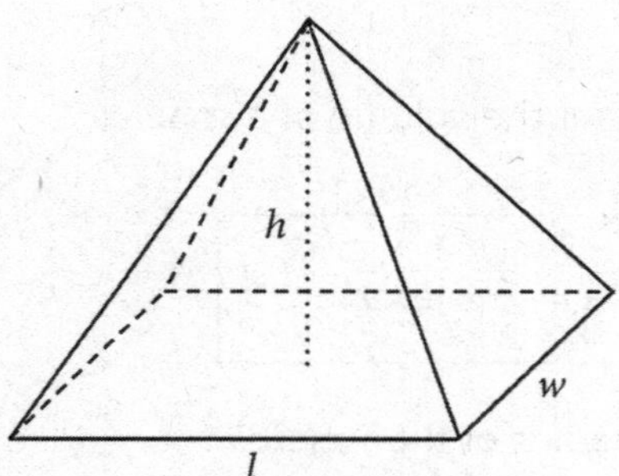

The formula for the volume of a right pyramid:

$$\text{Volume} = \frac{1}{3} \times (l \times w) \times h$$

The $(l \times w)$ is the area of the pyramid's quadrilateral base, and h is the height of the pyramid.

A pyramid's height is the distance from the apex straight down to the base.

You can think of volume as the amount of space that can fill an object. For example, the volume of a sphere whose radius is 4 is equal to the amount of space inside a perfectly spherical ball whose radius is 4. You could measure the volume in real life by making a small hole at the top of the ball, filling the ball with water, and then pouring the water into measuring cups.

SOLVING AREA AND VOLUME QUESTIONS

Try It Out! **Complete the following sample question.**

A circle has been drawn on a coordinate plane. Its center is at (2, 4) and one of the points on the circle is at (7, 4). Find the equation of the circle and the circle's area and circumference. For the same circle, what is the length of an arc corresponding to an interior angle of 36°? What is the area of a sector corresponding to the same interior angle?

Step 1: Write down the general formulas you will need to solve for the shape's parameters. For example, if asked to find the area of a triangle, you would write down "area = $\frac{1}{2}bh$."

Radius of the circle (distance formula) ____________________

Equation of the circle ____________________

Area of the circle ____________________

Circumference of the circle ____________________

Arc length ____________________

Sector area ____________________

Step 2: Using the question stem and the formulas you wrote down in Step 1, solve for the parameters.

Radius of the circle (distance formula) ____________________

____

____

Equation of the circle ____________________

____

____

Area of the circle ____________________

____

Circumference of the circle ________________________________

____

Arc length ________________________________

____

____

Sector area ________________________________

24

____

____

Step 3: Review your answer

Try It Out! **Complete the following sample question.**

Your friend heard a theory that one of the Great Pyramids was filled with water in ancient times. You wanted to find out how much water it would take to fill such a huge structure. You looked up the dimensions of the pyramid and found out that the base is a rectangle with a width of 730 feet and a length of 760 feet. If the height of the pyramid in ancient times (before wind erosion) was estimated to be 150 feet, how much water could it hold?

Step 1: Write down the general formulas you will need to solve for the shape's parameters.

Volume of a pyramid ________________________________

Step 2: Using the question stem and the formulas you wrote down in Step 1, solve for the parameters.

Volume of a pyramid ________________________________

____

____

Step 3: Review your answer.

Try It Out! **Work through the following multiple-choice question.**

The diameter of a circle is 14 cm. The circle is the base of a right cone. If the volume of the cone is 735π, what is its height?

A) 15 cm

B) 30 cm

C) 45 cm

D) 60 cm

Step 1: Write down the general formulas you will need to solve for the shape's parameters.

Volume of a right cone: Volume $= \frac{1}{3} \times (\pi r^2) \times h$

Step 2: Using the question stem and the formulas you wrote down in Step 1, solve for the parameters.

Volume of a right cone: Given: circular base diameter = 14 cm
volume of cone = 735π
Find: height of cone

If the circle's diameter is 14 cm, its radius is $\frac{14 \text{ cm}}{2} = 7$ cm.

$$\frac{1}{3} \times \pi r^2 \times h = \text{Volume}$$
$$\frac{1}{3} \times \pi(7)^2 \times h = 735\pi$$
$$\frac{1}{3} \times 49\pi \times h = 735\pi$$

Solving for h:

$$h = \frac{735\pi \times 3}{49\pi}$$

$h = 45$ cm

Choice (C) is the correct answer.

Step 3: Review your answer.

Plugging in 45 for h into the original equation yields two equal sides.

$$\frac{1}{3} \times 49\pi \times 45 = 735\pi$$

$735\pi = 735\pi$ ✓

This worked solution would resemble the following:

The diameter of a circle is 14 cm. The circle is the base of a right cone. If the volume of the cone is 735π, what is its height?

A) 15 cm

B) 30 cm

C) 45 cm

D) 60 cm

Straightforward math:

$$\frac{1}{3} \times \pi(7)^2 \times h = 735\pi$$

$$\frac{1}{3} \times 49\pi \times h = 735\pi$$

$$h = \frac{735\pi \times 3}{49\pi}$$

$$h = 45 \text{ cm}$$

Choice (C) is correct.

Use the Kaplan Method to answer the following questions. Use the hints provided as needed.

1. Find the circumference of a circle whose area is 81π.

   A) 9π

   B) 15π

   C) 18π

   D) 22π

 *First, find the radius using the area, then solve for the circumference.*

2. What is the pyramid's volume in the figure below?

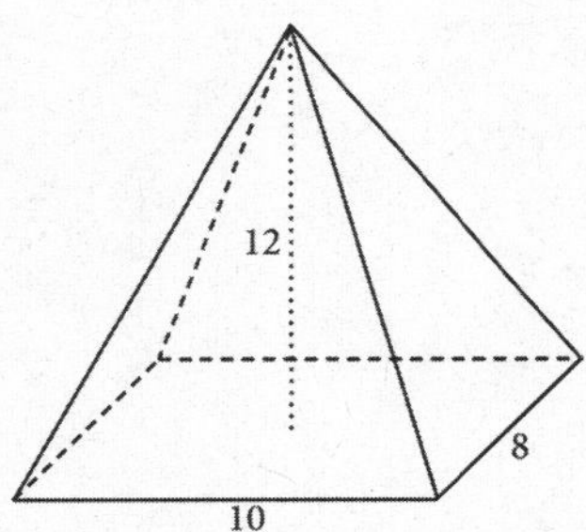

   A) 120

   B) 320

   C) 480

   D) 960

hint *Remember to use the formula for right pyramids.*

3. A circle has been plotted on a coordinate plane, and a diameter has been drawn across it through the circle's center. If the two endpoints of the diameter are at (2, 3) and (5, 7), what is the circle's radius?

   A) 1

   B) 2.5

   C) 5

   D) 6.5

hint *You can use the distance formula to find the diameter, then divide by 2 to find the radius. You could also plot the points on a coordinate plane and connect them to form the diameter. You would then make a right triangle with this diameter as the hypotenuse, and solve using the Pythagorean theorem. Is it a special right triangle?*

24

24

Use the Kaplan Method as you solve the following questions on your own.

1. What is the equation of the circle in the figure below?

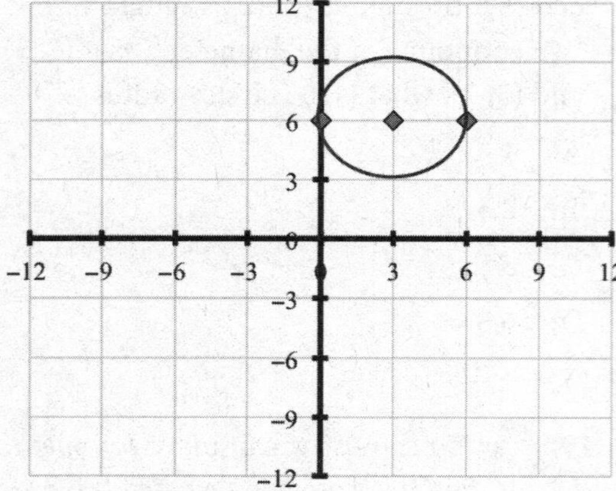

A) $(x-6)^2+(y-3)^2=9$
B) $(x-6)^2+(y-3)^2=12$
C) $(x-3)^2+(y-6)^2=12$
D) $(x-3)^2+(y-6)^2=9$

2. What is the volume of a sphere whose equator is a circle with an area of 144π?

A) 576π
B) 683π
C) $2{,}304\pi$
D) $4{,}608\pi$

3. What is the area of a triangle whose height is 33 and whose base is one-third its height?

A) 181.5
B) 235.2
C) 316.8
D) 363.0

Use the Kaplan Method as you solve the following questions for homework.

1. What is the sphere's volume in the figure below (rounded to the nearest ones place)? The area refers to the dashed circle.

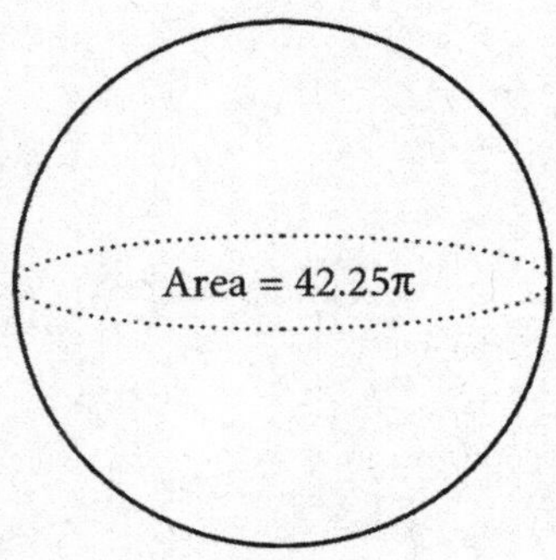

A) 56π
B) 92π
C) 288π
D) 366π

2. The diameter of a circle whose area is 25π is the base of a triangle. If the triangle's height is 10, what is the triangle's area?

A) 25
B) 50
C) 100
D) 200

3. A circle's circumference is 17π. What is the length of the circle's arc corresponding to a central angle of 36°?

A) 0.9π
B) 1.7π
C) 5.6π
D) 8.5π

The following questions are similar to what you would encounter on a college admissions test such as the SAT or ACT. Apply the Kaplan Method and your knowledge of area and volume to answer the following questions.

24

1. What is the base of a triangle whose height is π and whose area is equal to the 135° sector area of a circle with a diameter of 20?

   A) 13

   B) 40

   C) 75

   D) 115

2. What is the area of an equilateral triangle whose sides are 6 cm?

   A) $4.5\sqrt{2}$ cm^2

   B) $4.5\sqrt{3}$ cm^2

   C) $9\sqrt{2}$ cm^2

   D) $9\sqrt{3}$ cm^2

PART TWO

Science

UNIT FIVE

Science

IN THIS UNIT, YOU WILL LEARN HOW TO:

1. Map Science passages using the Kaplan Method
2. Apply the Kaplan Method for Science to answer questions
3. Distinguish among independent variables, dependent variables, and constants
4. Analyze independent variables, dependent variables, and constants within experiments
5. Locate data in a table
6. Organize, interpret, and analyze data in a table
7. Interpret the results of experimental procedures
8. Apply an interpretation to accompanying questions
9. Apply the Kaplan Method for Paired Passages to Conflicting Viewpoints passages
10. Evaluate viewpoints in scientific passages
11. Compare and contrast viewpoints in Science passages

CHAPTER 25

The Kaplan Method for Science

CHAPTER OBJECTIVES

By the end of this chapter, you will be able to:

1. Map Science passages using the Kaplan Method
2. Apply the Kaplan Method for Science to answer questions

THE KAPLAN METHOD FOR SCIENCE

Step 1: Map the passage

- If the passage includes an experiment:
  - Underline the Purpose
  - Put brackets around the Method
  - Star the Results
- If the passage provides straightforward data:
  - Circle keywords
  - Underline key phrases

Step 2: Examine the figures provided

- Locate variables in the figures
- Identify trends and patterns

Step 3: Find support for the answer in the passage

- Identify keywords in the question stem
- Locate the corresponding data in the passage
- Match it to the correct answer

Step 1: Map the passage

Step 1 of the Kaplan Method for Science instructs you to identify and mark the **Purpose**, **Method**, and **Results** of an experiment. Locating and labeling each of these will save you time as you answer the questions. As you read, underline the Purpose, put brackets around the Method, and put a star next to the Results of the experiment.

The Purpose of an experiment explains **why the experiment was conducted**. To identify the Purpose, look for phrases such as "in order to investigate" or "to study." Understanding the purpose of an experiment will help you answer questions about what researchers are testing, as well as why.

> ✔ **Helpful Hint**
>
> **Some experiments provide straightforward Results and focus more on these than on the Purpose. So if you cannot easily locate a Purpose to underline, move right along to the Method.**

The Method describes **what the experimenters did** and outlines the setup of an experiment, which includes what the experimenters varied, what they kept the same, what changed, and how they measured the changes.

- Independent variables: What was intentionally varied
- Dependent variables: What was measured
- Controlled variables (constants): What was kept the same throughout the experiment

Understanding the Method of an experiment will help you answer questions about a single variable, multiple variables, and relationships among variables.

> ✔ **Helpful Hint**
>
> **Some passages do not provide detailed information about the variables in the introductory text, but you will be able to locate those variables in the figures provided during Step 2 of the Kaplan Method.**

The Results of an experiment show **how the experiment turned out**. The Results may be discussed in the text and will likely be displayed in graphs, tables, charts, and diagrams. Keywords in question stems will direct you to the specific area within the Results that provides support for the correct answer.

25

Step 2: Examine the figures provided

Step 2 of the Kaplan Method requires you to examine the results to locate variables and identify trends and patterns. The setup, or the Method, of an experiment provides information about the independent, dependent, and controlled variables that the Results represent with tables, graphs, and diagrams. This visual display of the Results will help you identify trends and relationships among the variables such as:

- Direct:
    - As the independent variable increases, the dependent variable increases.
    - As the independent variable decreases, the dependent variable decreases.
    - Example: ______________________________
- Inverse:
    - As the independent variable decreases, the dependent variable increases.
    - As the independent variable increases, the dependent variable decreases.
    - Example: ______________________________
- Fluctuating:
    - As the independent variable steadily increases or decreases, the dependent variable fluctuates between increasing and decreasing values.
    - Example: ______________________________
- Non-correlative:
    - The variables do not share a relationship
    - Example: ______________________________

Step 3: Find support for the answer in the passage

Like in reading passages, you will always find support for the correct answer to a given science question in its corresponding passage. Look for keywords and key phrases (e.g., "According to Figure/Table 1", "What was intentionally varied in Experiment 2") to help determine where you need to look to find that support.

Try It Out! **Use the Kaplan Method for Science to answer the following multiple-choice questions.**

Researchers conducted a study on a pride of lions in a zoo setting in order to determine the correlation, if any, between food consumption of female lions and estrogen levels. The researchers provided five female lions 12.0 kg of food each once per day. The blood estrogen levels were measured, in picograms per milliliter (pg/mL), one hour before each feeding. The lions' estrogen levels are listed is found in Table 1, and the corresponding consumed portions of each 12.0 kg food serving provided to each of the five lions in Table 2.

hint *Underline the Purpose, bracket the Method, and star the Results.*

Table 1

	Blood Estrogen Levels (pg/mL)				
Day	**Lion 1**	**Lion 2**	**Lion 3**	**Lion 4**	**Lion 5**
1	112.0	68.3	71.0	81.3	114.7
2	88.2	143.9	134.4	92.6	91.9
3	78.0	137.9	127.5	45.9	78.3
4	137.0	80.5	81.4	118.0	128.3

hint *Compare to the blood estrogen levels to the corresponding daily food consumption. What kind of pattern do you see?*

Table 2

	Daily Food Consumption (kg)				
Day	**Lion 1**	**Lion 2**	**Lion 3**	**Lion 4**	**Lion 5**
1	6.5	10.3	10.2	7.9	6.3
2	7.3	4.1	5.1	7.1	7.2
3	9.9	4.6	5.7	12.0	9.8
4	4.7	8.3	7.8	6.1	5.8

hint *If food consumption increased as estrogen levels increased, there is a direct relationship between the variables. If food consumption decreased as estrogen levels increased, there is an inverse relationship between the variables.*

1. The lowest blood estrogen level of any lion during the course of the four days was
   A) 4.1.
   B) 12.0.
   C) 45.9.
   D) 143.9.

hint *The keywords "estrogen level" indicate that the answer is in Table 1. The word "lowest" directs you to find the smallest value in the entire table.*

✔ Helpful Hint

You can eliminate answer choices that are from the wrong part of the passage. For example, if a question stem directs you to Table 1, you don't need to spend time looking at Table 2.

2. Which of these statements best describes the changes in the blood estrogen level of lion 4 over the course of the four days?

   A) The blood estrogen level increased on days 2 and 3 but decreased on day 4.

   B) The blood estrogen level decreased on day 2, increased on day 3, and decreased on day 4.

   C) The blood estrogen level decreased on days 2 and 3 but increased on day 4.

   D) The blood estrogen level increased on day 2, decreased on day 3, and increased on day 4.

hint *The keywords "estrogen levels" indicate that the answer is in Table 2; "lion 4" directs you to closely read the corresponding column.*

3. As the blood estrogen level of lion 1 decreased, its food consumption

   A) decreased only.

   B) increased only.

   C) increased, then decreased.

   D) decreased, then increased.

hint *The keywords "food consumed" and "blood estrogen levels" indicate that you need to compare the data in both tables. The words "lion 1" direct you to closely read the corresponding columns.*

Use the Kaplan Method to answer the following multiple-choice questions. Use the hints provided as needed.

Colonies of *Staphylococcus aureus* bacteria grow exponentially. During what is called the "doubling time", each cell doubles in size and then divides into two cells of the original size. Doubling times can range from 20 minutes (when nutrients are very abundant) to several hours (when nutrients are scarce). Many cell characteristics, including size and the rate at which protein is generated in ribosomes (a type of structure within a cell), will change as the doubling time changes.

Table 1 compares doubling time to the average mass of a cell and its ribosome count.

hint *Underline the Purpose, bracket the Method, and star the Results.*

Table 1

Doubling Time (minutes)	Average Mass of a Cell (micrograms)	Ribosomes (per cell)
300	0.15	2,000
100	0.21	6,900
50	0.33	15,800
25	0.83	64,900

Table 2 shows the corresponding changes in the DNA and RNA contents of the cells. For example, when the doubling time is 25 minutes, 3.2% of the weight of the cells consists of DNA molecules, and 32% consists of RNA molecules. Most of the RNA (24% out of the 32%) consists of rRNA (ribosomal RNA), the form which ribosomes use for making proteins. Thus, the cells are presumably producing new proteins far more rapidly than when the doubling time is longer.

Table 2

Doubling Time (minutes)	DNA (% of total weight)	rRNA (% of total weight)	Total RNA (% of total weight)
300	4.1	4	12
100	3.8	9	18
50	3.5	14	22
25	3.2	24	32

1. According to Tables 1 and 2, as the number of ribosomes per cell increased, the percentage of rRNA

   A) increased only.

   B) decreased only.

   C) increased, then decreased.

   D) decreased, then increased.

hint *The number of ribosomes is given in Table 1, and the percentage of rRNA is given in Table 2. Because both of these tables contain the doubling time, it would be possible to create a table containing all three of these quantities.*

25

2. Based on the information in Table 2, as the doubling time increases by a factor of 2, the percentage of DNA
   - A) decreases by more than a factor of 2.
   - B) decreases by less than a factor of 2.
   - C) increases by less than a factor of 2.
   - D) increases by more than a factor of 2.

hint *According to Table 2, as the doubling time doubles from 25 to 50 minutes, the percentage of DNA increases from 3.2 to 3.5.*

3. Which of the following lists the substances in Table 2 in order of decreasing mass in a cell that is dividing every 300 minutes?
   - A) DNA, rRNA, total RNA
   - B) total RNA, DNA, rRNA
   - C) rRNA, total RNA, DNA
   - D) total RNA, rRNA, DNA

hint *Locate the row you need in Table 2, then arrange the values for DNA, rRNA, and total RNA in order of decreasing mass.*

Use the Kaplan Method to answer the following multiple-choice questions on your own.

A physics student mounts a 10 cm spring and a meter stick to the top of a table and compresses the spring to 5 cm as shown in Figure 1.

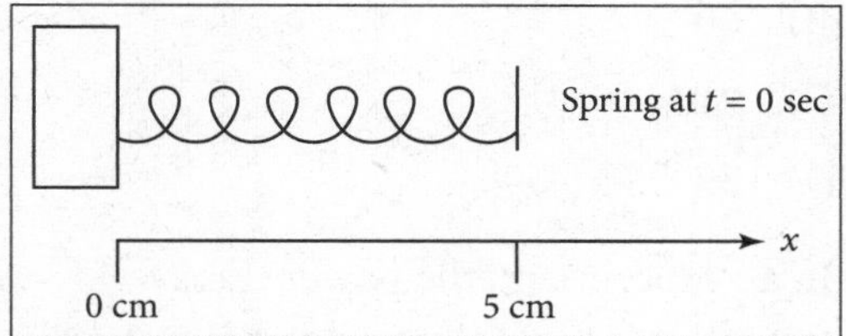

Figure 1

When the student releases the spring, a timer-controlled camera takes a picture of it every 0.5 seconds. The student records the length of the spring at each time point from the photographs and then calculates the potential energy of the spring relative to its potential energy before release. The results are shown in Table 1.

The results of the first 3 seconds of the experiment are shown in Table 1. The student measured the length of the spring in each photograph and used the change in length to calculate the potential energy of the spring (relative to its potential value at time 0).

Table 1

Time (seconds)	Length (cm)	Potential Energy
0.0	5.0	1.00
0.5	5.5	0.90
1.0	6.5	0.70
1.5	8.0	0.40
2.0	10.0	0.00
2.5	12.0	0.40
3.0	13.5	0.70

1. Based on the information in Table 1, the potential energy dropped to one-half of its original value
   A) between 0.0 and 0.5 seconds.
   B) between 0.5 and 1.0 seconds.
   C) between 1.0 and 1.5 seconds.
   D) between 1.5 and 2.0 seconds.

2. If an error in the timer had caused the camera to photograph the spring at 2.8 seconds after release rather than 3.0 seconds, the length of the spring would have been closest to
   A) 11.9 cm.
   B) 12.0 cm.
   C) 12.8 cm.
   D) 13.6 cm.

3. The experiment is designed to determine how
   A) a spring's length changes as its potential energy changes.
   B) the spring's length changes over time after the spring is compressed and released.
   C) time changes as the spring's length changes.
   D) the spring's length and potential energy change over time after the spring is compressed and released

Use the Kaplan Method as you answer the following multiple-choice questions for homework.

The thermal conductivity of a material, Kappa, is a constant that indicates how readily the material conducts heat. For instance, if one side of a solid with a high thermal conductivity, such as a metal pot, is heated, the other side will quickly become warm as well.

Thermal conductivity can be determined from the rate at which power is transferred across a material of a given thickness when there is a constant temperature difference between the two sides:

$$\frac{\text{Kappa (in watts per meter per °C)} = \text{power (in watts)}}{\text{(1 meter thickness * 1°C temperature difference)}}$$

Table 1 lists thermal conductivities for various solids, in watts per meter per °C.

Table 1

Material	Kappa
Aluminum	210
Copper	390
Water	0.6

The electrical conductivity of a material, Sigma, is a constant that indicates how readily the material conducts electricity. Table 2 lists electrical conductivities for various materials, in Sigmas per meter.

Table 2

Material	Sigmas per meter
Aluminum	38
Copper	60
Water	0.001

1. The highest thermal conductivity recorded (in watts per meter per °C) was

   A) 0.001.

   B) 60.

   C) 210.

   D) 390.

2. In an experiment, the power transferred across a 0.5-meter-long sample is 500 watts. How much power should be expected to transfer across a different material with the same length but a Kappa value two times greater?

   A) 1000 W

   B) 500 W

   C) 250 W

   D) 125 W

The following questions are similar to what you would encounter on a college admissions test such as the SAT or ACT. Apply the Kaplan Method for Science to answer the following questions.

Titration is a procedure often used in chemistry to determine the concentration of a chemical species in a water solution. Many titrations involve adding an acidic solution to a basic solution (or vice versa), in which the acid and base react to form water. A substance known as an indicator is used to determine when all the acid or base in a solution has been consumed.

Experiment 1

15.0 ml of 0.2M H_2SO_4 solution (sulfuric acid) is placed in Buret A. 50.0 ml of a potassium hydroxide (KOH) solution of unknown concentration is placed in Buret B. The sulfuric acid is allowed to run into the Erlenmeyer flask, and three drops of phenolphthalein are added to the flask. The base is added drop by drop until the phenolphthalein turns a very faint pink color. This is considered the endpoint of the titration. The experiment is repeated three more times using other concentrations of potassium hydroxide (KOH). The results of this experiment are summarized in Table 1.

Table 1

Trial #1	Concentration H_2SO_4 (M)	Volume H_2SO_4 (ml)	Starting Volume KOH (ml)	Ending Volume KOH (ml)
1	0.2	15.0	50.0	25.4
2	0.2	15.0	50.0	15.1
3	0.2	15.0	50.0	8.4
4	0.2	15.0	50.0	11.6

Experiment 2

A second titration was done with a setup similar to that in Figure 1. In this case, an iodine solution is placed in Buret A, and various fruit juices are placed in Buret B. Once the fruit juice was placed in the flask, several drops of a starch solution were added. This solution would turn a blue-black color once the endpoint of the titration was reached. The chemical reaction is: Ascorbic Acid + I2 $\rightarrow$ 2I- + dehydroascorbic acid.

The results of this experiment are summarized in Table 2.

Table 2

Juice	Concentration Iodine Solution (M)	Volume Iodine Solution (ml)	Starting Volume Juice (ml)	Ending Volume Juice (ml)
Apple	0.5	15.0	50.0	12.7
Cranberry	0.5	15.0	50.0	35.5
Orange	0.5	15.0	50.0	43.8
Grape	0.5	15.0	50.0	29.3

1. One of the students doing Experiment 2 hypothesized that orange juice has the most vitamin C (ascorbic acid) of all the juices tested. Assuming that using less juice indicates the presence of more vitamin C, is this hypothesis supported from the experiment?
   A) No, because when compared to orange juice, the higher ending volume of apple juice indicates that less apple juice was used to reach the endpoint.
   B) No, because when compared to apple juice, the higher ending volume of orange juice indicates that less orange juice was used to reach the endpoint.
   C) Yes, because when compared to orange juice, the higher ending volume of apple juice indicates that less apple juice was used to reach the endpoint.
   D) Yes, because when compared to apple juice, the higher ending volume of orange juice indicates that less orange juice was used to reach the endpoint.

2. Assuming that the molarity of H_2SO_4 equals the concentration of KOH times the volume of KOH used over the original volume of H_2SO_4, which of the following equations would calculate the molarity of the base in Trial 1?

   A) $x = \frac{0.2(15)}{15.1}$

   B) $x = \frac{0.2(15)}{24.6}$

   C) $x = \frac{0.2(15)}{25.4}$

   D) $x = \frac{0.2(15)}{50}$

CHAPTER 26

Experimental Variables and Graphing

CHAPTER OBJECTIVES

By the end of this chapter, you will be able to:

1. Distinguish among independent variables, dependent variables, and constants
2. Analyze independent variables, dependent variables, and constants within experiments

THE KAPLAN METHOD FOR SCIENCE

Step 1: Map the passage

- If the passage includes an experiment:
    - Underline the Purpose
    - Put brackets around the Method
    - Star the Results
- If the passage provides straightforward data:
    - Circle keywords
    - Underline key phrases

Step 2: Examine the figures provided

- Locate variables in the figures
- Identify trends and patterns

Step 3: Find support for the answer in the passage

- Identify keywords in the question stem
- Locate the corresponding data in the passage
- Match it to the correct answer

INDEPENDENT VARIABLES, DEPENDENT VARIABLES, AND CONSTANTS

While marking the **Purpose**, **Method**, and **Results** of an experiment, examine the Method closely. The Method describes **what the experimenters did** and outlines the setup of an experiment, which includes what the experimenters varied, what they kept the same, and how they measured the changes.

- Independent variables: What was intentionally varied
- Dependent variables: What was measured
- Constants: What was kept the same throughout the experiment

For example, a group of scientists might be interested in discovering how temperature is related to the speed of a chemical reaction. They propose a hypothesis: the warmer two solutions are, the faster they will react chemically. Within this experiment, the **independent variable** is temperature; scientists will set the temperature to different levels so they can see how it affects the reaction speed. The **dependent variable** is the speed of the reaction; this is what the scientists will measure after each change of the independent variable. The outcome here—the speed of the reaction—*depends* on the temperature.

Constants are the other aspects of the experiment. In order to say that the temperature change is responsible for a change in reaction time, the scientists must keep these other aspects constant. In this example, the constants might be the amount of each solution used, the type of solutions used, the container used in the experiment, etc. Everything about the experiment must remain unchanged *except for the independent variable.*

✔ Helpful Hint

Think about what the scientists change in experiments. Those variables will be your independent variables.

ANSWERING QUESTIONS ABOUT VARIABLES

Understanding the method of an experiment will help you answer questions about a single variable, multiple variables, or the relationships among variables. In the example above, the scientists **varied** the temperature (independent variable), **measured** time (dependent variable), and **controlled** the quantity of the solutions used. In a second experiment, the scientists want to study how the quantity of Solution 2 affects the speed of the reaction.

A. What should the scientists intentionally vary? ______________________

B. What should the scientists measure? ______________________

C. What should the scientists keep constant? ______________________

If a passage does not provide detailed information about the variables in the introductory text, you'll be able to locate the variables within the Results. The Results of the experiments will include the values for the independent variable(s) and the measurement of the dependent variable(s) at each of those values. After you put a star next to the Results, you are ready for **Step 2: Examine the figures provided.**

✔ Helpful Hint

The things that remain the same in each new experiment are controls. They remain constant so the researcher knows the one variable he or she changed is the reason a different outcome resulted.

GRAPHICAL REPRESENTATION OF VARIABLES

Graphical representations of variables include tables, graphs, and diagrams. The results of an experiment can be represented in a variety of ways, each of which highlights the types of variables, as well as trends among the variables. As you examine the figures in Step 2, first identify each variable, and then analyze any trends.

✔ Helpful Hint

Whenever you see a graphical image in Science, ask yourself the following questions: What does this show? What are the units of measurement? What patterns do I see?

Diagrams

You should also expect to see diagrams or figures that explain an experimental setup or phenomenon researchers are studying. When you see a diagram in a Science passage, spend enough time to get a general understanding of how the apparatus was used to collect the data or conduct an experiment.

Try It Out! **Read the introductory information and answer the questions about the diagram.**

Hooke's Law states that the force *F* required to extend or compress a spring some distance is proportional to that distance. When measuring the force *F* applied to the spring, the equation for Hooke's Law is:

$$F = k \cdot x$$

where *x* is the distance the spring is extended or compressed, and *k* is a constant expressing the stiffness of the spring. Two students perform two activities in order to study the relative stiffness of three different springs.

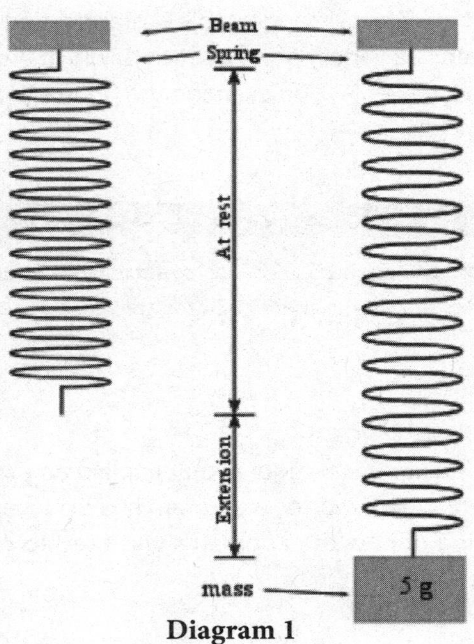

Diagram 1

What is included in Diagram 1?

___

What does the diagram demonstrate?

___

✔ Helpful Hint

Don't worry about understanding every detail. If there is a question about a diagram, you can look more closely at the diagram when you answer the question.

Tables

Tables contain information about multiple variables, using rows and columns to organize the data. To analyze a table, first look at the row headings and determine what data sets are being compared. Then look at the column headings to see what categories are being compared.

Try It Out! **Read the Activity 1 description and answer the questions about the table.**

Activity 1

The apparatus shown in Diagram 1 was used to measure the extension of each 10 cm spring of unknown stiffness. The top of each 10 cm spring was suspended from a beam, and a 1 g mass was attached to the bottom. After waiting for five minutes, the students measured the extension of each spring from its "at rest" position. The process was repeated with four additional masses on each spring. The results are shown in Table 1 and Figure 1.

Table 1

Mass (g)	Extension (cm)		
	Spring 1	Spring 2	Spring 3
1 g	0.5	1.0	2.0
2 g	1.0	2.0	4.0
3 g	1.5	3.0	6.0
4 g	2.0	4.0	8.0
5 g	2.5	5.0	10.0

Table 1 displays the data from Activity 1 in four columns. The first column, **Mass**, is the independent variable. The units of mass are grams (**g**). The next three columns collectively called **Extension** contain the measurements in centimeters (**cm**). The distance each spring extends depends on how much mass is added to the spring. As the mass increases, the extension increases.

Which variable did the students intentionally change?

____

What is the dependent variable?

____

What is the constant?

____

What type of relationship exists between mass and extension?

____

26

✔ Helpful Hint

Look for patterns in your figures and tables to help you anticipate questions about how the independent and dependent variables are related.

Graphs

Graphs provide graphical representations of data. Typically, scientists plot the independent variable on the *x*-axis and the dependent variable on the *y*-axis.

Try It Out! **Review the Activity 1 description and answer the questions about the graph.**

Activity 1

The apparatus shown in Diagram 1 was used to measure the extension of each 10 cm spring of unknown stiffness. The top of each 10 cm spring was suspended from a beam, and a 1 g mass was attached to the bottom. After waiting for five minutes, the students measured the extension of each spring from its "at rest" position. The process was repeated with four additional masses on each spring. The results are shown in Table 1 and Figure 1.

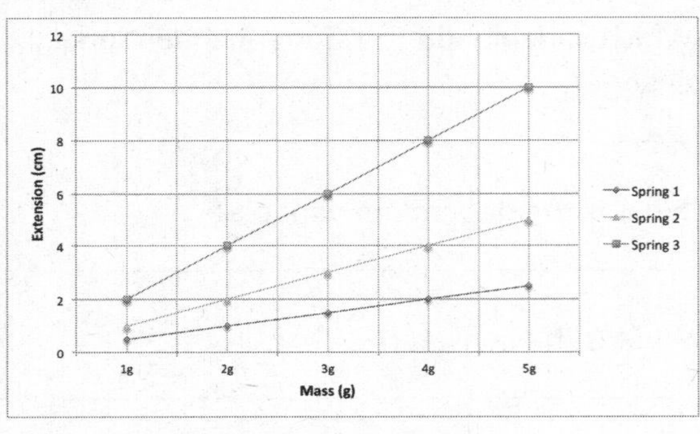

Figure 1

Figure 1 presents the results from Activity 1 as a graph in the *xy*-coordinate plane. The **independent** variables are plotted on the *x*-axis, and the **dependent** variables are plotted on the *y*-axis. Note that each of the **constants**, the springs, is plotted on its own line. When the results are displayed on multiple lines, make sure you identify which line goes with which data set.

Which line has the greatest slope?

____

What does the slope represent?

____

26

Apply the Kaplan Method for Science to answer the following multiple-choice questions.

Hooke's Law states that the force *F* required to extend or compress a spring some distance is proportional to that distance. When measuring the force *F* applied to the spring, the equation for Hooke's Law is:

$$F = k \cdot x$$

where *x* is the distance the spring is extended or compressed, and *k* is a constant expressing the stiffness of the spring. Two students perform two activities in order to study the relative stiffness of three different springs.

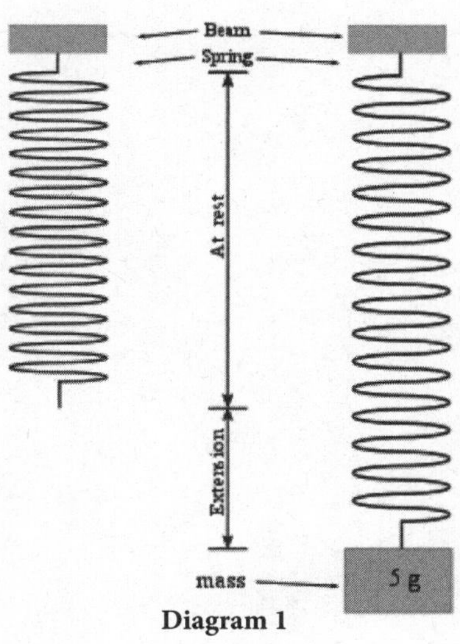

Diagram 1

Activity 1

The apparatus shown in Diagram 1 was used to measure the extension of each 10 cm spring of unknown stiffness. The top of each 10 cm spring was suspended from a beam, and a 1 g mass was attached to the bottom. After waiting for five minutes, the students measured the extension of each spring from its "at rest" position. The process was repeated with four additional masses on each spring. The results are shown in Table 1 and Figure 1.

Table 1

Mass (g)	Extension (cm)		
	Spring 1	Spring 2	Spring 3
1 g	0.5	1.0	2.0
2 g	1.0	2.0	4.0
3 g	1.5	3.0	6.0
4 g	2.0	4.0	8.0
5 g	2.5	5.0	10.0

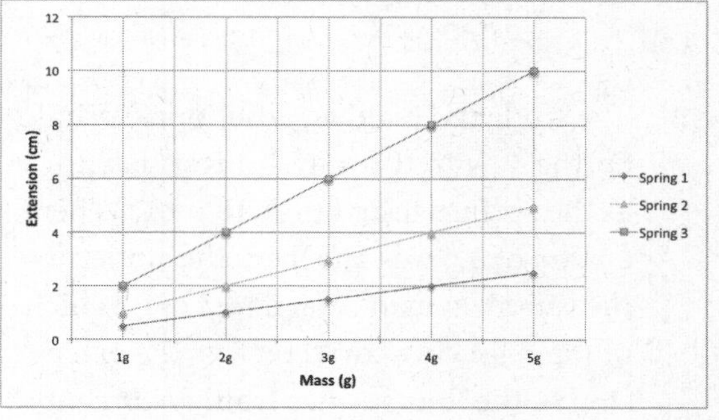

Figure 1

Activity 2

The students then used the equation for Hooke's Law to determine the relative value of *k* for each of the springs tested. For the unit of force, the students used the dyne, which is the force required to accelerate 1 g of mass 1 cm/sec^2. The results are shown in Figure 2.

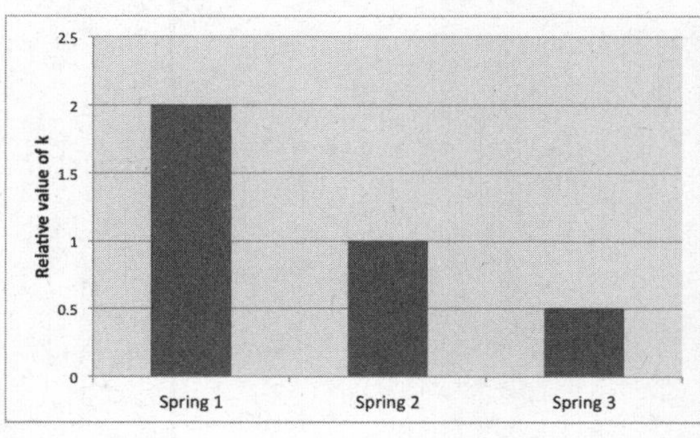

Figure 2

1. Based on the results of Activity 1, as the added mass increases, the measured extension

   A) increases only.

   B) decreases only.

   C) increases, then decreases.

   D) decreases, then increases.

hint *The question tells you to look at the results for Activity 1, which are found in Table 1 and Figure 1. As the mass increases, what happens to the extension?*

2. The students tested an additional spring, Spring 4, with the same "at rest" length as the springs tested in Activity 1. When a mass of 3 g was attached, the students measured an extension of 2.5 cm. Which of the following correctly lists the extension of the four springs from *greatest to least?*

   A) Spring 1, Spring 4, Spring 2, Spring 3

   B) Spring 1, Spring 2, Spring 4, Spring 3

   C) Spring 3, Spring 4, Spring 2, Spring 1

   D) Spring 3, Spring 2, Spring 4, Spring 1

hint *In Table 1, look in the row containing the data for a mass of 3 g. At 3 g, where is there an extension of 2.5 cm?*

3. Based on the results of Activity 2, which of the following is most likely to be the value of k for Spring 4?

   A) 0.3

   B) 0.6

   C) 1.2

   D) 2.4

hint *Look in Figure 2 for a value that falls between Spring 1 and Spring 2.*

Use the Kaplan Method to answer the following multiple-choice questions. Use the hints provided as needed.

Butylated hydroxytoluene, or BHT, is a chemical compound that is often added to packaged foods to preserve their color and flavor. Foods high in fat and oils, such as potato chips, often contain BHT. Students conducted two experiments to measure BHT.

Experiment 1

Five solutions, each containing a different amount of BHT, were prepared. A coloring agent that binds with the BHT to form a colored compound that absorbs light of a specific wavelength was added to each solution, and each solution was diluted to 100 mL. A separate solution was prepared in the same manner, but no BHT was added. A *colorimeter* (a device that measures how much light of a selected wavelength is absorbed by a sample) was used to measure the *absorbance* of each solution. The absorbances were corrected by subtracting the absorbance of the separate solution from each reading (see Table 1 and Figure 1).

Underline the Purpose, bracket the Method, and star the Results.

Table 1

Concentration of BHT (ppm*)	Measured Absorbance	Corrected Absorbance
0.0	0.015	0.000
2.5	0.080	0.065
5.0	0.146	0.131
7.5	0.212	0.197
10.0	0.278	0.263
12.5	0.343	0.328

*ppm is parts per million

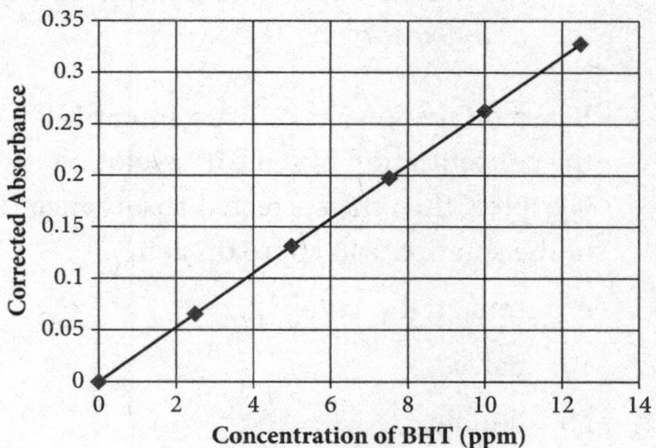

Figure 1

hint *Evaluate each figure carefully. What does it show? What are the units of measurement? What patterns do you see in the figure? What is the independent variable? What is the dependent variable?*

Experiment 2

100 g of plain potato chips and 50 mL of ethanol were pureed in a blender, and the resulting mixture was filtered. The filtered liquid was added to the sample solution. The coloring agent was added, and the solution was diluted to 100 mL. The procedure was repeated for several types of potato chips, and the absorbances were measured (see Table 2).

Table 2

Potato Chip Flavor	Corrected Absorbance	Concentration of BHT (ppm*)
Plain	0.040	1.5
Barbecue	0.243	9.3
Cheddar	0.315	12.1
Ranch	0.275	10.6
Salt and vinegar	0.099	3.8

hint *What does Table 2 show? How does it relate to the Method of Experiment 2? What Results did the students obtain in Experiment 2?*

1. Based on the Results of Experiment 1, if the concentration of BHT in a solution is tripled, then the corrected absorbance of the solution will approximately

   A) remain the same.

   B) halve.

   C) double.

   D) triple.

hint *What is the corrected absorbance at a concentration of 2.5? How does that compare to the absorbance at 7.5, or three times 2.5?*

26

2. A sample of sour cream and onion potato chips was also measured in Experiment 2, and its corrected absorbance was determined to be 0.298. Which of the following correctly lists barbecue, cheddar, and sour cream and onion in *increasing* order of BHT concentration?

   A) Cheddar, barbecue, sour cream and onion

   B) Barbecue, cheddar, sour cream and onion

   C) Sour cream and onion, cheddar, barbecue

   D) Barbecue, sour cream and onion, cheddar

hint *Use Table 2 to find where sour cream and onion potato chips fit. Arrange them from smallest to largest.*

3. Based on the results of Experiment 1, if a solution with a concentration of 6.25 ppm BHT had been tested, the corrected absorbance would have been closest to which of the following values?

   A) 0.050

   B) 0.163

   C) 0.247

   D) 0.285

hint *Use the graph in Figure 1 to locate a concentration of 6.25 ppm on the x-axis. Move your pencil vertically to find 6.25 on the line. Read horizontally to find the corresponding value on the y-axis.*

4. Based on the results of Experiments 1 and 2, if the measured absorbances for the potato chips tested in Experiment 2 were compared with their corrected absorbances, the measured absorbances would be

   A) lower for all the potato chips tested.

   B) higher for all the potato chips tested.

   C) lower for some of the potato chips tested but for the others.

   D) the same for all of the potato chips tested.

hint *Compare the measured absorbances in Experiment 1 to their corrected values. Are the measured absorbances higher or lower? Is there any reason why that would change in Experiment 2?*

Use the Kaplan Method to answer the following multiple-choice questions on your own.

The ozone (O_3) layer is located in the stratosphere. Ozone is an important key to healthy life on Earth, as it helps protect us from the sun's ultraviolet rays. Unfortunately, when located in the troposphere, the layer in which we live, ozone can pose a number of concerns. In addition to being a breathing hazard, ozone at the tropospheric level acts as a greenhouse gas, contributing to the apparent rise in global temperatures over the past 50 years. The presence of nitrogen oxides (NO and NO_2) in the troposphere is one of the factors in ozone formation. The burning of fossil fuels tends to produce nitrogen oxides which will, in turn, lead to ozone production. This is particularly problematic during AM and PM rush hours, when a major portion of all working professionals is headed to and from work. NO_2 produces ozone according to the balanced equation $NO_2 + O_2 \Rightarrow NO + O_3$. Scientists looked at the effects of two types of transportation that use internal combustion engines on the production of nitrogen oxides and ozone by conducting two studies.

Study 1

In order to understand the effect of airplanes on the production of nitrogen oxides and ozone, samples of the upper troposphere were collected at altitudes of 9 to 12 km, the altitude of typical commercial aircraft. These samples were collected hourly, and the times of commercial flights passing through the sample area were noted. The results of this study are summarized in Table 1 and Figure 1.

Table 1

Flight #	Time in Target Area	Flight #	Time in Target Area
1	5:45 AM	11	1:30 PM
2	6:03 AM	12	2:20 PM
3	7:20 AM	13	3:10 PM
4	7:40 AM	14	3:45 PM
5	7:50 AM	15	4:08 PM
6	8:10 AM	16	4:41 PM
7	8:47 AM	17	5:15 PM
8	10:17 AM	18	5:58 PM
9	10:50 AM	19	6:40 PM
10	11:37 AM	20	7:20 PM

Figure 1

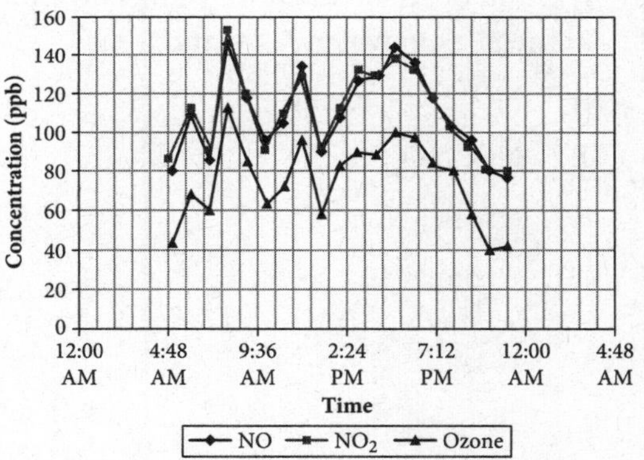

Study 2

Scientists wanted to explore a possible link between car exhaust and nitrogen oxides and ozone. They took air samples near an urban highway at various times on a typical workday. The results of this study are summarized in Figure 2.

Figure 2

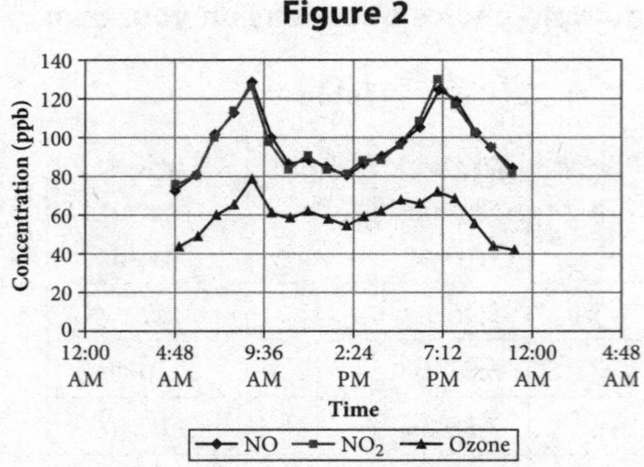

1. According to Study 1, when was the NO_2 concentration the greatest?
   A) 5:00 AM
   B) 8:00 AM
   C) 1:30 PM
   D) 4:45 PM

2. According to the results of Study 1, which of the following lists the three gases analyzed in order of ascending concentration at the peak between 7 AM and 8 AM?
   A) NO_2, NO, ozone
   B) NO, NO_2, ozone
   C) Ozone, NO, NO_2
   D) Ozone, NO_2, NO

3. Based on the results of both studies, which of the following could be a logical conclusion?
   A) Nitrogen oxides are increased by the use of the internal combustion engine.
   B) Nitrogen oxides are decreased by the use of the internal combustion engine.
   C) Increasing ozone levels tend to trap heat, raising average global temperature.
   D) Decreasing ozone levels tend to trap heat, raising average global temperature.

Use the Kaplan Method to answer the following multiple-choice questions for homework.

Geologists describe the orientation of sedimentary rock layers using two angles: "dip" and "strike." The dip indicates how far from perfectly horizontal the rock layer is tilted, and the strike indicates the compass direction along which the rock layer has been tilted. For example, a dip of 1 degree indicates that a rock layer is nearly horizontal: it slopes downward at an angle of only 1 degree. The highest dip value possible is 90 degrees, which corresponds to a perfectly vertical rock layer. A strike of 1 degree indicates that the rock layer is tilted along a line running 1 degree east of north (i.e., almost due north), a strike of 90 degrees indicates that the rock layer is tilted along a line running 90 degrees east of north (i.e., due east), and so forth.

Within a mountain range, strike values are typically similar. For instance, a map will show that the Allegheny Mountains run from southwest to northeast, and the strikes of rock layers within this area are often approximately the same (a value of approximately 45 degrees, corresponding to northeast). In addition, near the outer edge of a mountain range, rock layers will generally be tilted much less than near the center of the range.

Table 1 shows the dips and strikes measured at several points in a square mile of the Allegheny Mountains.

Table 1

Location	Dip	Strike
1	20	44
2	43	46
3	11	39
4	49	42
5	31	44

Figures 1 and 2 show how the average dip and average strike vary at 25-mile intervals along a particular north-south line in the Alleghenies.

Figure 1

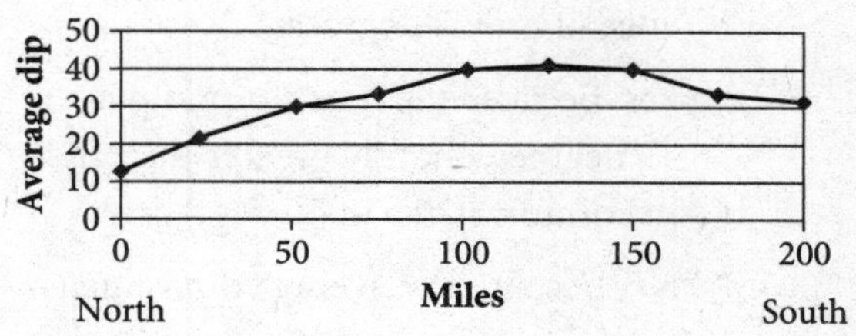

Figure 2

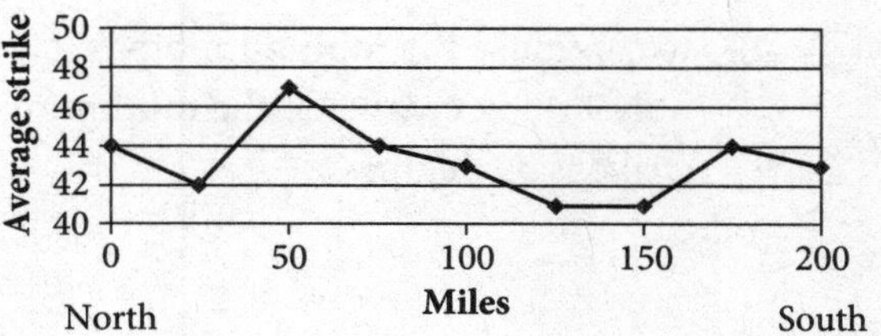

1. According to Figure 1, from north to south, the average dip

   A) increases only.

   B) decreases only.

   C) increases, then decreases.

   D) decreases, then increases.

26

2. The dip values in Table 1 were expected to vary more than the strike values. Does the actual data support this?

   A) Yes, because the dip values range from 11 to 49 degrees, a difference of 38 degrees; while the strike values range from 39 to 46 degrees, a difference of only 7 degrees.

   B) Yes, because the maximum dip is 49 degrees, slightly greater than the maximum strike of 46 degrees.

   C) No, because the average dip value is approximately 31 degrees, while the average strike value is approximately 43 degrees.

   D) No, because the minimum dip is only 11 degrees, while the minimum strike is 39 degrees.

The following questions are similar to what you would encounter on a college admissions test such as the SAT or ACT. Apply the Kaplan Method and your knowledge of experiment variables and graphing to answer the following questions.

Hypertension is a medical condition in which a person's blood pressure is significantly above normal ranges. With each heartbeat, a person's blood pressure rises from a lower value, termed the diastolic pressure, to an upper value, termed the systolic pressure, and then drops back to the lower value again. Thus, when a doctor determines a patient's blood pressure, both the systolic and diastolic pressures are usually reported. However, a single value, which may be termed the "weighted mean pressure," can also be calculated. This value can be approximated using the following formula:

Weighted mean pressure = 1/3 × systolic pressure + 2/3 × diastolic pressure

Thus, the weighted mean pressure lies between the systolic and diastolic pressures, but it is closer to the diastolic pressure because the blood pressure remains near this value for most of each heartbeat.

The typical systolic and diastolic pressures (recorded at a doctor's office) for males and females are shown in Tables 1 and 2, respectively. Additionally, the ratio between the pressures and the difference between the pressures have been calculated.

Table 1

Blood pressure data from male patients				
Age	**Systolic**	**Diastolic**	**Systolic – Diastolic**	**Systolic/ Diastolic**
0	89	60	30	1.50
20	111	76	37	1.48
40	117	80	38	1.46
60	130	83	49	1.58
80	140	86	58	1.65

Table 2

Blood pressure data from female patients				
Age	**Systolic**	**Diastolic**	**Systolic – Diastolic**	**Systolic/ Diastolic**
0	91	61	29	1.48
20	114	77	35	1.46
40	120	82	37	1.46
60	134	85	47	1.57
80	147	89	54	1.63

1. Does the information in Tables 1 and 2 support the hypothesis that males typically have higher blood pressures than females of the same age?

   A) Yes, because at each age, males have lower systolic pressures than females and lower diastolic pressures than females.

   B) Yes, because at each age, males have higher systolic pressures than females and higher diastolic pressures than females.

   C) No, because at each age, males have lower systolic pressures than females and lower diastolic pressures than females.

   D) No, because at each age, males have higher systolic pressures than females and higher diastolic pressures than females.

26

2. In Table 1, as the difference between systolic and diastolic pressures in males increases, the ratio between the two pressures
   A) increases only.
   B) decreases only.
   C) increases, then decreases.
   D) decreases, then increases.

3. Based on the information given, a person's hypertension risk probably
   A) decreases with age and is higher in males than females.
   B) decreases with age and is lower in males than females.
   C) increases with age and is higher in males than females.
   D) increases with age and is lower in males than females.

CHAPTER 27

Reading and Analyzing Data Tables

CHAPTER OBJECTIVES

By the end of this chapter, you will be able to:

1. Locate data in a table
2. Organize, interpret, and analyze data in a table

THE KAPLAN METHOD FOR SCIENCE

Step 1: Map the passage.

- If the passage includes an experiment:
    - Underline the Purpose.
    - Put brackets around the Method.
    - Star the Results.
- If the passage provides straightforward data:
    - Circle keywords.
    - Underline key phrases.

Step 2: Examine the figures provided

- Locate variables in the figures.
- Identify trends and patterns.

Step 3: Find support for the answer in the passage

- Identify keywords in the question stem.
- Locate the corresponding data in the passage.
- Match it to the correct answer.

LOCATING DATA IN A TABLE

The first step of the Kaplan Method includes underlining the **Purpose**, putting brackets around the **Method**, and starring the **Results** of an experiment. After you put a star next to the Results, you are ready for **Step 2: Examine the figures provided.** If the Results include a table, the accompanying questions will require you to locate data within the table.

	Pounds of beans 100 *Phaseolus vulgaris* (garden bean) plants will produce when provided with daily sunlight exposure of:				
	2 hours	**4 hours**	**6 hours**	**8 hours**	**10 hours**
Day 50	0 lb	0 lb	0 lb	10 lb	7 lb
Day 60	0 lb	5 lb	10 lb	43 lb	44 lb
Day 70	0 lb	1 lb	2 lb	6 lb	12 lb

The table above shows that the number of beans a garden plant will produce varies according to daily sunlight exposure. Questions that ask you to locate data in a table require you to pinpoint specific values. You don't need to interpret the Results to answer these questions; instead, you can put your finger directly on the information you need or make small calculations such as addition or subtraction to identify the correct answer.

Try It Out! **Using the data in the table, answer the following questions.**

A. Which daily sunlight exposure resulted in the highest bean yield on Day 60? ____________

B. On which day of measurement did the scientists record the lowest yield for daily sunlight exposure of 8 hours? ____________

27

C. On which day of measurement did the scientists record the lowest yield for daily sunlight exposure of 10 hours? ____________

D. Which daily sunlight exposure amount resulted in the highest total bean yield? ____________

INTERPRETING AND ANALYZING DATA IN A TABLE

Some questions will require you to use the data in a table to identify the independent variables, dependent variables, and constants.

- Independent variables: What was intentionally varied
- Dependent variables: What was measured
- Constants: What was kept the same throughout the experiment

Once you have determined each variable, look for common relationships among those variables, including direct, inverse, fluctuating, and noncorrelative relationships.

- Direct:
  - As the independent variable increases, the dependent variable increases OR as the independent variable decreases, the dependent variable decreases.
- Inverse:
  - As the independent variable decreases, the dependent variable increases OR as the independent variable increases, the dependent variable decreases.
- Fluctuating:
  - As the independent variable steadily increases or decreases, the dependent variable fluctuates between increasing and decreasing values.
- Noncorrelative
  - The variables do not share a relationship.

	Yield from 100 Garden Bean Plants				
	2 hours of daily sunlight	**4 hours of daily sunlight**	**6 hours of daily sunlight**	**8 hours of daily sunlight**	**10 hours of daily sunlight**
Day 50	0 lb	0 lb	0 lb	7 lb	10 lb
Day 60	0 lb	5 lb	10 lb	43 lb	44 lb
Day 70	0 lb	0 lb	2 lb	6 lb	12 lb

Try It Out! **Using the data in the table, answer the following questions.**

27

A. Which variable was intentionally varied? ______________

B. Which variable was measured? ______________

C. What was kept constant? ______________

D. As the sunlight exposure increases, the amount of beans produced ______________.

E. The relationship between daily sunlight exposure and bean yield is ______________.

F. Based on the information in the table, 100 garden bean plants would produce how many pounds of beans if provided with a daily sunlight exposure of 1 hour? ______________

G. If, on Day 80, the bean plants given daily sunlight exposure of 4 hours produced 5 lb of beans, the relationship between daily sunlight exposure and bean yield would be ______________.

Try It Out! **Apply the Kaplan Method for Science to answer the following multiple-choice questions.**

Four of the most common volcanoes are cinder cone, composite, shield, and lava cone. Some information regarding these volcano types is found in Table 1.

Table 1

Volcano Type	Lava Type	Eruption Type
Cinder cone	Basalt warm	Gentle
Composite	Cool ashy	Varied
Shield	Warm ashy	Gentle
Lava cone	Basalt cool	Strong

hint *Note that the values in the second column are not arranged in ascending or descending order, nor are the values in the third column. Table 1 shows the lava type and eruption type for several different types of volcanoes. Note the column headings of this table.*

27

The data from several previous eruptions are shown below in Table 2.

Table 2

Volcano Type	Lava Deposition Rate (L/h)	Total Lava Depth (m)
Cinder cone	120	40
Composite	230	60
Shield	100	14
Lava cone	310	30

hint *Note that the values in the second column are not arranged in ascending or descending order, nor are the values in the third column. The shield volcano has the lowest lava deposition rate and the lowest total lava depth. However, the lava cone volcano has the highest lava deposition rate but the second-lowest total lava depth. Hence, the relationship here is non-correlative—there is no consistent relationship between these two variables.*

✔ Helpful Hint

Don't spend too much time looking for intricate patterns in the data. Just look for general trends and move on. If you need to look more deeply at a pattern within a figure, wait for a question to prompt you to do so.

1. What type of volcano is most likely to have a strong eruption?

   A) Cinder cone

   B) Composite

   C) Shield

   D) Lava cone

hint *Table 1 gives us information about the properties of different types of volcanoes, and this question asks us about the strength of eruptions of different types of volcanoes. Consult Table 1. What type has the strongest eruption?*

2. Which of the following correctly lists the volcano types in *decreasing* order of total lava depth?

   A) Composite, cinder cone, lava cone, shield

   B) Composite, lava cone, cinder cone, shield

   C) Shield, composite, cinder cone, lava cone

   D) Shield, lava cone, cinder cone, composite

hint *The question prompts us to look at Table 2 and put the types of volcanoes in reverse order, starting with the greatest lava depth.*

3. Based on the information in Tables 1 and 2, cool lava

   A) has a higher deposition rate than warm lava.

   B) has a lower deposition rate than warm lava.

   C) has an equal deposition rate to warm lava.

   D) has a deposition rate that cannot be determined.

hint *Use Table 1 to determine which type of lava is associated with each volcano type. Then match that information to the lava deposition rates in Table 2.*

Use the Kaplan Method to answer the following multiple-choice questions. Use the hints provided as needed.

Soap molecules often consist of long chains of hydrocarbons ending in negatively charged ions. In water, the soap molecules form clusters called micelles. Soaps are able to remove dirt particles from surfaces by trapping them in the centers of the micelles.

Experiment 1

A science fair student designs an experiment to measure the cleaning power of sodium oleate, a chemical that can be used as a soap. In the experiment, eight white T-shirts were stained with either dirt or ketchup. After the shirts were cleaned under varying conditions, the student rated how visible the stains were and reported the average for the shirts in Table 1.

Table 1

Cleaning Power of Sodium Oleate		
Scoops of soap	Ketchup	Dirt
0	4	4
1	4	4
2	3	3
4	2	1
8	1	1
1 = Clean, 2 = Slightly Dirty, 3 = Dirty, 4 = Very Dirty		

Experiment 2

To demonstrate that the cleaning action is due to the oleate and not to the sodium, the student measures the cleaning power of potassium oleate, using four scoops of the soap to clean a T-shirt stained with ketchup and a T-shirt stained with soil. The results of the experiment are reported in Table 2.

Table 2

Cleaning Power of Potassium Oleate		
Scoops of soap	Ketchup	Dirt
4	2	1
1 = Clean, 2 = Slightly Dirty, 3 = Dirty, 4 = Very Dirty		

hint *Evaluate each figure carefully. What does it show? What are the units of measurement? What patterns do you see in the figure?*

1. In Experiment 1, what is the independent variable?
   A) The type of soap used
   B) The amount of soap used
   C) The brand of ketchup used
   D) The number of shirts used

hint *Look at Experiment 1's Method and Results. The Results in Table 1 show how much ketchup and dirt remained after washing the T-shirts with zero to eight scoops of soap.*

2. In Experiment 1, what is the minimum number of scoops of sodium oleate required to produce a change in stain visibility?

   A) 0

   B) 1

   C) 2

   D) 4

hint *Question 2 requires us to use the key at the bottom to decipher what rates as a measurable result. There, we see that before a T-shirt had been cleaned with sodium oleate, it was rated "4—very dirty." How many scoops did it take to change that?*

3. Based on the results from Table 1, the student would most likely have rated a T-shirt stained with soil and cleaned with 12 scoops of sodium oleate as

   A) clean.

   B) slightly dirty.

   C) dirty.

   D) very dirty.

hint *Looking at Table 1, we see that as we use more scoops of soap, the T-shirts become cleaner/less dirty. When we used eight scoops, the T-shirts were rated as "clean" for both dirt and ketchup. What would happen if we used even MORE soap?*

Use the Kaplan Method to answer the following multiple-choice questions on your own.

A chemist investigating the influence of molecular weight and structure on the boiling point (transition from liquid to gaseous state) of different compounds recorded the data in the following tables. Two types of compounds were investigated: organic carbon compounds (shown in Table 1) and inorganic compounds (shown in Table 2).

Table 1

Straight-Chain Hydrocarbons		
Molecular formula	**Molecular weight* (g/mol)**	**Boiling point (°C)**
CH_4	16	−162
C_2H_6	30	−88
C_3H_8	44	−42
C_4H_{10}	58	0
C_5H_{12}	72	36
C_8H_{18}	114	126
$C_{20}H_{42}$	282	345

Table 2

Other Substances (Polar and Non-Polar)		
Molecular formula	**Molar weight (g/mol)**	**Boiling point (°C)**
N_2*	28	−196
SiH_4*	32	−112
GeH_4*	77	−90
Br_2*	160	59

1. An unknown organic compound with a boiling point of 0°C is likely to have a molecular weight closest to which of the following?
   A) 61
   B) 75
   C) 88
   D) 108

2. Given that room temperature is 20°C, which of the following straight-chain hydrocarbons would be a gas at room temperature?
   A) C_4H_{10}
   B) C_5H_{12}
   C) C_8H_{18}
   D) $C_{20}H_{42}$

3. Based on the data in Table 1, the boiling point of the straight-chain hydrocarbon C_6H_{14} (molecular weight 86 g/mol) is most likely
   A) 30°C.
   B) 70°C.
   C) 130°C.
   D) 350°C.

27

4. Based on the data in Table 2, as molecular weight increases, the boiling points of inorganic substances
   A) increase.
   B) decrease.
   C) remain constant.
   D) vary randomly.

Use the Kaplan Method to answer the following multiple-choice questions for homework.

Atoms of the elements hydrogen (H) and helium (He) make up over 98% of the atoms in the solar system. Only six other elements are present in abundances between 0.05% and 1%, and, together with H and He, these are called the "major elements." The other 89 stable elements are even less abundant and are called the "minor elements."

In addition, elements with even atomic numbers are usually more abundant than neighboring elements with odd atomic numbers.

Table 1 shows an estimate of the abundance of each element in the Solar System.

Table 1

Element	Atomic #	Abundance (%)
H	1	91.03
He	2	7.24
C	6	0.41
N	7	0.11
O	8	0.79
Ne	10	0.10
Mg	12	0.05
Si	14	0.05
All other elements	> 14	< 0.05

1. The abundances in Table 1 were calculated to the nearest
   A) 1%.
   B) 0.1%.
   C) 0.01%.
   D) 0.001%.

2. Which of the following statements best describes how the abundances of the eight major elements listed in the table change with increasing atomic number?
   A) The abundances always decrease or remain constant as the atomic number increases.
   B) The abundances usually decrease or remain constant as the atomic number increases.
   C) The abundances usually increase or remain constant as the atomic number increases.
   D) The abundances always increase or remain constant as the atomic number increases.

3. According to Table 1, as the atomic number increases from 6 to 7 to 8, the abundances
   A) decrease, then increase.
   B) increase, then decrease.
   C) increase only.
   D) decrease only.

4. Based on the data in Table 1, an element with an atomic number of 16 would have an abundance that is
   A) greater than 0.41%.
   B) less than 0.41%.
   C) greater than 0.05%.
   D) less than 0.05%.

27

The following questions are similar to what you would encounter on a college admissions test such as the SAT or ACT. Apply the Kaplan Method and your knowledge of reading and analyzing data tables to answer the following questions.

Two students are doing various activities using a Spec 20. A Spec 20 is a device that can measure the transmittance and absorbance of solutions at various wavelengths of light.

Activity 1

The students insert a "blank" curvette into the sample holder and set the dial for 0% transmittance. They then place solutions of increasing chlorophyll concentration into the Spec 20 and record the transmittance at four wavelengths. The results are summarized in Table 1.

Table 1

Concentration Chlorophyll (M)	Transmittance (%) at 250 nm	Transmittance (%) at 350 nm	Transmittance (%) at 450 nm
0.2	73	68	52
0.6	56	52	45
1.2	40	36	35
1.4	29	27	23

Activity 2

The students are given a prepared solution of chlorophyll and are asked to determine the correct chlorophyll concentration. According to Beer's Law, the absorbance (A) of a substance equals the wavelength of the light (b) times the molar absorbance of the material (a) times the concentration (C): $A = abC$. At a wavelength of 450 nm, $a = 0.2$. The students test three samples of the prepared solution, and their results are summarized in Table 2.

Table 2

Sample	Absorbance
1	59
2	57
3	61

Activity 3

The students are given a sample 0.2 M solution of a red food dye and asked to determine the absorbance of the material. They insert a blank into the Spec 20, set it to 0 transmittance, and then run the sample at 3 wavelengths. The results are summarized in Table 3.

Table 3

Wavelength (nm)	Transmittance (%)
350	65
450	55
650	35

1. If the samples in Activity 3 were run at a wavelength of 400 nm, the transmittance would most likely be closest to

   A) 70%.

   B) 60%.

   C) 45%.

   D) 30%.

2. According to the results of Activity 1, chlorophyll has the highest transmittance at a wavelength of

   A) 250 nm.

   B) 350 nm.

   C) 450 nm.

   D) 550 nm.

3. What concentration of chlorophyll in Activity 1 had a transmittance of 52% at 350 nm?

   A) 0.2 M

   B) 0.6 M

   C) 1.2 M

   D) 1.4 M

4. The students in Activity 1 are given an unknown concentration of chlorophyll. According to Figure 1, if the sample transmits 40% at a wavelength of 450 nm, its concentration is closest to

   A) 1.7.

   B) 1.3.

   C) 1.1.

   D) 0.9.

CHAPTER 28

Analyzing Experiments

CHAPTER OBJECTIVES

By the end of this chapter, you will be able to:

1. Interpret the results of experimental procedures
2. Correctly interpret and answer accompanying questions

THE KAPLAN METHOD FOR SCIENCE

Step 1: Map the passage

- If the passage includes an experiment:
  - Underline the Purpose.
  - Put brackets around the Method.
  - Star the Results.
- If the passage provides straightforward data:
  - Circle keywords.
  - Underline key phrases.

Step 2: Examine the figures provided

- Locate variables in the figures.
- Identify trends and patterns.

Step 3: Find support for the answer in the passage

- Identify keywords in the question stem.
- Locate the corresponding data in the passage.
- Match it to the correct answer.

ANALYZING EXPERIMENTS

When analyzing an experiment, it is important to consider the **Purpose**, **Method**, and **Results** of that experiment.

Analyzing Purpose

An experiment is designed to answer a scientist's question about something. Finding the answer to that question is the Purpose of the experiment.

Experiment	Stated Purpose	Rephrased as a Question
1	To study the effects of adding various amounts of the solute NaCl (table salt) on the boiling point of water.	Does adding salt to water change the boiling point?
2	To investigate the relationship between the solubility of NaCl (the solute) and the temperature of water (the solvent).	Will more salt dissolve in warmer water?

Analyzing Method

In the table above, both experiments involve adding salt to water, but each experiment answers a different questions. To analyze the Method, think about what you need to do in order to answer the question that each experiment is designed to answer. What should you vary intentionally? What should you measure? What should be kept constant?

Experiment	Variable to Vary Intentionally (Independent)	Variable to Measure (Dependent)	Constant
1	The amount of salt added to tap water	The temperature of the water salt solution	The initial quantity of water The salt used (NaCl) Atmospheric pressure
2	The temperature of the water salt solution	The amount of salt that dissolves in the water	The initial quantity of water The salt used (NaCl) Atmospheric pressure

28

Analyzing Results

Step 2 of the Kaplan Method for Science directs you to identify the relationships between the variables. When you are analyzing the Results of an experiment, use those relationships to help you to answer the question asked in the Purpose.

Experiment 1		
Solution	**NaCl Added gms**	**Boiling Point °C**
Tap water	0.0	100.15
1	0.6	100.25
2	3.0	100.65
3	6.0	101.15
4	12.0	102.15

Experiment 2 (gms NaCl Dissolved/100 gms H_2O)						
	0°C	20°C	40°C	60°C	80°C	100°C
NaCl	35	36	36	37	38	39

Try It Out! Use the Kaplan Method for Science to answer the following multiple-choice questions.

1. According to the results of Experiment 1, which of the following conclusions can be made about the effect of NaCl on the boiling point of water?

   A) The addition of NaCl had no effect on the boiling point of water.
   B) The addition of NaCl lowered the boiling point of water.
   C) The addition of NaCl initially raised and then lowered the boiling point of water.
   D) The addition of NaCl raised the boiling point of water.

hint *Review the Purpose and your question in Table 1, and look at the results in Table 3.*

2. In order to learn more about the relationship between NaCl solubility in water and water temperature, what experiment should the researchers from Experiment 2 perform next?

   A) Measuring the solubility every 5°C instead of every 20°C
   B) Testing the solubility of NaCl in different solvents at the same temperatures
   C) Testing the solubility of different solutes in water at the same temperatures
   D) Testing the solubility of different solutes in different solvents at the same temperatures

hint *Pay attention to which variables the question tells you stay the same. What remains to test?*

3. If the researchers in Experiment 1 re-ran the experiment using distilled water that boiled at 100°C, the boiling points measured would be

   A) higher for all the solutions tested.

   B) lower for all the solutions tested.

   C) higher for some and lower for other solutions tested.

   D) the same for all solutions tested.

hint *Does the tap water boil at a higher temperature? What will using distilled water do to the results of the experiment?*

28

Use the Kaplan Method to answer the following multiple-choice questions. Use the hints provided as needed.

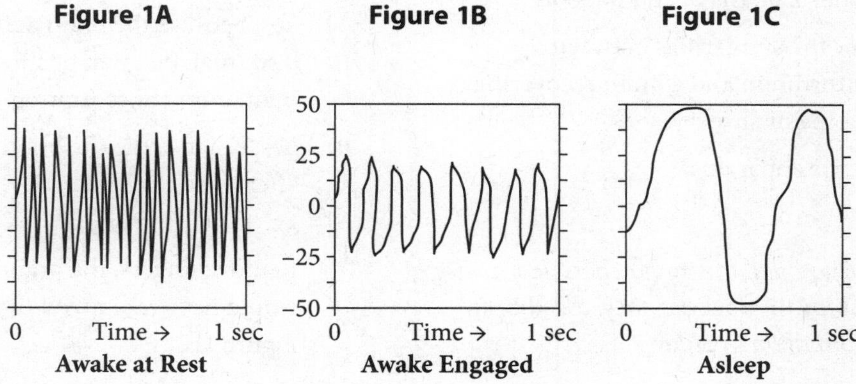

Study 1

The electrical activity of a healthy human volunteer's brain is recorded using EEG electrodes attached to her scalp. The results are shown in the figures. In Figure 1A, when the volunteer is awake but resting, the voltage varies with an amplitude (height from the bottom to the top of a peak) of approximately 50 microvolts (from –25 to +25 microvolts) and a frequency of approximately 10 cycles per second. This frequency and amplitude are both characteristic of "alpha waves." In Figure 1B, the volunteer is concentrating on a task, and the voltage peaks occur approximately 20 times per second, characteristic of "beta waves." In Figure 1C, the volunteer is asleep, and the peaks occur less than 2 times per second, characteristic of "delta waves."

Study 2

The electrical activity of a patient recovering from major surgery is measured using the same procedure as in Study 1. At the time marked as 0, the patient is asked to move his fingers. The patient's fingers do not move, but the doctors examine the EEG recording for evidence of a change. If a change occurred, the patient must have been aware of the sound and may have attempted to understand it or even respond to it. The results of the study are shown in Figure 2.

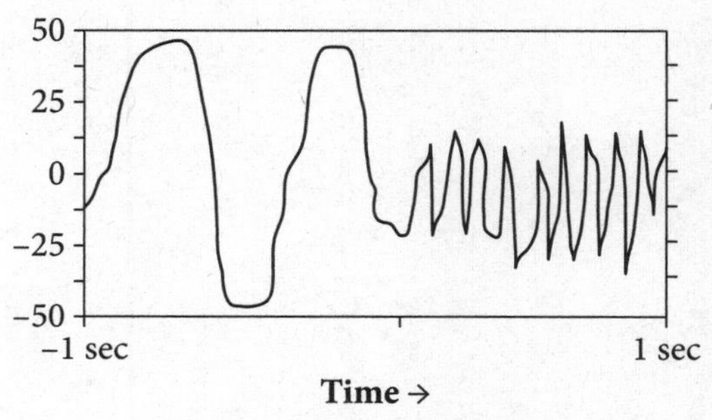

Figure 2

1. The purpose of Study 1 is to
   A) learn more about the electrical activity of a healthy human brain.
   B) establish a basis of comparison.
   C) show the similarities between a healthy brain and a brain recovering after major surgery.
   D) test the apparatus.

hint *What did the researchers learn in Study 1? How did they use that information in Study 2?*

2. Based on the information in Figure 2, from −1 sec to 0 sec, the recorded EEG most nearly resembles
   A) a healthy brain that is awake and concentrating.
   B) a healthy brain that is awake and resting.
   C) a healthy brain that is awake and watching television.
   D) a healthy brain that is deeply asleep.

hint *Use the information in the question stem to determine which section of Figure 2 you should examine.*

3. According to the results in Study 1 and Study 2, is it logical for the researchers to conclude that the patient in Study 2 was aware of the researcher's request?
   A) Yes, because the brain activity after 0 sec matched that of a healthy human brain concentrating.
   B) Yes, because the the brain activity after 0 sec changed.
   C) No, because if the patient attempted to move fingers, the brain activity would have resembled the activity in Figure 1B.
   D) No, because the patient's fingers did not move.

hint *If the researchers find the result that they have hypothesized, then they can logically make the conclusion.*

28

Use the Kaplan Method to answer the following multiple-choice questions on your own.

Before the development of modern techniques for measuring the molecular weights of extremely large molecules, scientists often expressed the sizes of such molecules in Svedberg units. This unit indicates the sedimentation coefficient (S) of the molecules, or how fast they will settle to the bottom of a solution. (1 Svedberg unit is defined as a sedimentation coefficient of 10–13 seconds.) The higher the sedimentation coefficient, the more rapidly the molecule settles.

It is also possible to measure the diffusion coefficient (D) of a molecule, which indicates the rate at which the molecule diffuses through a solution. For instance, if a drop of dye is placed in water, the color will gradually spread further and further from the point at which the dye was added. If the diffusion coefficient of the molecule in the dye is high, the color will spread rapidly, and if the diffusion coefficient is low, the color will spread slowly. Table 1 lists molecular weights, sedimentation coefficients and diffusion coefficients for several large molecules.

Table 1

Molecule	Molecular Weight	S (in Svedberg units)	D (in cm^2/s)
Albium	68,500	4.6	6.1
Aldolase	149,100	7.4	4.4
Catalase	221,600	11.2	4.3
Cytochrome C	13,370	1.7	11.4
Urease	482,700	18.6	3.5

The data from these proteins are plotted in Figures 1 and 2.

Figure 1

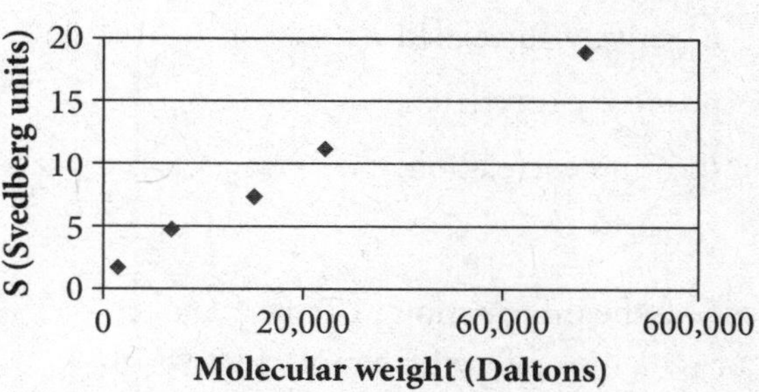

Figure 2

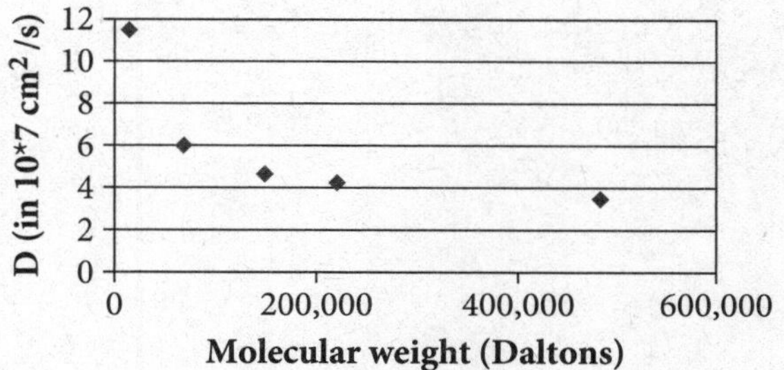

1. If the sedimentation coefficient (S) of an unknown molecule is determined to be 9.3, the molecular weight of that molecule is

   A) less than urease and greater than catalase.

   B) less than catalase and greater than aldolase.

   C) less than aldolase and greater than albumin.

   D) less than albumin and greater than cytochrome c.

2. Based on the information in Table 1 and Figures 1 and 2, the sedimentation coefficient and the diffusion coefficient are
   A) negatively correlated.
   B) positively correlated.
   C) show no correlation.
   D) equal.

3. Based on the information in Table 1 and Figure 2, a molecule with a molecular weight of 100,000 has a diffusion rate closest to
   A) 2.
   B) 3.
   C) 4.
   D) 5.

Use the Kaplan Method to answer the following multiple-choice questions for homework.

A local university hosts a domino tournament each year to encourage collaboration between the art and science departments. Students design and set up elaborate designs of upright dominoes that will then be knocked over after pushing on the first domino. Exhibitions are judged on design, topple speed, complexity, and spectator votes. A group of art and engineering students was interested in determining the optimal parameters before constructing a design.

Experiment 1

The students selected one brand of dominoes and placed 75 dominoes in a line. Each trial had a different spacing distance ranging from 0.2 cm to 2.0 cm apart, and the students recorded the distance traveled by the falling dominoes and the time it took them to fall. Data for these tests are found in Table 1 and Figure 1.

Table 1

Spacing (cm)	Time (s)	Total Distance (cm)	Velocity (cm/s)
0.2	1.6	84	52.5
0.4	1.9	91	47.9
0.6	2.1	104	49.5
0.8	2.2	118	53.6
1	2.6	123	47.3
1.2	2.8	130	46.4
1.4	2.9	145	50.0
1.6	3.1	160	51.6
1.8	3.2	177	55.3
2	3.4	189	55.5

Figure 1

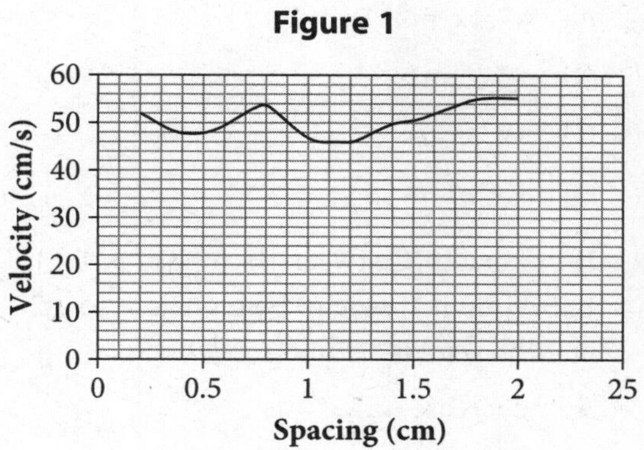

Experiment 2

A second series of tests was carried out using four brands of dominoes. The students determined the average mass of an individual domino before conducting the tests. In these tests, 75 dominoes were placed 0.5 cm apart, and the students recorded the distance traveled by the falling dominoes and the time it took them to fall. Table 2 and Figure 2 provide information about this second series of tests.

Table 2

Brand	Avg. mass of a single domino
Warner's	3.5
Apex	4.2
Robin	2.8
Gilbert	5.1

Figure 2

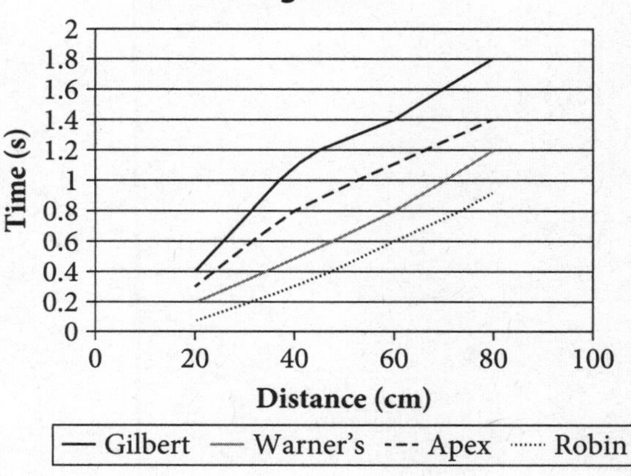

28

1. In Experiment 1, what is the domino velocity at a spacing of 1.0 cm?
   A) 47.3 cm/s
   B) 53.6 cm/s
   C) 123 cm/s
   D) 130 cm/s

2. If the spacing between dominoes in Experiment 1 were to be increased to 2.2 cm, the velocity would most likely
   A) decrease only.
   B) increase only.
   C) decrease, then increase.
   D) increase, then decrease.

3. The Robin and Gilbert brand dominoes used in the second test were set up in a 100 cm line and allowed to fall as indicated in the second test. Which of the following statements will most likely be true of the time they take to completely fall?
   A) Robin dominoes will fall at a slower rate than Gilbert dominoes.
   B) Robin dominoes will fall at a faster rate than Gilbert dominoes.
   C) Both brands of dominoes will fall at approximately the same rate.
   D) The answer cannot be determined from the information provided.

4. Suppose that a set of dominoes were tested in the same manner as the second test performed in which dominoes of various masses were toppled. Based upon the information presented in Table 2 and Figure 2, how long would it take a domino chain with an average mass of 4.7 g to fall a distance of 60 cm?
   A) 0.8 s
   B) 1.0 s
   C) 1.3 s
   D) 2.1 s

The following questions are similar to what you would encounter on a college admissions test such as the SAT or ACT. Apply the Kaplan Method and your knowledge of analyzing experiments to answer the following questions.

The solute of a solution is the substance that is dissolved by the solvent. A student wishes to discover what effects, if any, pressure and temperature have on the solubility of various substances in water.

Experiment 1

At a constant pressure of 770 torr, a student tested the solubility of five substances at different temperatures. The student started with 100 g of water and gradually added the solutes, in five separate trials, until no more of that solute could dissolve. All of the solutes tested in this experiment were in the solid state unless otherwise indicated. The results of this experiment are summarized in Table 1.

Table 1

Temperature (°C)	0	20	40	60	80	100
Solutes	Solubility (g solute/100 g water)					
Na_2SO_4	5	19	45	48	82	101
NaCl	35	36	37	38	39	40
$Ca(NO_2)_3$	5	10	12	20	28	33
$Ce_2(SO_4)_2$ (g)	18	10	6	4	2	1
Na_2HSO_4	8	28	49	65	83	—

Experiment 2

At a constant temperature of 25°C, the student tested the solubility of four compounds at different pressures. The student gradually increased the pressure of the solutions while determining the effect on solubility. The solvents tested were in either solid or gaseous state. The results of this experiment are summarized in Table 2.

Table 2

Pressure (torr)	150	300	450	600	750	900
Solutes	Solubility (g solute/100 g water)					
CO_2 (g)	20	39	59	78	98	117
NH_3 (g)	7.5	15	23	30	38	45
SO_2 (g)	14	27	41	53	68	80
$LiNO_3$ (s)	51	49	52	50	49	51

1. According to the information in Tables 1 and 2, the solubility of a gas varies
   A) directly with temperature and indirectly with pressure.
   B) directly with pressure and indirectly with temperature.
   C) directly with both temperature and pressure.
   D) indirectly with both temperature and pressure.

2. According to the information in Table 1, is the nature of the change in solubility of NaCl with increasing temperature consistent with that of the other solid solutes tested?
   A) Yes, because it varies indirectly with temperature.
   B) Yes, because it more than doubles as the temperature increases.
   C) No, because it varies indirectly with temperature.
   D) No, because it shows relatively little variance as the temperature increases.

28

CHAPTER 29

Evaluating Conflicting Viewpoints

CHAPTER OBJECTIVES

By the end of this chapter, you will be able to:

1. Apply the Kaplan Method for Paired Passages to Conflicting Viewpoints passages
2. Evaluate viewpoints in scientific passages
3. Compare and contrast viewpoints in scientific passages

THE KAPLAN METHOD FOR PAIRED PASSAGES

- **Step 1:** Read and map Passage 1, and then answer its questions
- **Step 2:** Read and map Passage 2, and then answer its questions
- **Step 3:** Answer questions about both passages

EVALUATING VIEWPOINTS IN SCIENTIFIC PASSAGES

Conflicting Viewpoints passages present two or more explanations for the same phenomenon, such as dinosaur extinction. Scientists draw different conclusions from the same data provided in the introductory paragraph, which, in the case of dinosaur extinction, could be fossils, evidence of meteors, or volcanic activity.

As you read each viewpoint, ask yourself:

- How does the scientist interpret the evidence given in the introduction?
- What evidence does the scientist offer to support the suggested theory?

After you evaluate each viewpoint, you will be able to answer questions that ask you to clarify viewpoints, as well as questions that ask about additional information that may support or contradict a viewpoint. Questions that provide additional information certainly do go beyond the scope of the passage presented, but the correct answer will be directly based on the information provided.

✔ Helpful Hint

Read the first scientist's viewpoint and answer questions that ask just about that scientist. Then read the second scientist's viewpoint, and answer questions about that viewpoint. Finally, answer questions about more than one viewpoint.

Comparing and Contrasting Viewpoints in Scientific Passages

In addition to evaluating each viewpoint separately, you will compare and contrast the viewpoints. Common questions include:

- Which of the following statements are the scientists most likely to agree with?
- Which of the following statements would the scientists disagree about?
- How would Scientist 1 respond to the statement ". . ." by Scientist 2?
- Scientist 1 and Scientist 2 disagree on the point that . . .

When answering questions about what the scientists will agree upon, focus on the introductory information. Any data provided in the introduction is accepted as valid by all of the scientists—the scientists disagree only about the conclusions that can be drawn from that valid data. Correct answers reflect that the scientists agree upon the validity and accuracy of the information provided in the introduction. For questions about disagreement, identifying each scientist's viewpoint first will help you analyze what the scientists do not agree upon.

Try It Out! **Apply the Kaplan Method for Paired Passages to answer the following multiple-choice questions.**

Although there is good evidence that rivers and even lakes temporarily existed on Mars when that planet was much younger, astronomers are still debating whether a temporary ocean ever existed in a large depression in the northern plains.

Two scientists discuss the evidence for an ocean.

hint *What is the topic or issue the scientists are discussing in this passage? What question do they hope to answer?*

Scientist 1

Satellite data show a feature that resembles some of the shorelines surrounding Earth's oceans: a terrace, "Shoreline A," that is almost always at the same elevation wherever it is visible. There are also three more features resembling those found in some of Earth's oceans. First, there is some evidence for additional terraces at other elevations (representing earlier or later times when the sea level was at that higher or lower elevation for a long period of time). Second, the surface is much smoother inside Shoreline A than outside the shoreline, exactly as is the case in Earth's present oceans. Third, there are features resembling river channels leading into the depression. Therefore, an ocean was present in the northern plains of Mars at one point in time.

hint *Scientist 1 argues in the final sentence of his/her viewpoint that there was an ocean present in the northern plains of Mars at some point. What evidence does the scientist provide to support this conclusion?*

Scientist 2

In a few locations (near the Tharsis and Elysium volcanoes and near the Lyot crater), the elevation of the proposed Shoreline A is much higher than elsewhere. The situation is much worse for other potential shorelines in the area. For example, "Shoreline B" obviously cannot correspond to the boundary of an ancient ocean because its elevation varies by several kilometers from one end to the other. The surface of any body of water will, of course, be level—so its shore must also be at the same height at every point.

hint *Scientist 2 presents evidence to support a different conclusion. What does Scientist 2 believe? What evidence does he/she present to support that belief?*

✔ Helpful Hint

Underline the main idea of each scientist's viewpoint to help keep clear who said what.

1. Scientist 2's views differ from Scientist 1's views in that only Scientist 2 believes the shorelines of an ancient ocean must have
   - A) a surface that is at the same elevation at all points.
   - B) a surface that may be at different elevations at different points.
   - C) a depth that is the same at different points.
   - D) a depth that is different at different points.

hint *Questions about how the scientists differ will hinge on the main points each scientist presents. What is their main point of disagreement?*

2. Suppose that Scientist 1 is correct, and also that Shoreline A was formed when the ocean was at its maximum size. Which of the following statements is most consistent with these facts?
   - A) It may be possible to find other ancient shorelines inside and outside Shoreline A.
   - B) It may be possible to find other ancient shorelines inside Shoreline A, but not outside.
   - C) It may be possible to find other ancient shorelines outside Shoreline A, but not inside.
   - D) It will not be possible to find other ancient shorelines inside or outside Shoreline A.

hint *This question asks about Scientist 1 only, so review Scientist 1's point of view. Scientist 1 argues that Shoreline A was formed when the ocean was at its largest. If this is true, then you would not expect to find shorelines from even larger oceans. However, you may find other shorelines from within Shoreline A, because they may have formed when the ocean dried up.*

3. New research shows evidence of 17 deltas, similar to river deltas on Earth, all at the same elevation as the proposed elevation of Shoreline A. Based on the information provided, this research would most likely *weaken* the viewpoint(s) of
   A) Scientist 1 only.
   B) Scientist 2 only.
   C) both Scientist 1 and Scientist 2.
   D) neither Scientist 1 nor Scientist 2.

hint *When a question asks us whose argument would be weakened, review the argument each scientist makes: Scientist 1 = Yes ocean, and Scientist 2 = No ocean. Does the new research provide evidence for or against the ocean?*

4. Scientists 1 and 2 would likely agree that
   A) there is good evidence that Mars once had an ocean in its northern plains.
   B) there is no evidence that Mars did not have an ocean in its northern plain.
   C) there is good evidence that rivers and lakes once existed on Mars.
   D) there is no evidence that rivers and lakes once existed on Mars.

hint *When a question in a Conflicting Viewpoints passage asks what is true "according to the passage," first look at the introduction to see if it provides any clues to the answer. What information does the introductory paragraph provide?*

Use the Kaplan Method to answer the following multiple-choice questions. Use the hints provided as needed.

The planet Mars has two small moons, Phobos and Deimos, whose origins are puzzling. Two scientists debate how these moons were formed.

hint *What is the topic the scientists are debating in this passage?*

Scientist 1

Both moons are only half as dense as Mars, and much darker than that planet. In fact, they are slightly less than twice the density of ice, and they reflect only 7 percent of the light that strikes them, quite similar to black paint. Thus, they appear surprisingly different from the planet they supposedly formed around.

On the other hand, if either of these bodies were placed in the outer asteroid belt, it would be classified as just another typical "Type C" (or "carbonaceous chondrite") asteroid. Because Mars orbits just inside the asteroid belt, it is reasonable to suspect that the moons actually are asteroids whose orbits strayed too near Mars, allowing that planet to capture them. Astronomers already accept that a number of the moons of Jupiter, on the outer edge of the asteroid belt, are asteroids captured by this process.

hint *What does Scientist 1 believe? Underline the main idea. What evidence does Scientist 1 present to support this belief?*

Scientist 2

Even though it is not known why the compositions of the moons differ so greatly from that of Mars, every aspect of their orbits suggests that they were formed in orbit around Mars. Jupiter and the other gas giant planets are orbited by a number of captured asteroids, but the orbits of these bodies are distinct from the orbits of these planets' natural moons (ones that formed in orbit around the planet) in several ways. Captured asteroids typically have orbits with high eccentricity (i.e., their orbits are very noncircular) and high inclination (i.e., their orbits are tilted at a large angle to the planet's equator). Captured asteroids also typically orbit far from the planet and quite often in the opposite direction to the natural moons (counterclockwise rather than clockwise).

Phobos and Deimos have orbits with very low eccentricity (nearly circular), and those orbits are almost in the same plane as Mars' equator. Furthermore, they orbit very close to the planet and in the same direction as the natural moons of the other planets. All of these characteristics are typical of natural moons.

hint *What does Scientist 2 believe? Underline his/her main idea. What evidence does Scientist 2 present to support this belief?*

29

1. Which of the following statements best explains why Scientist 2 mentioned that the orbits of Phobos and Deimos are nearly circular?
   A) The orbits of natural moons typically have high inclinations.
   B) The orbits of captured asteroids are typically not circular.
   C) The orbits of natural satellites typically have high eccentricity.
   D) Highly eccentric orbits typically also have high inclinations.

hint *What does Scientist 2 think? What kind of evidence will Scientist 2 present?*

2. Earth's moon is much less dense than the Earth, and it is believed to have formed in orbit around the Earth. This finding would most likely weaken the viewpoint(s) of
   A) Scientist 1 only.
   B) Scientist 2 only.
   C) both Scientist 1 and Scientist 2.
   D) neither Scientist 1 nor Scientist 2.

hint *Which scientist cites density differences to support his/her position? If the moon is a natural satellite, whose position is weakened?*

3. The equator of the planet Uranus is tipped nearly perpendicular to the plane of its orbit. As Scientist 2 notes, the natural moons of Uranus would most likely orbit
   A) clockwise, in the same plane as the orbit of Uranus around the Sun.
   B) clockwise, in the same plane as the equator of Uranus.
   C) counterclockwise, in the same plane as the orbit of Uranus around the Sun.
   D) counterclockwise, in the same plane as the equator of Uranus.

hint *Which scientist discusses the orbit characteristics of natural moons? How do natural moons typically orbit?*

4. Both scientists would most likely agree with which of the following statements?
   A) Mars reflects less than 7 percent of the light that strikes it, and it is less dense than ice.
   B) Mars reflects less than 7 percent of the light that strikes it, and it is more than twice as dense as ice.
   C) Mars reflects more than 7 percent of the light that strikes it, and it is less dense than ice.
   D) Mars reflects more than 7 percent of the light that strikes it, and it is more than twice as dense as ice.

hint *What does Scientist 1 say about the characteristics of Phobos and Deimos? What does Scientist 2 say?*

Use the Kaplan Method to answer the following multiple-choice questions on your own.

A study of patients who have been taking the prescription drug rosiglitazone has raised doubts about this medicine's safety. Of the 6,241 patients who had taken the medicine for more than one year, 93 suffered heart attacks and 102 suffered heart failure. By comparison, only 84 cases of heart attacks and 62 cases of heart failure were reported among the 7,870 patients in the control group (who had the same illness but did not receive rosiglitazone).

Scientist 1

Based on the above results, the medicine appears to raise the risk of heart disease: 1 out of every 66 patients taking the medicine suffered heart attacks, versus only 1 in every 95 patients who were not taking the medicine. The risk of heart failure increased even more.

The best course of action would therefore be to stop the sale of this medicine while a larger follow-up study is performed to confirm the results.

Scientist 2

I agree that the results of the study are worrisome. As Scientist 1 noted, approximately 1.5 percent of the patients taking rosiglitazone experienced heart attacks, compared to approximately 1.1 percent of the patients not taking this medicine. However, such studies provide only an estimate of the true risks—and when the number of patients reporting a particular side effect is small, the estimates are likely to contain significant errors.

In this case, the differences between the two groups could be due to errors in the estimates. For example, consider the fraction of patients taking rosiglitazone who suffer heart attacks, which is estimated to be 93 out of every 6,241. According to the laws of statistics, the uncertainty in this risk estimate can be estimated simply by taking the square root of 93, which is approximately 10. There is actually 1 chance in 3 that the risk estimate is in error by more than this amount, so the true value could well be less than 83 out of every 6,241 (rather than 93). It is equally possible that the correct number in the other group is more than 93 out of 7,870 (rather than 84).

A larger follow-up study should be performed as soon as possible, but I would not advise banning use of rosiglitazone in the meantime. This medicine has been shown to be effective at preventing a dangerous illness, and patients would be harmed if they switch to a medicine that turns out to be less effective.

1. The percentage of patients in the control group who experienced heart failure is closest to which value?

   A) 0.1%

   B) 1%

   C) 10%

   D) 100%

2. According to Scientist 2, the uncertainty of the risk estimates in such a study will

   A) depend on the square of the number of patients reporting the effect.

   B) depend on the number of patients reporting the effect.

   C) depend on the square root of the number of patients reporting the effect.

   D) not depend on the number of patients reporting the effect.

3. Assume that a different study finds 100 cases of heart failure among 7,500 patients taking rosiglitazone and 200 cases among 15,000 patients not taking rosiglitazone. According to this study
   A) the medicine had no effect on the risk of heart failure.
   B) the medicine increased the risk of heart failure by a factor of 2.
   C) the medicine decreased the risk of heart failure by a factor of 2.
   D) the risks cannot be calculated because the sizes of the two groups are not comparable.

Use the Kaplan Method to answer the following multiple-choice questions for homework.

DNA, the genetic material within cells, stands for deoxyribonucleic acid. It consists of subunits called nucleotides, and each nucleotide has a nitrogenous base, a sugar, and at least one phosphate group. There are four different nitrogenous bases: guanine, cytosine, adenine, and thymine. Adenine and guanine are classified as purines due to their double ring structure, whereas thymine and cytosine have a single ring structure and are called pyrimidines. The sugar is a ribose that is missing two oxygen atoms, hence deoxyribose is a part of the name, and the ribose is bound to at least one phosphate group.

The structure of DNA has been known since 1953 when James Watson and Francis Crick first published the now famous double helix structure. The following chemical bonds are needed to create the double helix:

1. Phosphodiester bonds are formed between a phosphate group on one nucleotide and the sugar on the adjacent nucleotide.
2. Deoxyribose is bound to the nitrogenous base via a glycosidic bond.
3. Hydrogen bonds form between corresponding nitrogenous bases. Guanine will always form a hydrogen bond with cytosine, and adenine will always form a hydrogen bond with thymine.

Two scientists discuss possible causes of flexibility in the double helix structure.

Scientist 1

The double helix conformation of DNA, as suggested by Watson and Crick, is only one possible shape. In spite of the strong chemical bonds between nucleotides and within the backbone, DNA molecules are, in fact, very flexible. The double-stranded molecule can easily change its helical shape on a regular basis.

Scientist 2

While some small DNA molecules are flexible, the primary cause of changes in the helical conformation is due to hydration. Water molecules are electrostatically attracted to the highly negative sugar-phosphate backbone. Additionally, the hydrogen bonds between nitrogenous bases strengthen the interaction. Therefore, the helical conformation is influenced by the size, shape, and number of the water molecules that are transiently bound to DNA.

1. Based on the passage, what is true of the amount of adenine in a DNA molecule compared to the amount of thymine?
   - A) It is unrelated to the amount of thymine.
   - B) It is identical to the amount of thymine.
   - C) It is double the amount of thymine.
   - D) It is half the amount of thymine.
2. Which of the following experimental findings would support Scientist 2's hypothesis?
   - A) A dried sample of DNA has a different shape than a DNA sample that is in water.
   - B) A long DNA molecule has the same shape as a short DNA molecule.
   - C) A long DNA molecule has a different shape than a short DNA molecule.
   - D) A dried sample of DNA has the same shape as a DNA sample that is in water.

3. How does the opinion of Scientist 2 differ from Scientist 1?

   A) Scientist 2 believes that hydrogen bonding holds the nucleotides together.

   B) Scientist 2 believes that DNA molecules always have the double helix shape postulated by Watson and Crick.

   C) Scientist 2 believes that alternate helical shapes are due to phosphate and hydrogen bonds.

   D) Scientist 2 believes that water molecules are primarily responsible for changes in helical conformation.

The following questions are similar to what you would encounter on a college admissions test such as the SAT or ACT. Apply the Kaplan Method for Paired Passages to answer the following questions.

Two scientists are discussing possible origins of human life on Earth. While they agree that the earliest fossil evidence is that modern humans first appeared in Africa 130,000 years ago and that there is evidence of modern humans in the Near East approximately 90,000 years ago, they do not agree on the path that led to the evolution of modern humans. During the process of evolution, mutations of DNA appear in offspring. While many mutations are harmful and detrimental to the individual, a few may be helpful in the survival of that individual. DNA codes for useful traits are passed on to offspring, and, over very long periods of time, enough DNA changes accumulate for the group of organisms to evolve into a different species.

Scientist 1

The evolution of the "modern" humans, *Homo sapiens*, was a result of parallel evolution from populations of *Homo erectus* and an intermediary of some sort. This process occurred in Africa, Europe, and Asia with some genetic intermixing among some members of these populations. There is clear anatomical evidence for this theory when comparing certain minor anatomical structures of *Homo erectus* populations with modern humans from these areas. These anatomical differences are very minor, which is clear evidence that modern humans must have evolved separately in Africa, Europe, and Asia. This is the "Multi-Generational Hypothesis."

Scientist 2

If one looks at the evidence carefully, the only logical explanation is that a fairly small isolated population of people eventually evolved into the modern *Homo sapiens*. It is this population that would eventually spread across Asia, Africa, and Europe. As they spread, they displaced and replaced other humanoid populations. When one looks at DNA evidence of living humans, especially that of mitochondrial DNA, and the mutation rate of DNA, one can calculate when modern humans diverged from a common ancestor. Most of these calculations suggest that this divergence occurred approximately 200,000 years ago, which is much too recent for the hypothesis of Scientist 1 to be true. Molecular biology also suggests that the first modern humans evolved in Africa. This is the "Out of Africa Hypothesis."

1. Which of the following best states the basis for the belief of Scientist 1?

   A) Anatomical differences among groups in Asia, Africa, and Europe are evidence of separate evolutions.

   B) Anatomical similarities among groups in Asia, Africa, and Europe are evidence of a single evolution.

   C) Anatomical differences among groups in Asia, Africa, and Europe are evidence of a single evolution.

   D) Anatomical similarities among groups in Asia, Africa, and Europe are evidence of separate evolutions.

2. The presence of radiation has been shown to increase DNA mutation rate. If clear evidence were to be found that background radiation levels were four times greater than present day levels during that evolution of early humans, this discovery would most likely *weaken* the viewpoint(s) of

   A) Scientist 1 only.

   B) Scientist 2 only.

   C) both Scientist 1 and Scientist 2.

   D) neither Scientist 1 nor Scientist 2.

3. Scientist 2 would argue that a five-year drought occurring approximately 310,000 years ago is likely to have the strongest effect on

   A) populations of early humans living in Asia.

   B) populations of early humans living in Europe.

   C) populations of early humans living in Africa.

   D) populations of early nomadic humans.

PART THREE

Math and Science Progress Checks

MATH & SCIENCE PROGRESS CHECK 1

SECTION **1**

1. Ⓐ Ⓑ Ⓒ Ⓓ	6. Ⓐ Ⓑ Ⓒ Ⓓ	11. Ⓐ Ⓑ Ⓒ Ⓓ	16. Ⓐ Ⓑ Ⓒ Ⓓ
2. Ⓐ Ⓑ Ⓒ Ⓓ	7. Ⓐ Ⓑ Ⓒ Ⓓ	12. Ⓐ Ⓑ Ⓒ Ⓓ	17. Ⓐ Ⓑ Ⓒ Ⓓ
3. Ⓐ Ⓑ Ⓒ Ⓓ	8. Ⓐ Ⓑ Ⓒ Ⓓ	13. Ⓐ Ⓑ Ⓒ Ⓓ	18. Ⓐ Ⓑ Ⓒ Ⓓ
4. Ⓐ Ⓑ Ⓒ Ⓓ	9. Ⓐ Ⓑ Ⓒ Ⓓ	14. Ⓐ Ⓑ Ⓒ Ⓓ	19. Ⓐ Ⓑ Ⓒ Ⓓ
5. Ⓐ Ⓑ Ⓒ Ⓓ	10. Ⓐ Ⓑ Ⓒ Ⓓ	15. Ⓐ Ⓑ Ⓒ Ⓓ	20. Ⓐ Ⓑ Ⓒ Ⓓ

correct in Section 1

incorrect in Section 1

SECTION **2**

1. Ⓐ Ⓑ Ⓒ Ⓓ	6. Ⓐ Ⓑ Ⓒ Ⓓ	11. Ⓐ Ⓑ Ⓒ Ⓓ	16. Ⓐ Ⓑ Ⓒ Ⓓ
2. Ⓐ Ⓑ Ⓒ Ⓓ	7. Ⓐ Ⓑ Ⓒ Ⓓ	12. Ⓐ Ⓑ Ⓒ Ⓓ	17. Ⓐ Ⓑ Ⓒ Ⓓ
3. Ⓐ Ⓑ Ⓒ Ⓓ	8. Ⓐ Ⓑ Ⓒ Ⓓ	13. Ⓐ Ⓑ Ⓒ Ⓓ	18. Ⓐ Ⓑ Ⓒ Ⓓ
4. Ⓐ Ⓑ Ⓒ Ⓓ	9. Ⓐ Ⓑ Ⓒ Ⓓ	14. Ⓐ Ⓑ Ⓒ Ⓓ	19. Ⓐ Ⓑ Ⓒ Ⓓ
5. Ⓐ Ⓑ Ⓒ Ⓓ	10. Ⓐ Ⓑ Ⓒ Ⓓ	15. Ⓐ Ⓑ Ⓒ Ⓓ	20. Ⓐ Ⓑ Ⓒ Ⓓ

correct in Section 2

incorrect in Section 2

Section 1

30 Minutes—20 Questions

NO-CALCULATOR SECTION

Turn to Section 1 of your answer sheet to answer the questions in this section.

Directions: For this section, solve each problem and decide which is the best of the choices given. Fill in the corresponding oval on the answer sheet. You may use any available space for scratch work.

Notes:

1. Calculator use is NOT permitted.
2. All numbers used are real numbers.
3. All figures used are necessary to solving the problems that they accompany. All figures are drawn to scale EXCEPT when it is stated that a specific figure is not drawn to scale.
4. Unless otherwise indicated, the domain of a given function *f* is the set of all real numbers *x* for which *f*(*x*) is a real number.

1. If a hot air balloon rises to 1,000 ft above sea level, descends 150 ft, and then rises 100 ft, how many feet above sea level is the balloon?

A) 750

B) 850

C) 950

D) 1,050

2. Kayla walks $2\frac{1}{3}$ miles to school each day, and Luc walks $3\frac{3}{4}$ miles to school each day. How much farther is Luc's walk to school than Kayla's?

A) $1\frac{2}{7}$

B) $1\frac{1}{3}$

C) $1\frac{5}{12}$

D) $1\frac{1}{2}$

3. What is the greatest common factor among 28, 35, and 56?

A) 5

B) 7

C) 14

D) 28

4. Simplify $-36 \div (-15+6) + 2 \times 9^{\frac{1}{2}}$.

A) −9

B) −3

C) 10

D) 18

5. If $\frac{x}{5} = 15$, then what is the value of x?

A) −3

B) 10

C) 20

D) 75

6. What is the value of x that satisfies the equation $2x + 8 = 4x - 10$?

A) -9

B) -3

C) 3

D) 9

7. What is the equation of a line that has a slope of 2 and crosses the x-axis at $x = 9$?

A) $y = 2x - 18$

B) $y = 2x + 18$

C) $y = -2x + 18$

D) $y = -2x - 18$

8. What is the slope of the line in the xy-plane that passes through the points $(-3, -2)$ and $(2, 13)$?

A) -3

B) $-\frac{11}{5}$

C) $\frac{11}{5}$

D) 3

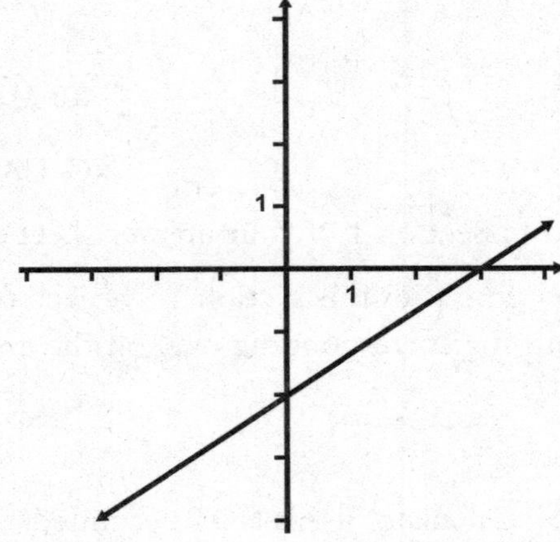

9. Which of the following equations best represents the line above?

A) $y = \frac{2}{3}x - 2$

B) $y = \frac{3}{2}x - 2$

C) $y = -\frac{2}{3}x + 2$

D) $y = -\frac{3}{2}x - 2$

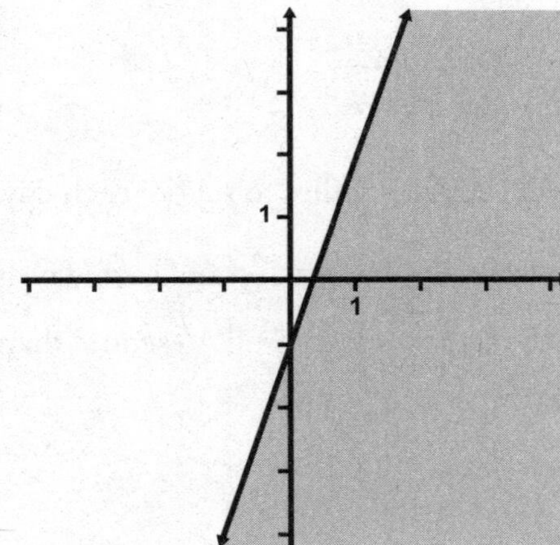

10. The graph above best represents which of the following inequalities?

A) $y \leq -3x + 1$

B) $y \geq -3x - 1$

C) $y \leq 3x - 1$

D) $y \geq 3x - 1$

11. Which of the following defines the solution set for the inequality $14 - 3x \leq 7$?

A) $x \geq \frac{7}{3}$

B) $x \leq \frac{7}{3}$

C) $x \geq -\frac{7}{3}$

D) $x \leq -\frac{7}{3}$

12. If $a = 3 + 10b$ and $c = 2 + 5b$, what is a in terms of c?

A) $2c - 17$

B) $2c - 1$

C) $2c + 1$

D) $2c + 13$

13. If (x, y) is the solution to the system of equations shown below, what is the value of $x + y$?

$$x + 4y = 20$$
$$x + 7y = 41$$

A) −13

B) −1

C) 1

D) 15

14. The solution to the system of equations $y = -2x - 1$ and $y = 2x + 3$ is best represented by which of the following graphs?

A)

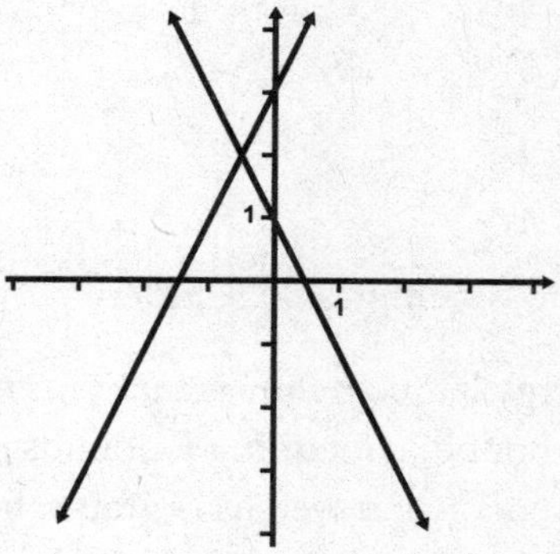

B)

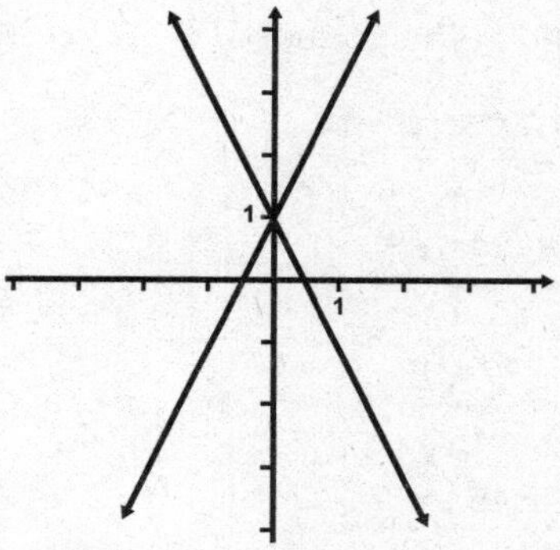

C)

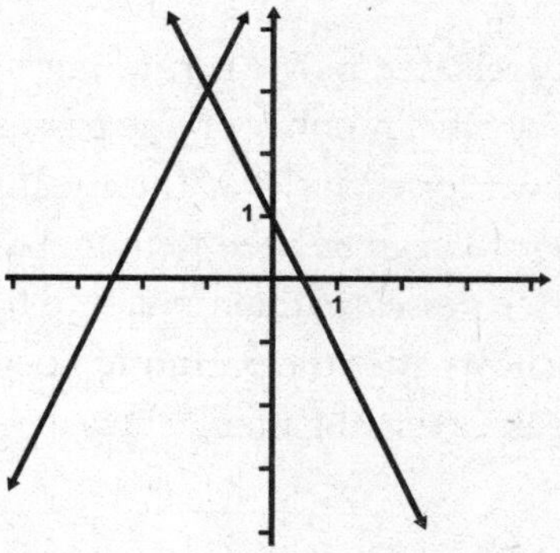

D)

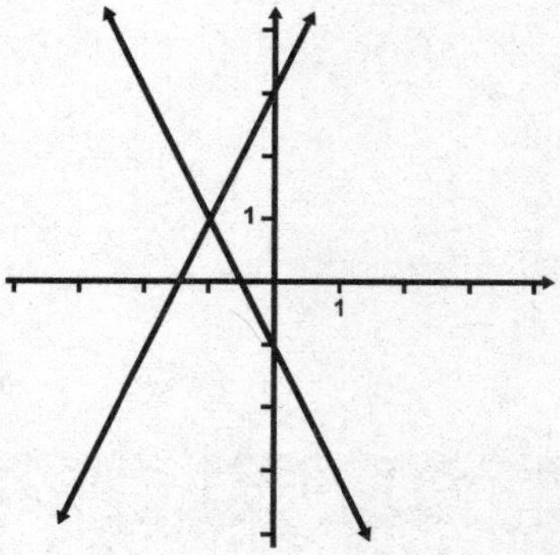

15. Which of the following represents the solution to the system of equations shown below?

$$y = x + 3$$
$$y = x^2 + 4$$

A) (0, 3)

B) (3, 4)

C) (0, 4)

D) The system has no solution.

16. An energy bar company is making energy bars from a hopper containing P pounds of dough. If each energy bar weighs G grams, how many energy bars E can be made from the hopper? (1 pound = 454 grams)

A) $E = \dfrac{P \times G}{454}$

B) $E = \dfrac{454 \times P}{G}$

C) $G = \dfrac{P \times E}{454}$

D) $G = \dfrac{454 \times P}{E}$

17. A newly released movie is running a promotion in which a number of free passes are given away for each show. The equation $15s + p = 135$ can be used to model the number of free passes, p, that remain to be given away s shows after the promotion began. How many passes remain after 7 shows?

A) 2

B) 7

C) 30

D) 105

18. Simplify $\dfrac{3^3 \times 9^{-2}}{3^2}$.

A) 3^{-3}

B) 3^{-2}

C) 3^2

D) 3^3

19. Which of the following is equivalent to $\left(5^{\frac{3}{2}}\right)^2$?

A) $\left(\sqrt{5^3}\right)^2$

B) $\left(\sqrt[3]{5^2}\right)^2$

C) $\left(\sqrt{5^2}\right)^3$

D) $\left(\sqrt[3]{5^2}\right)^3$

20. Simplify $\dfrac{(x^2 - 4x - 5)(x^2 + 4x - 5)}{(x^2 - 25)(x^2 - 1)}$.

A) $-25x$

B) $-1x$

C) 1

D) 25

IF YOU FINISH BEFORE TIME IS CALLED, YOU MAY CHECK YOUR WORK ON THIS SECTION ONLY. DO NOT TURN TO ANY OTHER SECTION IN THE TEST. **STOP**

Section 2

30 Minutes—20 Questions

CALCULATOR SECTION

Turn to Section 2 of your answer sheet to answer the questions in this section.

MATH

Directions: For this section, solve each problem and decide which is the best of the choices given. Fill in the corresponding oval on the answer sheet. You may use any available space for scratch work.

Notes:

1. Calculator use is permitted.
2. All numbers used are real numbers.
3. All figures used are necessary to solving the problems that they accompany. All figures are drawn to scale EXCEPT when it is stated that a specific figure is not drawn to scale.
4. Unless otherwise indicated, the domain of a given function f is the set of all real numbers x for which $f(x)$ is a real number.

Information:

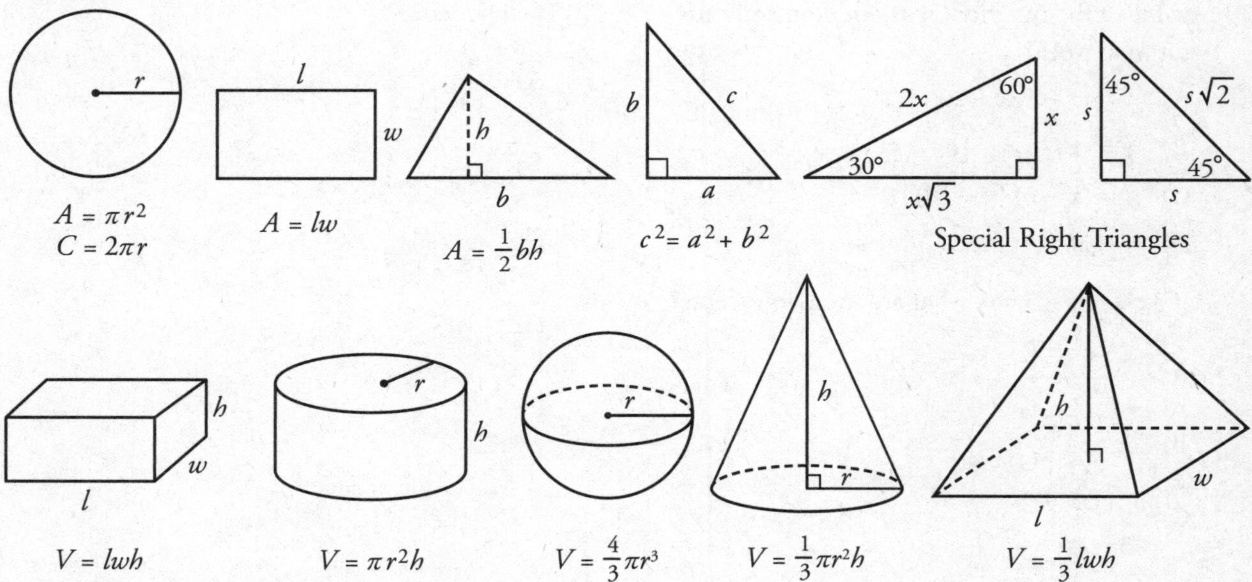

1. If $f(x - 2) = 2x^2 + 5$ for all values of x, what is the value of $f(-5)$?

   A) 3

   B) 23

   C) 55

   D) 103

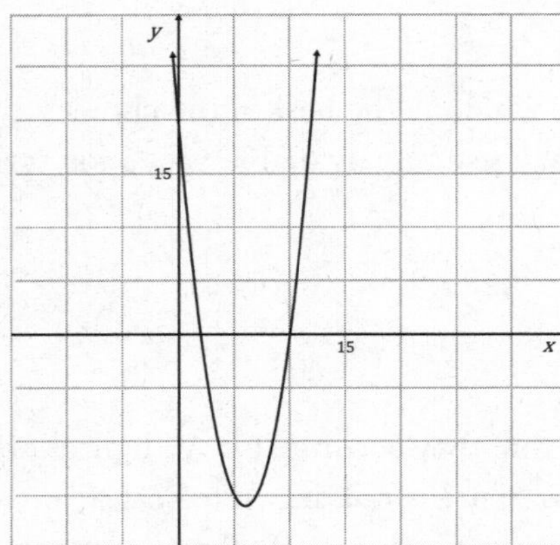

2. The following quadratic equations are all representations of the graph shown above. Which equation could you use to find the minimum value of the function, without doing any additional work?

   A) $y = x^2 - 12x + 20$

   B) $y = (x - 6)^2 - 16$

   C) $y = (x - 2)(x - 10)$

   D) $y - 20 = x^2 - 12x$

3. If $3x^2 - 2x - 5 = 0$, what are the x-intercepts?

   A) $\frac{-1 \pm \sqrt{14}}{3}$

   B) $\frac{1 \pm \sqrt{14}}{3}$

   C) $\frac{5}{3}, -1$

   D) $1, -\frac{5}{3}$

4. Mikaela drove for 5 hours and traveled 280 miles, and Jerome drove for 7 hours and traveled 350 miles. What was the difference in their rates (in miles per hour)?

   A) 2

   B) 6

   C) 35

   D) 50

5. An ink cartridge normally sells for \$30. If the cartridge goes on sale for \$24, what is the percentage off the original price?

   A) 20%

   B) 24%

   C) 25%

   D) 30%

6. If a sheet of origami paper is randomly chosen from a package that contains exactly 5 green sheets, 6 red sheets, and 7 blue sheets, what is the probability that the sheet of origami paper will be red?

   A) $\frac{5}{18}$

   B) $\frac{1}{3}$

   C) $\frac{7}{18}$

   D) $\frac{1}{2}$

Questions 7–8 refer to the following table.

Subject	Number of tutors	Number of students per tutor
U.S. History	6	7
Algebra II	8	4
Physics	3	2
American Literature	5	6

7. The table above shows the number of students at the library studying with a tutor in one of four subjects. Each subject has a number of tutors. For instance, there are 6 tutors for U.S. History. If all the students in the tutoring program are studying only one of the four subjects, how many students are in the tutoring program?

A) 19

B) 22

C) 104

D) 110

8. What is the average number of students per tutor?

A) 4

B) 4.5

C) 5

D) 5.5

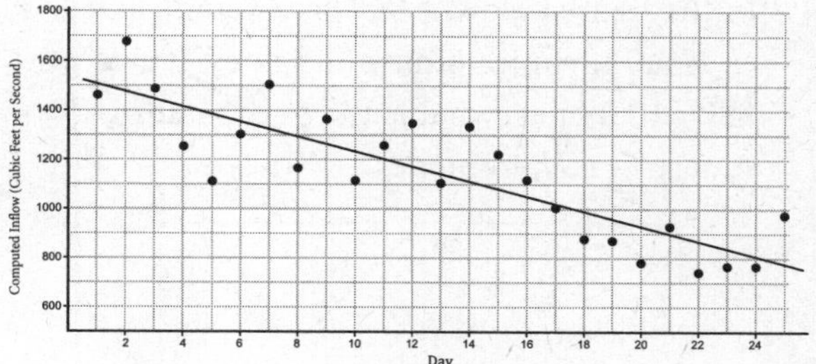

9. The scatterplot above shows the computed inflow of water into a lake in cubic feet per second over a period of 25 days. What was the approximate computed inflow, in cubic feet per second, on the day represented by the data point that is farthest from the line of best fit (shown)?

A) 1,100

B) 1,350

C) 1,500

D) 1,700

10. In the figure below, lines m and n are parallel, transversals r and s intersect to form an angle measure of $x°$, and 2 other angles are as marked. What is the value of x?

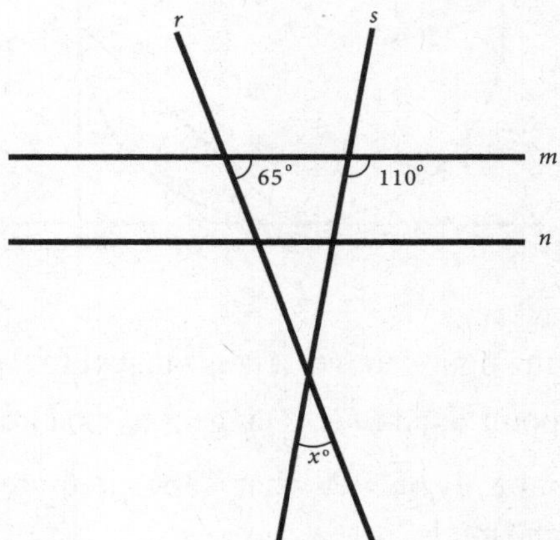

A) 15

B) 20

C) 45

D) 70

11. In the figure below, $ABCD$ is a square and E, F, G, H are the midpoints of its sides. If side $AB = 10$ inches, what is the perimeter of square $EFGH$, in inches?

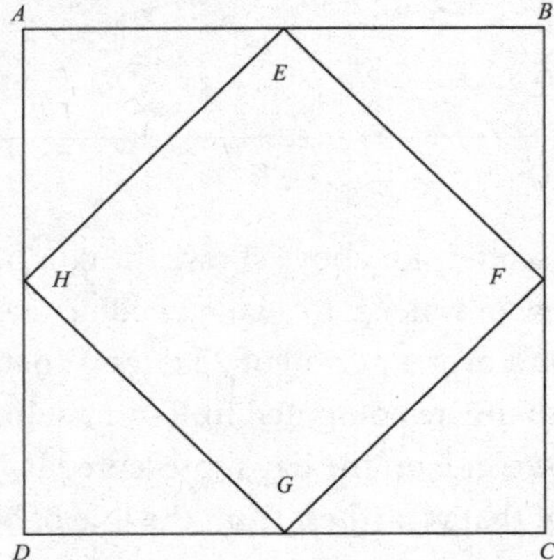

A) $20\sqrt{2}$
B) $20\sqrt{3}$
C) $25\sqrt{2}$
D) $25\sqrt{3}$

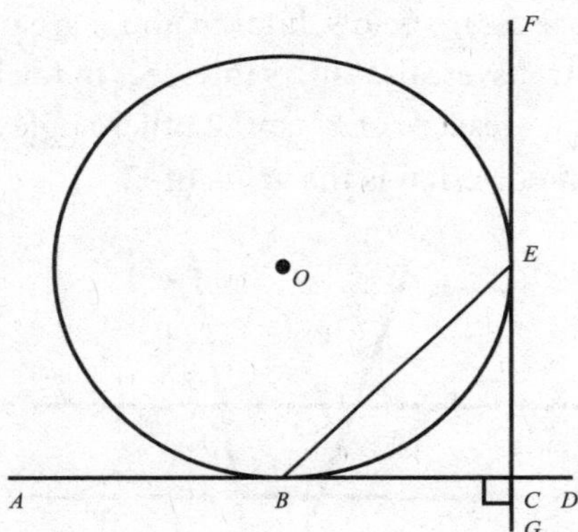

12. In the figure above, $\overline{AD}$ is tangent to the circle at point B, and $\overline{FG}$ is tangent to the circle at point E. If $\overline{BE} = 2$, what is the circumference of the circle?

A) 2π
B) $2\pi\sqrt{2}$
C) 4π
D) $4\pi\sqrt{2}$

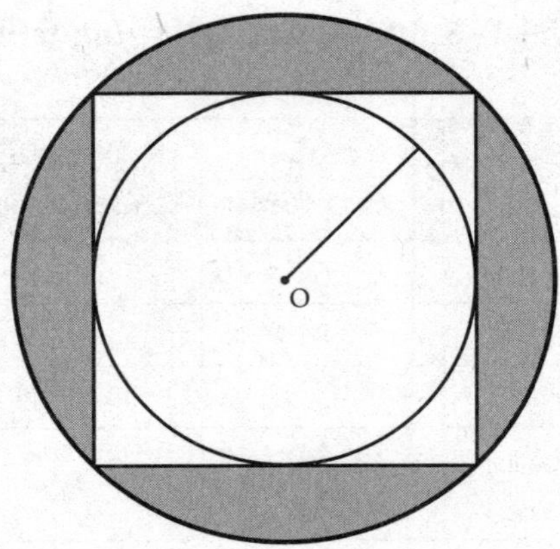

13. In the figure above, the smaller circle with a center at point O has a radius of 2 inches. What is the area of the shaded region?

A) $8\pi - 16$
B) $8\pi\sqrt{2} - 16$
C) $32\pi - 32$
D) $32\pi - 16$

14. A carton of milk completely fills a rectangular prism that has a square base with edges of length 4 inches and a height of 10 inches. If a carton of milk is poured into a cylindrical container that has a diameter of 8 inches, to what depth in inches will it fill the container?

A) $\frac{\pi}{10}$
B) $\frac{10}{\pi}$
C) 10
D) 10π

SCIENCE

Directions: After reading the passage, select the best answer to each question. Fill in the corresponding oval on the answer sheet. You may refer to the passages while answering the questions.

Although the pH (acidity) of pure water is approximately 7, the pH can change greatly if even a single drop of strong acid or strong base is added. Compounds that can act as weak acids or bases will minimize this change in pH, and such compounds are called buffers. Each buffer is most effective at a particular pH, referred to as the buffer's pK' value.

Study 1

A chemistry student performs three titrations—one of a carbonic acid solution, one with a phosphoric acid solution, and one with an ammonium solution. In each case, NaOH is gradually added, and the resulting pH is measured after each addition. The results are shown in Figure 1. As expected, the pH changes more and more slowly until it equals the indicated pK' value. (For instance, the phosphoric acid curve is closest to horizontal when the pH reaches the pK' of phosphoric acid, 7.2.) After this point, the pH changes more and more rapidly again.

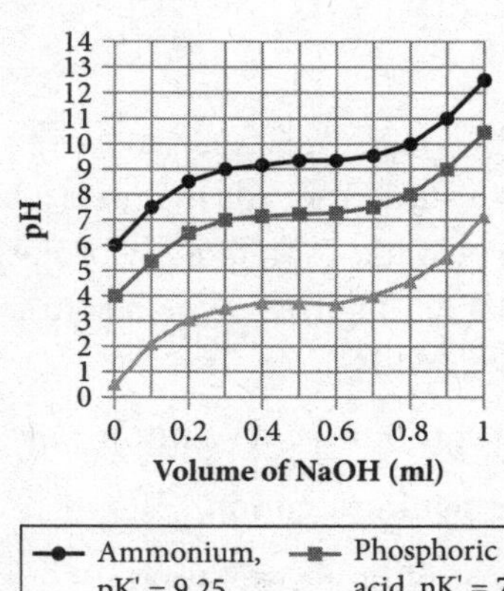

Figure 1

From the slopes of the curves, the student also calculated how the buffering ability of each compound varied with pH. The results are shown in Figure 2. Each curve reaches its maximum at the buffer's pK' value.

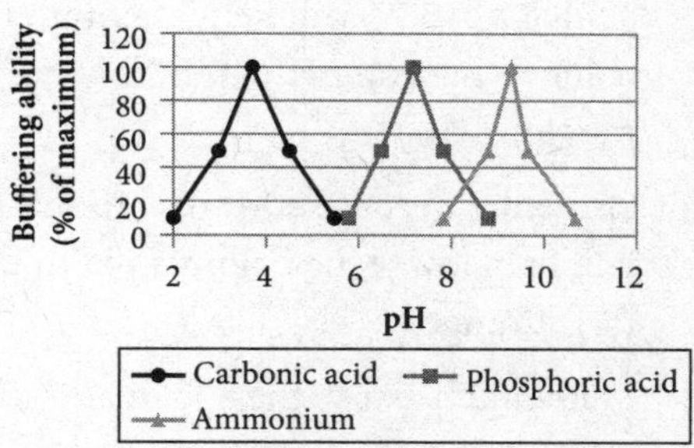

Figure 2

Study 2

The student performs a fourth titration, using the amino acid alanine. This compound contains multiple groups that can act as acids or bases. The results are shown in Table 1.

Table 1

Volume of NaOH (mL)	pH
0.1	0.5
0.3	2.1
0.5	2.2
0.7	2.8
0.9	4
1.1	7.9
1.3	9.5
1.5	9.9
1.7	10.0
1.9	11.5

15. Two students disagree on which buffering solution they would need to introduce to a colony of bacteria to keep the colony in a pH range of 3.5 to 4. Student 1 thinks they should add a buffered solution of carbonic acid, and Student 2 thinks they should add a buffered solution of ammonium. Which student's suggestion will most likely produce the desired result?

    A) Student 1 because the pK' of carbonic acid at pH 3.77 will help maintain the colony's natural pH within the optimal range.

    B) Student 1 because adding carbonic acid will help lower the colony's pH to the target range.

    C) Student 2 because the pK' of ammonium at pH 9.25 will counteract any lowering of the pH out of the target range.

    D) Student 2 because adding ammonium will help raise the colony's pH to the target range.

16. According to Figure 2, as the pH increases, the buffering ability of a particular compound

    A) increases only.

    B) decreases only.

    C) repeatedly increases and decreases.

    D) increases, then decreases.

17. In Figure 1, the titration curve for ammonium lies approximately

    A) 2 pH units higher than the curve for phosphoric acid.

    B) 4.5 pH units higher than the curve for phosphoric acid.

    C) 4.5 pH units lower than the curve for phosphoric acid.

    D) 2 pH units lower than the curve for phosphoric acid.

18. In Study 1, which of the variables did the student intentionally vary?

    A) The original concentration of each solution

    B) The indicated pK' of each solution

    C) The volume of NaOH added to each solution

    D) The starting pH of each solution

19. The pH of the alanine solution is closest to that of pure water when the volume of NaOH is how many mL?

    A) 0.3

    B) 0.7

    C) 1.1

    D) 1.5

20. Suppose a student needs to create a buffered solution of water for a biology project. Based on the data in Figure 2, which solution should the student add?

    A) The carbonic acid solution

    B) The alanine solution

    C) The ammonium solution

    D) The phosphoric acid solution

IF YOU FINISH BEFORE TIME IS CALLED, YOU MAY CHECK YOUR WORK ON THIS SECTION ONLY. DO NOT TURN TO ANY OTHER SECTION IN THE TEST.

MATH & SCIENCE PROGRESS CHECK 2

SECTION **1**

1. Ⓐ Ⓑ Ⓒ Ⓓ	6. Ⓐ Ⓑ Ⓒ Ⓓ	11. Ⓐ Ⓑ Ⓒ Ⓓ	16. Ⓐ Ⓑ Ⓒ Ⓓ
2. Ⓐ Ⓑ Ⓒ Ⓓ	7. Ⓐ Ⓑ Ⓒ Ⓓ	12. Ⓐ Ⓑ Ⓒ Ⓓ	17. Ⓐ Ⓑ Ⓒ Ⓓ
3. Ⓐ Ⓑ Ⓒ Ⓓ	8. Ⓐ Ⓑ Ⓒ Ⓓ	13. Ⓐ Ⓑ Ⓒ Ⓓ	18. Ⓐ Ⓑ Ⓒ Ⓓ
4. Ⓐ Ⓑ Ⓒ Ⓓ	9. Ⓐ Ⓑ Ⓒ Ⓓ	14. Ⓐ Ⓑ Ⓒ Ⓓ	19. Ⓐ Ⓑ Ⓒ Ⓓ
5. Ⓐ Ⓑ Ⓒ Ⓓ	10. Ⓐ Ⓑ Ⓒ Ⓓ	15. Ⓐ Ⓑ Ⓒ Ⓓ	20. Ⓐ Ⓑ Ⓒ Ⓓ

correct in Section 1

incorrect in Section 1

SECTION **2**

1. Ⓐ Ⓑ Ⓒ Ⓓ	6. Ⓐ Ⓑ Ⓒ Ⓓ	11. Ⓐ Ⓑ Ⓒ Ⓓ	16. Ⓐ Ⓑ Ⓒ Ⓓ
2. Ⓐ Ⓑ Ⓒ Ⓓ	7. Ⓐ Ⓑ Ⓒ Ⓓ	12. Ⓐ Ⓑ Ⓒ Ⓓ	17. Ⓐ Ⓑ Ⓒ Ⓓ
3. Ⓐ Ⓑ Ⓒ Ⓓ	8. Ⓐ Ⓑ Ⓒ Ⓓ	13. Ⓐ Ⓑ Ⓒ Ⓓ	18. Ⓐ Ⓑ Ⓒ Ⓓ
4. Ⓐ Ⓑ Ⓒ Ⓓ	9. Ⓐ Ⓑ Ⓒ Ⓓ	14. Ⓐ Ⓑ Ⓒ Ⓓ	19. Ⓐ Ⓑ Ⓒ Ⓓ
5. Ⓐ Ⓑ Ⓒ Ⓓ	10. Ⓐ Ⓑ Ⓒ Ⓓ	15. Ⓐ Ⓑ Ⓒ Ⓓ	20. Ⓐ Ⓑ Ⓒ Ⓓ

correct in Section 2

incorrect in Section 2

Section 1

30 Minutes—20 Questions

NO-CALCULATOR SECTION

Turn to Section 1 of your answer sheet to answer the questions in this section.

Directions: For this section, solve each problem and decide which is the best of the choices given. Fill in the corresponding oval on the answer sheet. You may use any available space for scratch work.

Notes:

1. Calculator use is NOT permitted.
2. All numbers used are real numbers.
3. All figures used are necessary to solving the problems that they accompany. All figures are drawn to scale EXCEPT when it is stated that a specific figure is not drawn to scale.
4. Unless otherwise indicated, the domain of a given function f is the set of all real numbers x for which $f(x)$ is a real number.

1. Simplify $24-(-34)$.

   A) -58

   B) -10

   C) 10

   D) 58

2. Simplify $\frac{1}{4}+\frac{5}{12}$.

   A) $\frac{1}{3}$

   B) $\frac{6}{16}$

   C) $\frac{7}{12}$

   D) $\frac{2}{3}$

3. Simplify $(2-5)\times 4-3\div 3$.

   A) -13

   B) -9

   C) -1

   D) 3

4. If $4+x=-14$, then what is the value of x?

   A) -18

   B) -10

   C) 10

   D) 18

5. What is the equation of the line in the xy-plane that passes through the points (2, 0) and (4, 2)?

   A) $y=x+2$

   B) $y=2x-2$

   C) $y=x-2$

   D) $y=2x$

6. Which of the following graphs represents the linear equation that has a slope of 2 and passes through the origin?

A)

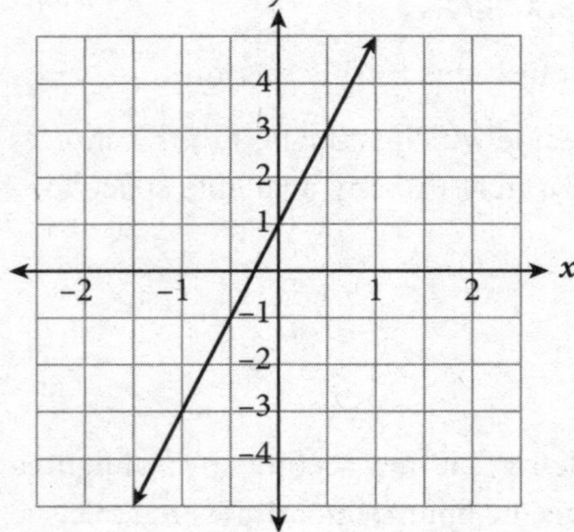

C)

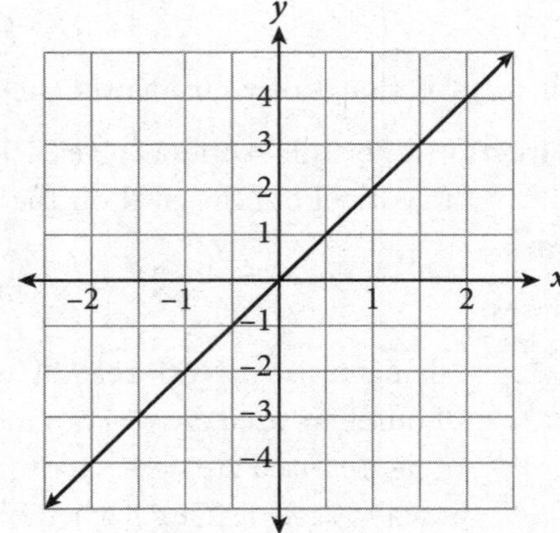

B)

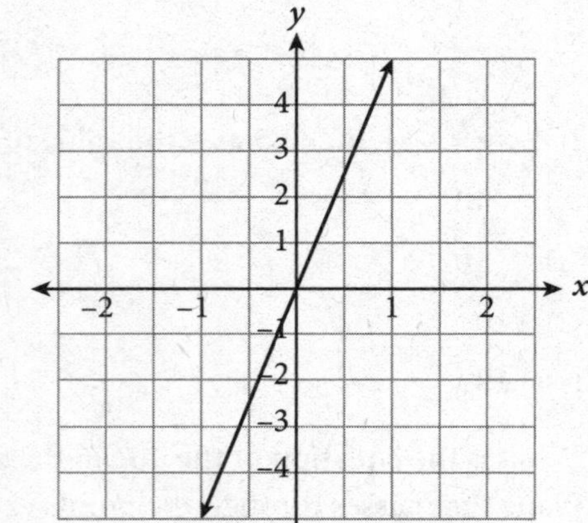

D)

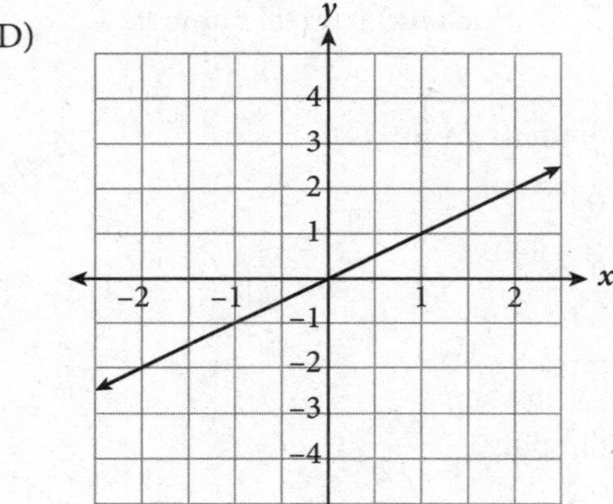

7. Which of the following defines the solution set for the inequality $12 + \frac{x}{4} < 3$?

A) $x = -12$

B) $x < -36$

C) $x < 60$

D) $x > 9$

8. If (x, y) is the solution to the system of equations shown below, what is the value of $\frac{x}{y}$?

$$x + y = 8$$
$$x - y = 4$$

A) 3

B) 6

C) 12

D) 16

9. If (x, y) is the solution to the system of equations shown below, what is the value of xy?

$$3x - 3 = 3y$$
$$x - 3y = 15$$

A) −42

B) −13

C) 13

D) 42

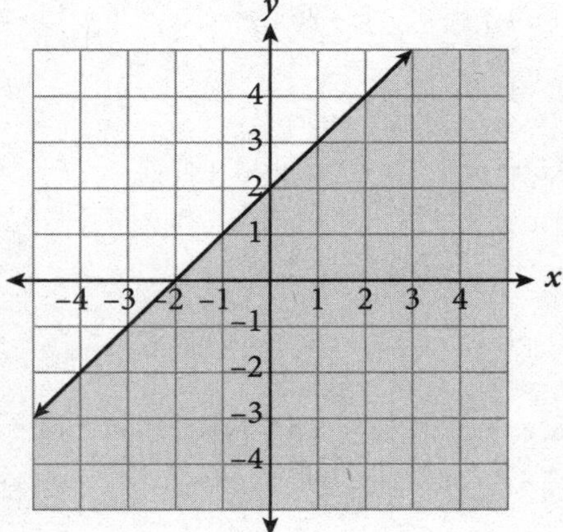

10. The graph above best represents which of the following inequalities?

A) $y \leq x - 2$

B) $y \leq x + 2$

C) $y \leq x$

D) $y \geq x + 2$

11. Yuriel and Hiro work at a lumberyard. Yuriel carries four times as many boards as Hiro does. If they combine their stock, together they can carry no more than 24 boards. If h represents the number of boards Hiro can carry, which of the following inequalities represents the number of boards Yuriel and Hiro can carry together?

A) $2h > 24$

B) $4h + 2h \geq 24$

C) $5h \leq 24$

D) $y + h \leq 24$

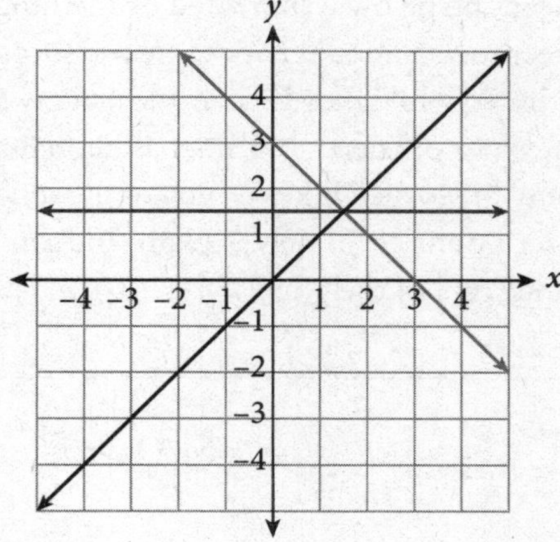

12. Which of the following represents the solution to the system of equations shown above?

A) $x = 2, y = 2$

B) $x = 1.5, y = 1.5$

C) $x = 1, y = 1$

D) Not enough information provided.

13. Erin's teacher instructed Erin to write an expression in which $x \leq -15$.

Erin's expression is: If x is divided by 2 and the quotient is then reduced by 14, the result is -32.

Does Erin's equation meet her teacher's requirement?

A) Yes, Erin's equation meets her teacher's requirement.

B) No, Erin's equation does not meet her teacher's requirement.

C) It depends on the domain of x.

D) There is not enough information provided.

14. The graph below was created by the ranger of Greenrock National Park to help visitors keep hydrated while they hike. It shows how much water visitors need to drink based on how many miles they hike. Which of the following descriptions accurately explains the slope and y-intercept of the graph?

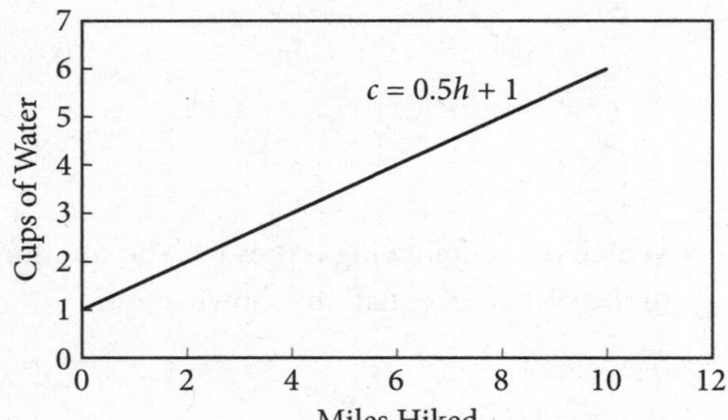

A) For every half-mile visitors hike, they need to drink 1 cup of water.

B) For every half-mile visitors hike, they need to drink half a cup of water.

C) Visitors need to drink 1 cup of water before they start their hike. For every 2 miles visitors hike, they need to drink an additional 1 cup of water.

D) Visitors need to drink 2 cups of water before they start their hike. For every mile visitors hike, they need to drink an additional 1 cup of water.

15. Simplify $\frac{(x^{-2})(x^3)}{x^5}$.

A) x

B) x^2

C) x^{-4}

D) x^{-5}

16. Solve for x.

$$y = 12 - 4x$$
$$y = x^2$$

A) $x = 2, x = -6$

B) $x = 0, x = -2$

C) $x = 2$

D) $x = -4$

17. What is the value of x that satisfies the equation $4\sqrt{x} - 32 = -26$?

A) 1

B) $\frac{3}{2}$

C) $\frac{9}{4}$

D) 4

18. If $\frac{x^2 + 4x}{x} = (x + 4)(x + 3)$, what is one value of x?

A) -3

B) -2

C) 2

D) 3

19. The function $6x + 2f(x) = 4$ is best represented by which of the following graphs?

A)

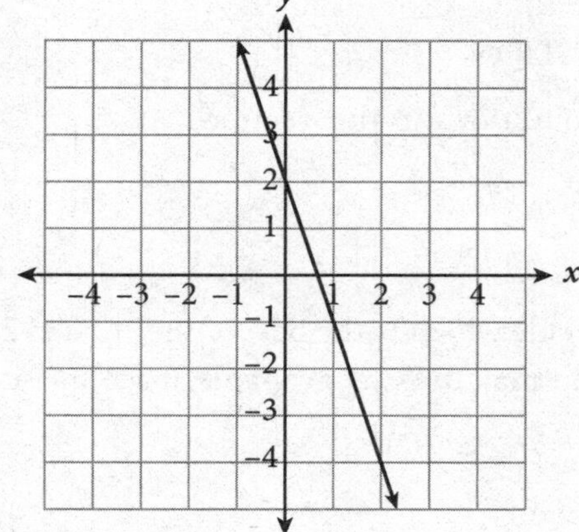

C)

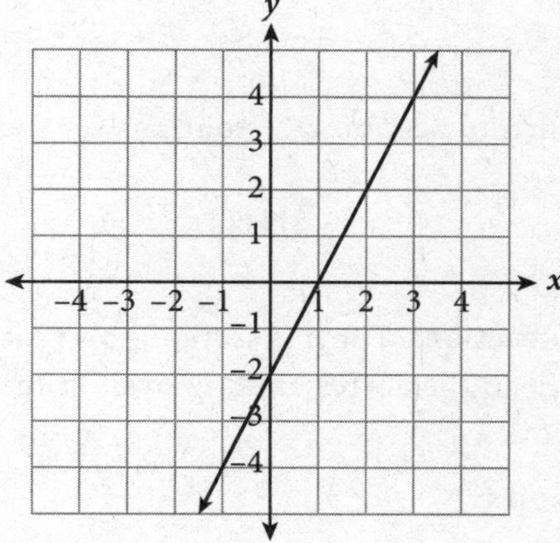

B)

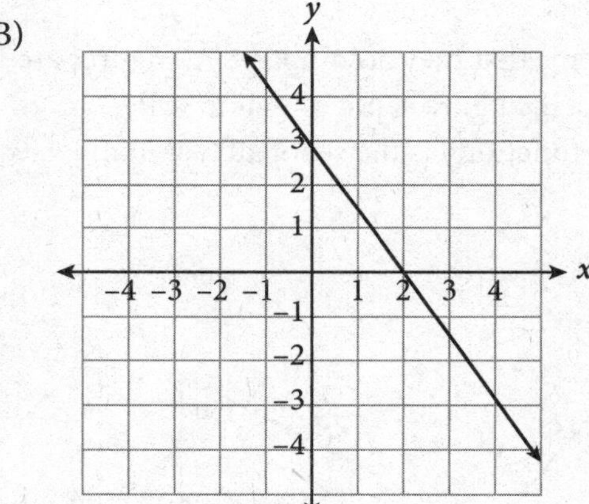

D)

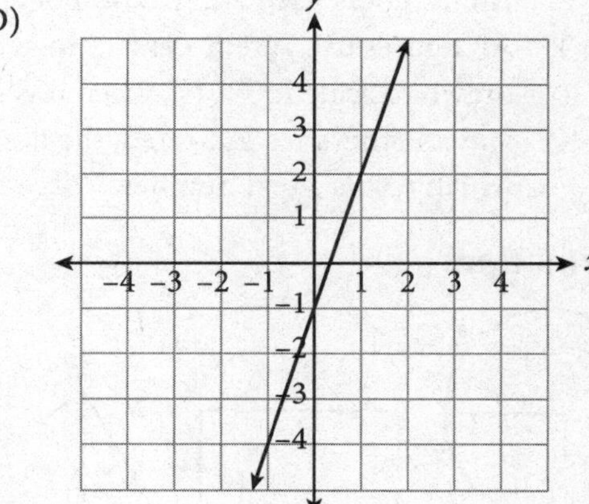

20. Which of the following values of x satisfies the equation $x^2 - 5x = 24$?

A) −8

B) −5

C) 5

D) 8

IF YOU FINISH BEFORE TIME IS CALLED, YOU MAY CHECK YOUR WORK ON THIS SECTION ONLY. DO NOT TURN TO ANY OTHER SECTION IN THE TEST.

STOP

Section 2

30 Minutes—20 Questions

CALCULATOR SECTION

Turn to Section 2 of your answer sheet to answer the questions in this section.

MATH

Directions: For this section, solve each problem and decide which is the best of the choices given. Fill in the corresponding oval on the answer sheet. You may use any available space for scratch work.

Notes:

1. Calculator use is permitted.
2. All numbers used are real numbers.
3. All figures used are necessary to solving the problems that they accompany. All figures are drawn to scale EXCEPT when it is stated that a specific figure is not drawn to scale.
4. Unless otherwise indicated, the domain of a given function *f* is the set of all real numbers *x* for which *f*(*x*) is a real number.

Information:

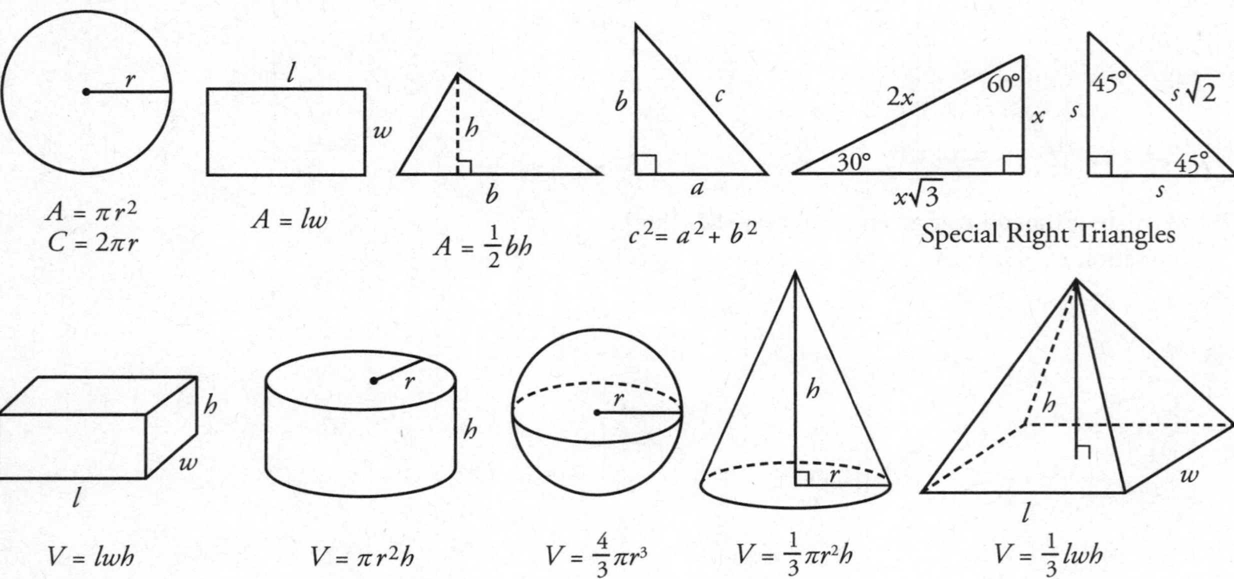

1. For every 2 hours Jake studies, he takes a 20-minute break to do something fun, such as playing games on his phone or taking his dog for a walk. If Jake studied for 26 hours total in February, how many minutes did he spend taking study breaks that month?

   A) 200 minutes

   B) 260 minutes

   C) 400 minutes

   D) 520 minutes

2. In Lake Pannaw there are 80 fish total: 60 edible catfish and 20 poisonous red herrings. If Ava goes fishing in Lake Pannaw, what is the probability that Ava will catch a poisonous fish?

   A) 20%

   B) 25%

   C) 33%

   D) 75%

3. The conversion rate between gold and silver in the capital city is 3 pieces of silver for every 1 gold piece. It's Saturday, and Adam is planning to walk to the marketplace to buy 6 chickens. Chickens cost 2 gold pieces each and can only be bought using gold. Adam's income is paid in silver, so Adam must first go to the bank and convert his earnings to gold. How much silver should Adam bring to the bank to purchase the 6 chickens?

   A) 12 silver pieces

   B) 22 silver pieces

   C) 24 silver pieces

   D) 36 silver pieces

Questions 4–5 refer to the following information.

A singing troupe consists of 15 baritones and 10 tenors. The table lists the number of singers in each category who are able to perform the songs "Blue Eyes," "Flowers," and "July."

Singing Range	"Blue Eyes"	"Flowers"	"July"
Baritones (15 total)	3	11	12
Tenors (10 total)	7	7	5

4. What percentage of the baritones are able to sing "Blue Eyes"?

   A) 15%

   B) 20%

   C) 35%

   D) 50%

5. Which percentage is the greatest?

   A) The percentage of total singers who can sing "Flowers"

   B) The percentage of tenors who can sing "Blue Eyes"

   C) The percentage of baritones who can sing "July"

   D) The percentage of total singers who can sing "July"

6. Four-sevenths of the citizens on the alien space colony Ganymede are able to photosynthesize their own sugars from sunlight. If there are 42,000 citizens living on Ganymede, how many of them can photosynthesize?

   A) 12,000

   B) 18,000

   C) 24,000

   D) 28,000

7. A sociologist wanted to find out how often tourists use the cameras on their smartphones. He surveyed 10 tourists by counting how many photos they had stored on their phones. The data set includes 2, 3, 22, 22, 26, 28, 34, 40, 55, and 120.

   What are the median, mean, mode, and range of the data set?

   A) median = 26
      mean = 35.2
      mode = 28
      range = 10

   B) median = 28
      mean = 40.2
      mode = 22
      range = 10

   C) median = 27
      mean = 35.2
      mode = 22
      range = 118

   D) median = 27
      mean = 33.2
      mode = 28
      range = 118

8. A spider plant can reproduce itself hundreds of times during its lifespan. When one of its flowers buds, the flower can be transplanted into new soil to produce an entirely new spider plant. Paul is a spider-plant aficionado. In year 1, he started with just 1 spider plant. By the end of that year, he had increased the number of spider plants in his home by 700%, just by replanting the flower buds. In year 2 he overwatered them, and 6 of his plants died. After this unfortunate event, what fraction remained of the total number of spider plants he had at the end of year 1?

   A) $\frac{1}{8}$

   B) $\frac{1}{6}$

   C) $\frac{1}{4}$

   D) $\frac{1}{2}$

Questions 9–10 refer to the following information.

The scatterplot shows the daily percentage of positive online reviews posted for a new restaurant.

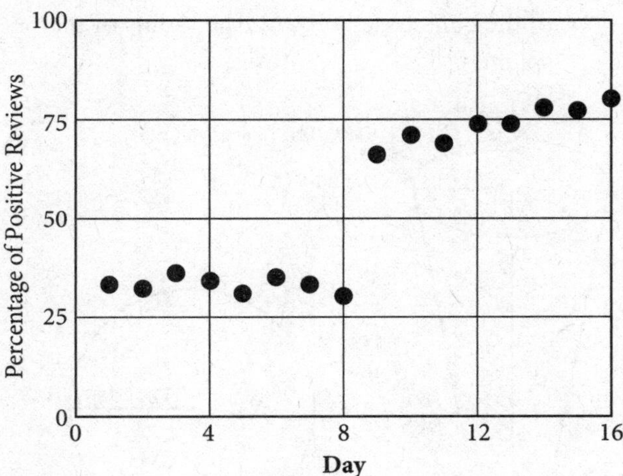

9. If a trend line was fit to the first 8 days' data points, what would the slope of this line be?

A) $m = 0$

B) $m =$ undefined

C) $m = 1$

D) $m = -1$

10. On the eighth day, the restaurant owner hired a floor manager to make sure every table was being served quickly and that customers were happy with their orders. Nothing else changed between days 8 and 9, so the owner assumed this decision caused the jump in positive reviews. What was the percentage gain from day 8 to day 16?

A) 100%

B) 133%

C) 167%

D) 200%

11. What is the value of c in the triangle below?

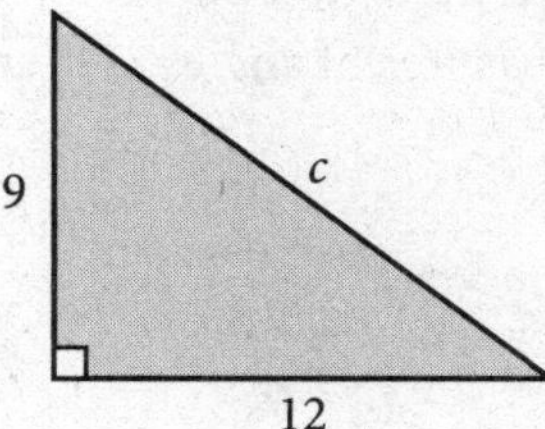

A) 10

B) 15

C) 24

D) 32

12. In the figure below, line segment BC bisects the rectangle. Find the value of x.

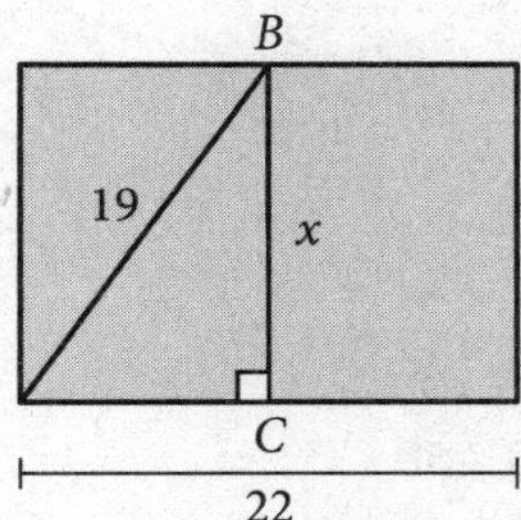

A) 11

B) 13.3

C) 15.5

D) 18

13. The circumference of the circle below is 20π. The gray triangles denote parallel lines. What are the measures of angles a, b, and c in degrees?

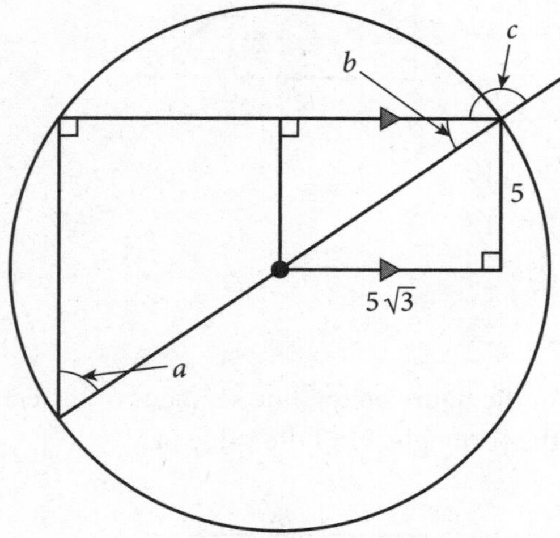

A) 45, 45, 60

B) 45, 45, 90

C) 60, 30, 120

D) 60, 30, 150

14. Remy is making kinetic sand sculptures in art class. She plans to pour the sand into two molds: a sphere for a clown head and a cone for a clown hat. Calculate the total volume of sand Remy will need to pour into the molds based on the following diagram. The area of the cone base is 100π. The radius of the sphere is 12.

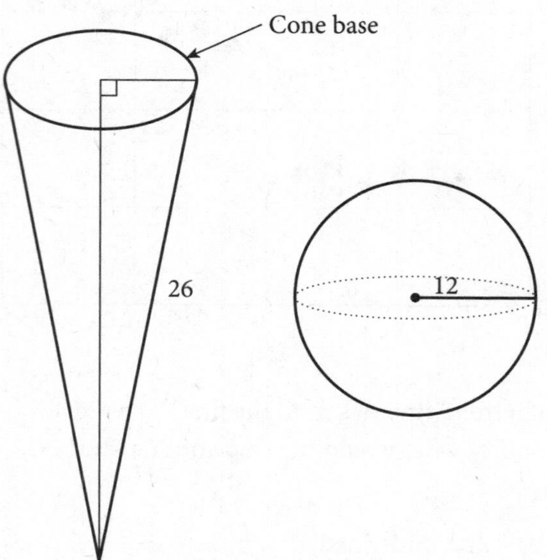

A) $1{,}208\pi$

B) $1{,}860\pi$

C) $2{,}304\pi$

D) $3{,}104\pi$

SCIENCE

Directions: After reading the passage, select the best answer to each question. Fill in the corresponding oval on the answer sheet. You may refer to the passages while answering the questions.

Gasoline efficiency is a very important topic in today's society. Gasoline is a distillation product of petroleum, along with diesel fuel, jet fuel, kerosene, and other substances. The process of distillation separates liquids by their boiling points. Generally speaking, liquids with a smaller molecular mass will have lower boiling points than those with higher molecular mass. The "octane level" of gasoline, essentially a ratio that determines how quickly gasoline will burn, can be increased by the addition of side chains of carbons, thus lowering the speed at which the gasoline can burn. Car manufacturers design different car engines to burn gasoline at different speeds, thus requiring varying levels of octane.

A student is trying to determine what factors contribute to greater fuel efficiency. The student's chemistry teacher believes that using a higher-octane gasoline in an engine designed for lower octane will not improve fuel efficiency, but the student's brother believes that all cars should use 91 octane to improve fuel efficiency. The student conducts the following two experiments to determine which of these two hypotheses are true.

Experiment 1

The student recruits three of his friends to join him in the experiment. According to the owners' manuals, two of the cars should use 87 octane, one should use 89 octane, and the last 91 octane. Each of the four students fill a car with one octane level, drive the same 50-mile route and record the mileage in miles per gallon (mpg). They then repeat this process for the other two levels of octane. The results of this experiment are summarized in Table 1.

Table 1—Average Temperature of 29°C

Car	Recommended Octane Level	Mileage with 87 Octane (mpg)	Mileage with 89 Octane (mpg)	Mileage with 91 Octane (mpg)
1	87	27	24	22
2	87	28	26	24
3	89	18	23	22
4	91	16	18	21

Experiment 2

The area the students live in experiences a heat wave in which the average high temperature is 38°C for nine days. During the time of the first experiment, the average temperature had been 29°C. The students repeat the procedure of the first experiment to determine if air temperature affects gas mileage. The results of this experiment are found in Table 2 and Figure 1.

Table 2—Average Temperature of 38°C

Car	Recommended Octane Level	Mileage with 87 Octane (mpg)	Mileage with 89 Octane (mpg)	Mileage with 91 Octane (mpg)
1	87	24	22	21
2	87	25	23	22
3	89	17	21	20
4	91	16	17	19

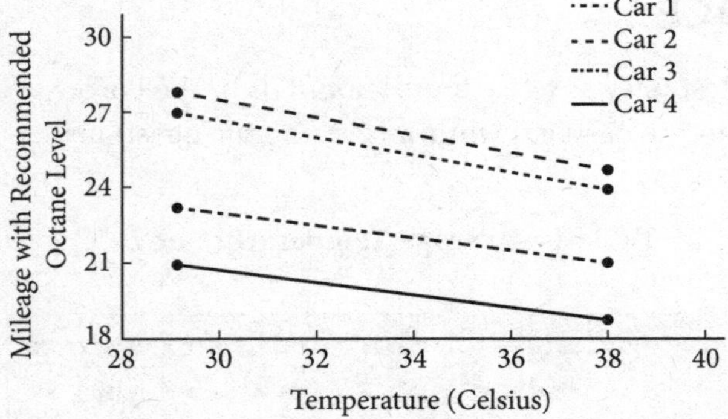

Figure 1

15. With which of the following statements would both the student's chemistry teacher and brother likely agree?

    A) Using 91-octane fuel will improve gas mileage in all cars.

    B) A fuel with an octane level higher than the manufacturer's recommendation may reduce gas mileage.

    C) The octane rating of fuel will affect a car's gas mileage.

    D) The effects of temperature on mileage can be offset by increasing the octane level of the fuel used.

16. Do the results of Experiment 1 support the student's brother's hypothesis that all cars should use 91 octane to improve fuel efficiency?

    A) Yes, because Cars 3 and 4 had their best mileage using the 91 octane gasoline.

    B) Yes, because Cars 1 and 2 did not have their best mileage using 91 octane gasoline.

    C) No, because Cars 3 and 4 had their best mileage using the 91 octane gasoline.

    D) No, because Cars 1 and 2 did not have their best mileage using 91 octane gasoline.

17. According to the results of Experiments 1 and 2, during which season would gas mileage most likely be the lowest?

    A) Spring

    B) Summer

    C) Fall

    D) Winter

18. According to the results of Experiments 1 and 2, which of the following produces the highest gas mileage in Car 1?

    A) Using 91-octane fuel at an average temperature of 38°C

    B) Using 87-octane fuel at an average temperature of 38°C

    C) Using 91-octane fuel at an average temperature of 29°C

    D) Using 87-octane fuel at an average temperature of 29°C

19. Which of the following statements is most consistent with the data in Figure 1?

    A) The mileage for Car 2 was 3 mpg lower at a higher average temperature.

    B) The mileage for Car 2 was 3 mpg higher at a higher average temperature.

    C) The mileage for Car 2 was 9 mpg lower at a higher average temperature.

    D) The mileage for Car 2 was 9 mpg higher at a higher average temperature.

20. To learn more about the effect of temperature on gas mileage, what experiment should the student perform next?

    A) Repeat Experiment 1 with four different cars with the same three recommended octane ratings.

    B) Repeat Experiment 1 with four different cars with three different recommended octane ratings.

    C) Repeat Experiment 1 with four different cars all using 91-octane fuel.

    D) Repeat Experiment 1 at average temperatures of 24°C and 34°C.

IF YOU FINISH BEFORE TIME IS CALLED, YOU MAY CHECK YOUR WORK ON THIS SECTION ONLY. DO NOT TURN TO ANY OTHER SECTION IN THE TEST.

MATH & SCIENCE PROGRESS CHECK 3

SECTION **1**

1. Ⓐ Ⓑ Ⓒ Ⓓ	6. Ⓐ Ⓑ Ⓒ Ⓓ	11. Ⓐ Ⓑ Ⓒ Ⓓ	16. Ⓐ Ⓑ Ⓒ Ⓓ	☐ # correct in Section 1
2. Ⓐ Ⓑ Ⓒ Ⓓ	7. Ⓐ Ⓑ Ⓒ Ⓓ	12. Ⓐ Ⓑ Ⓒ Ⓓ	17. Ⓐ Ⓑ Ⓒ Ⓓ	
3. Ⓐ Ⓑ Ⓒ Ⓓ	8. Ⓐ Ⓑ Ⓒ Ⓓ	13. Ⓐ Ⓑ Ⓒ Ⓓ	18. Ⓐ Ⓑ Ⓒ Ⓓ	
4. Ⓐ Ⓑ Ⓒ Ⓓ	9. Ⓐ Ⓑ Ⓒ Ⓓ	14. Ⓐ Ⓑ Ⓒ Ⓓ	19. Ⓐ Ⓑ Ⓒ Ⓓ	
5. Ⓐ Ⓑ Ⓒ Ⓓ	10. Ⓐ Ⓑ Ⓒ Ⓓ	15. Ⓐ Ⓑ Ⓒ Ⓓ	20. Ⓐ Ⓑ Ⓒ Ⓓ	☐ # incorrect in Section 1

SECTION **2**

1. Ⓐ Ⓑ Ⓒ Ⓓ	6. Ⓐ Ⓑ Ⓒ Ⓓ	11. Ⓐ Ⓑ Ⓒ Ⓓ	16. Ⓐ Ⓑ Ⓒ Ⓓ	☐ # correct in Section 2
2. Ⓐ Ⓑ Ⓒ Ⓓ	7. Ⓐ Ⓑ Ⓒ Ⓓ	12. Ⓐ Ⓑ Ⓒ Ⓓ	17. Ⓐ Ⓑ Ⓒ Ⓓ	
3. Ⓐ Ⓑ Ⓒ Ⓓ	8. Ⓐ Ⓑ Ⓒ Ⓓ	13. Ⓐ Ⓑ Ⓒ Ⓓ	18. Ⓐ Ⓑ Ⓒ Ⓓ	
4. Ⓐ Ⓑ Ⓒ Ⓓ	9. Ⓐ Ⓑ Ⓒ Ⓓ	14. Ⓐ Ⓑ Ⓒ Ⓓ	19. Ⓐ Ⓑ Ⓒ Ⓓ	
5. Ⓐ Ⓑ Ⓒ Ⓓ	10. Ⓐ Ⓑ Ⓒ Ⓓ	15. Ⓐ Ⓑ Ⓒ Ⓓ	20. Ⓐ Ⓑ Ⓒ Ⓓ	☐ # incorrect in Section 2

Section 1

30 Minutes—20 Questions

NO-CALCULATOR SECTION

Turn to Section 1 of your answer sheet to answer the questions in this section.

Directions: For this section, solve each problem and decide which is the best of the choices given. Fill in the corresponding oval on the answer sheet. You may use any available space for scratch work.

Notes:

1. Calculator use is NOT permitted.
2. All numbers used are real numbers.
3. All figures used are necessary to solving the problems that they accompany. All figures are drawn to scale EXCEPT when it is stated that a specific figure is not drawn to scale.
4. Unless otherwise indicated, the domain of a given function *f* is the set of all real numbers *x* for which *f*(*x*) is a real number.

1. A hiker stopped for lunch at an altitude of 2,000 feet. After lunch she climbed to the summit at 3,250 feet. From there, she descended to her car at 550 feet. What was the total vertical distance she traveled after lunch until she reached her car?

   A) 3,950 feet

   B) 4,000 feet

   C) 5,050 feet

   D) 5,400 feet

2. Michala recorded the rainfall her garden received over a four-week period last summer. If during weeks 1–4 her garden received $5\frac{1}{3}$, $1\frac{1}{8}$, $2\frac{1}{2}$, and $\frac{1}{6}$ inches respectively, how many total inches of rain did her garden receive in that time period?

   A) $8\frac{3}{8}$

   B) $8\frac{2}{3}$

   C) $8\frac{5}{6}$

   D) $9\frac{1}{8}$

3. Simplify $-26 \div (-17+4) + 3 \times 2^2$.

   A) -14

   B) -11

   C) 11

   D) 14

4. What is the value of x that satisfies the equation $7x = 4(11 - x)$?

   A) -24

   B) -4

   C) 4

   D) 24

5. What is the equation of a line that crosses the x-axis at $x = -3$ and crosses the y-axis at $y = -2$?

   A) $y = -\frac{2}{3}x - 2$

   B) $y = -\frac{3}{2}x - 2$

   C) $y = \frac{2}{3}x - 2$

   D) $y = \frac{3}{2}x - 2$

6. Which of the following statements best describes the equation below?

$$4x - 2y - 7 = 15$$

A) A line with a negative slope $m = -2$ and a y-intercept $y = 11$

B) A line with a negative slope $m = -2$ and a y-intercept $y = 6$

C) A line with a positive slope $m = 2$ and a y-intercept $y = -11$

D) A line with a positive slope $m = 2$ and a y-intercept $y = -6$

7. Which of the following inequalities defines the solution set for the inequality $9x < 3x - 2 < 9x + 6$?

A) $\frac{1}{3} < x < \frac{4}{3}$

B) $-\frac{1}{3} < x < \frac{4}{3}$

C) $-\frac{4}{3} < x < \frac{1}{3}$

D) $-\frac{4}{3} < x < -\frac{1}{3}$

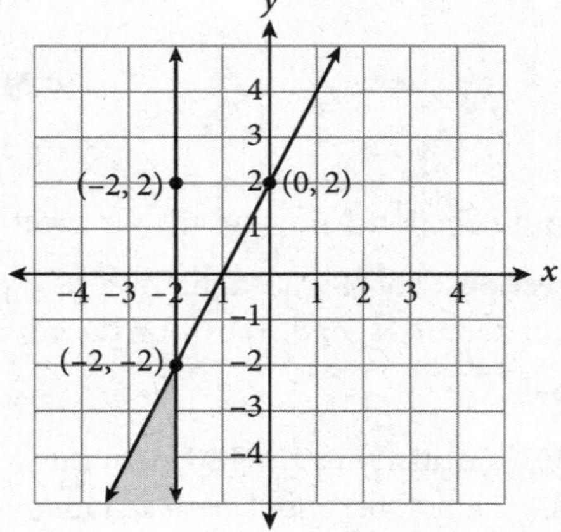

8. Which of the following systems of inequalities is represented by the shaded region of the graph above?

A) $y \geq 2x + 2$ and $x \geq -2$

B) $y \geq 2x + 2$ or $x \geq -2$

C) $y \leq 2x + 2$ and $x \leq -2$

D) $y \leq 2x + 2$ or $x \leq -2$

9. If $z = 7 + \frac{4}{3}y$ and $x = \frac{4}{3}y + 3$, what is z in terms of x?

A) $x + 4$

B) $x + 6$

C) $x + 10$

D) $x + 16$

10. Which ordered pair (x, y) satisfies the system of equations shown below?

$$4x + 3y = 9$$
$$2x - y = 7$$

A) (15, 23)

B) (10, 3)

C) (5, −2)

D) (3, −1)

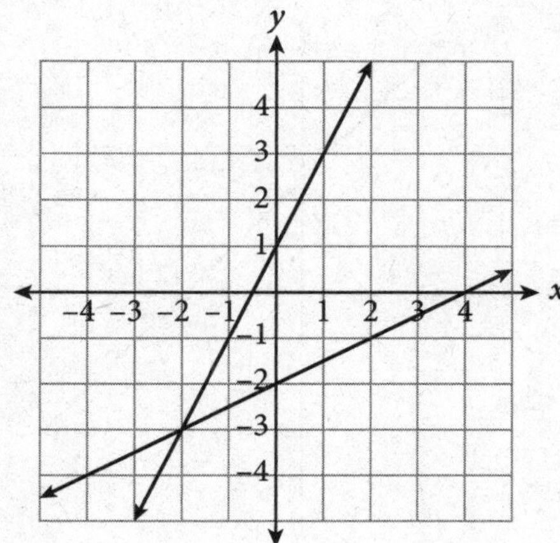

11. The graph above plots the equations $y = 2x + 1$ and $y = \frac{1}{2}x - 2$. Which ordered pair (x, y) represents the point of intersection?

A) $(-3, -2)$

B) $(-2, -3)$

C) $\left(-\frac{4}{3}, -\frac{2}{3}\right)$

D) $\left(-\frac{3}{2}, -\frac{4}{3}\right)$

12. At a bottled-water facility, a bottling machine fills and caps 30 bottles per minute. If each bottle contains 0.5 liters, which of the following equations expresses the total number of liters (L) of water used to fill the bottles (B) during an 8-hour production shift?

A) $$\frac{\left(30\frac{\text{bottles}}{\text{minute}}\right)\left(60\frac{\text{minutes}}{\text{hour}}\right)}{2\frac{\text{bottles}}{\text{liter}}}$$

B) $$\left(2\frac{\text{bottles}}{\text{liter}}\right)\left(30\frac{\text{bottles}}{\text{minute}}\right)\left(8\frac{\text{hours}}{\text{shift}}\right)$$

C) $$\frac{\left(30\frac{\text{bottles}}{\text{minute}}\right)\left(8\frac{\text{hours}}{\text{shift}}\right)}{2\frac{\text{bottles}}{\text{liter}}}$$

D) $$\frac{\left(30\frac{\text{bottles}}{\text{minute}}\right)\left(60\frac{\text{minutes}}{\text{hour}}\right)\left(8\frac{\text{hours}}{\text{shift}}\right)}{2\frac{\text{bottles}}{\text{liter}}}$$

13. Samantha sets the flow of water filling a 60-gallon tank at 5 gallons per hour. If the tank is full after 8 hours, how many gallons were in the tank when Samantha began to fill it?

A) 0

B) 5

C) 10

D) 20

14. Currently, Marco waters his garden with a sprinkler irrigation system that delivers 12 gallons per minute and needs to operate 3 hours per week to supply sufficient water to his garden. He is considering switching to a drip irrigation system that would deliver 2 gallons per minute and require 2 hours per week to supply sufficient water to his garden. If Marco makes the switch, how many gallons of water will he save per week?

A) 2,400

B) 2,160

C) 1,920

D) 240

15. Simplify $\frac{x^2y^3x^5}{\sqrt{x}}$.

A) $x^{\frac{13}{2}}y^3$

B) $x^{\frac{19}{2}}$

C) $x^{\frac{7}{2}}y^3$

D) $x^{14}y^6$

16. Simplify $\frac{(x^2y^2)^2}{(xy)^4}$.

A) x^2y^2

B) x^4y^4

C) 4

D) 1

17. Simplify $\frac{2x^2+6x+4}{x^2+6x+8}$.

A) $\frac{2x+2}{x+4}$

B) $\frac{2x+4}{x+8}$

C) $\frac{2x+1}{x+4}$

D) $\frac{2x+2}{x+8}$

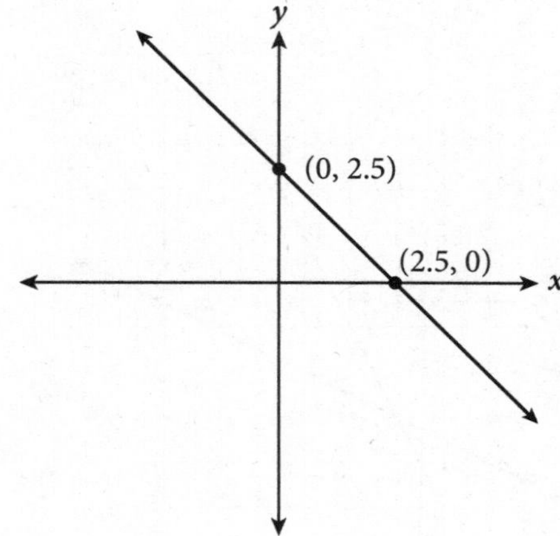

18. Which of the following equations best represents the line above?

A) $f(x) = x + 2.5$

B) $x = f(x) - 2.5$

C) $x = 2.5 + f(x)$

D) $f(x) = 2.5 - x$

19. If $x > 0$, which of the following represents the solution to the system of equations shown below?

$$x^2 - 4x - 5 = 0$$
$$y^2 - xy - x = 0$$

A) $x = 1, y = \{6.32, 1.68\}$

B) $x = 4, y = \{4.11, 9.34\}$

C) $x = 5, y = \{5.85, -0.85\}$

D) $x = 8, y = \{8.32, -1.62\}$

20. What is the value of x that satisfies the following system of equations?

$$3x - 15 = y$$
$$(x+4)(x-3) = (x-6)(x+7)$$

A) $x = 2.33$

B) $x = 6$

C) $x = 12$

D) No solution

IF YOU FINISH BEFORE TIME IS CALLED, YOU MAY CHECK YOUR WORK ON THIS SECTION ONLY. DO NOT TURN TO ANY OTHER SECTION IN THE TEST. **STOP**

Section 2

30 Minutes—20 Questions

CALCULATOR SECTION

Turn to Section 2 of your answer sheet to answer the questions in this section.

MATH

Directions: For this section, solve each problem and decide which is the best of the choices given. Fill in the corresponding oval on the answer sheet. You may use any available space for scratch work.

Notes:

1. Calculator use is permitted.
2. All numbers used are real numbers.
3. All figures used are necessary to solving the problems that they accompany. All figures are drawn to scale EXCEPT when it is stated that a specific figure is not drawn to scale.
4. Unless otherwise indicated, the domain of a given function *f* is the set of all real numbers x for which $f(x)$ is a real number.

Information:

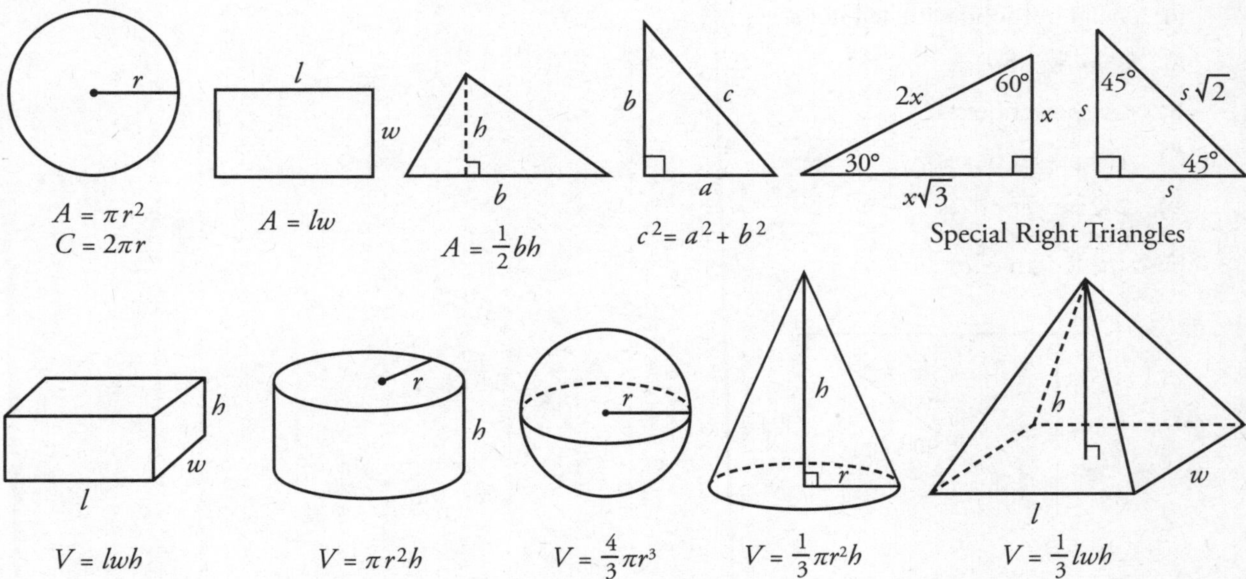

1. Find the value of a.

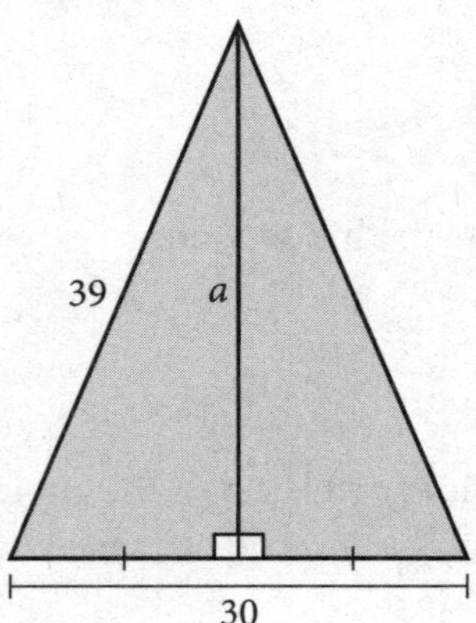

A) 15
B) 24
C) 36
D) 41

2. For every 4 houses in a particular suburban neighborhood, 1 electrical power box is required. How many power boxes are required for a neighborhood with 484 houses?

A) 85 power boxes
B) 121 power boxes
C) 164 power boxes
D) 242 power boxes

3. Find the length of b.

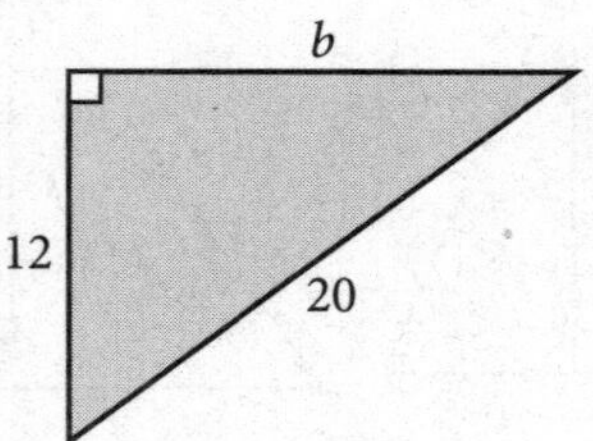

A) 14
B) 16
C) 18
D) 20

4. A psychologist wanted to find how many times people in different age groups check their smart phones for new calls, texts, emails, or other social updates. He selected several samples of individuals for each age group. The data from one survey sample of smart phones users aged 21–30 years can be found below. What are the mean and median number of smart phone checks, and what are the mode and range of the data set?

4, 5, 7, 8, 8, 8, 8, 15, 17, 18, 22, 24, 26, 29, 34

A) mean = 13.5, median = 17, mode = 8, range = 34
B) mean = 15.5, median = 15, mode = 8, range = 30
C) mean = 15.5, median = 17, mode = 4, range = 34
D) mean = 13.5, median = 15, mode = 4, range = 30

Questions 5–6 refer to the following information.

The chart depicts how many babies were born each month in a rural county.

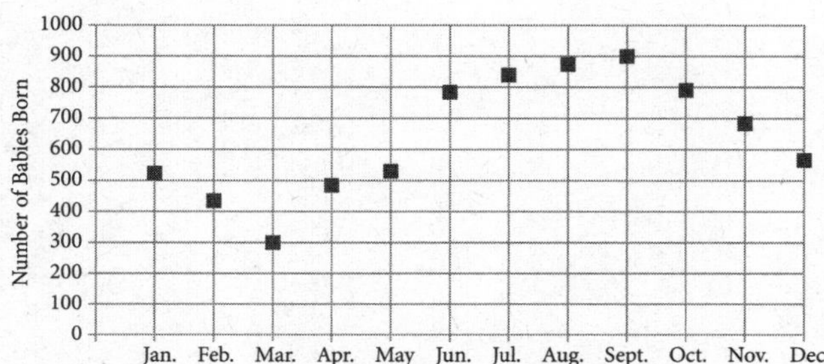

5. What is the percent increase of babies born from March to September?

   A) 100%

   B) 150%

   C) 200%

   D) 250%

6. The average length of a pregnancy is 40 weeks. In this particular county, during which season (summer, fall, winter, spring) did the greatest number of pregnancies begin?

   A) Summer

   B) Fall

   C) Winter

   D) Spring

7. Find the measures of angles x and y.

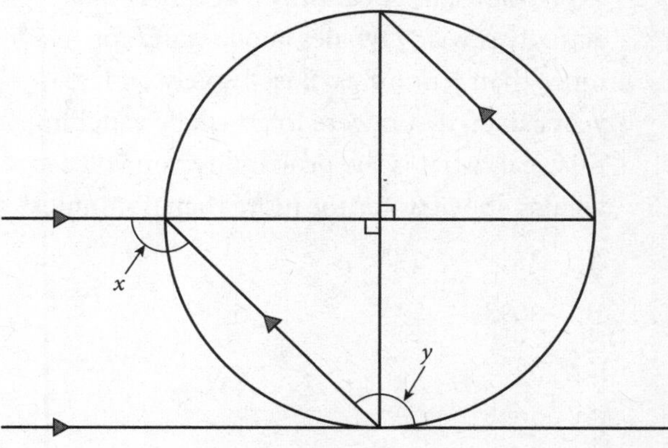

   A) $x = 145°, y = 145°$

   B) $x = 115°, y = 155°$

   C) $x = 135°, y = 135°$

   D) $x = 155°, y = 115°$

8. By the end of July, Justin wants to buy new set of headphones that costs $120. Luckily the headphones are on sale at a discount at the local store. Every Friday he gets an allowance of $15 from his parents. He also earns $10 on weekends helping his neighbor garden. He has no other money saved up to use this month. There are four Fridays and four weekends in July. After he collects all his earnable money in July, Justin has just enough cash to buy the headphones. What was the store's discount rate?

   A) 13.33%

   B) 16.67%

   C) 33.33%

   D) 50.00%

9. Although many boats go on whale-watching expeditions, last year only 84 of 210 boats actually saw any whales above water for more than 5 minutes. Based solely on last years' data, if you were to go whale watching this year, what is the probability you will see whales above water for more than 5 minutes?

   A) 25%

   B) 30%

   C) 35%

   D) 40%

10. If James drove for two hours at 60 miles per hour and then was stuck in traffic for half an hour at an average speed of 26 miles per hour, how many miles did James travel in all?

    A) 133 miles

    B) 154 miles

    C) 166 miles

    D) 182 miles

Questions 11–12 refer to the following information.

The table below shows in a particular year how many organic farms were in operation based on geographic region.

Northwest	Southwest	Central North	Central South	Northeast	Southeast
2,400	3,300	2,000	1,600	1,700	2,800

11. What percentage of total organic farms were located in the Central North region?
    A) 11.6%
    B) 14.5%
    C) 16.8%
    D) 18.4%

12. Which of the following statements about the table is true?
    A) The southern regions have more organic farms than the northern regions.
    B) Of west, central, and east regions, the central region has the most organic farms.
    C) The Southwest has more organic farms than the Central South and Northeast combined.
    D) The east regions have more organic farms than the west regions.

13. According to a national park map, there is a lodge directly east of the front entrance. The distance between the front entrance and the lodge is 4.5 centimeters. The map's legend states that every 1 centimeter on the map corresponds to 1.8 miles. How many miles east would one need to hike to get to the lodge?
    A) 8.1 miles
    B) 9.0 miles
    C) 10.3 miles
    D) 12.1 miles

14. Find the volume of the cone, the length of arc AB, and the equation of the circle (the base of the cone). The center of the circle is at point (1, 1). The measure of angle a is 30°. The area of the shaded right triangle cross-section of the cone is 15.

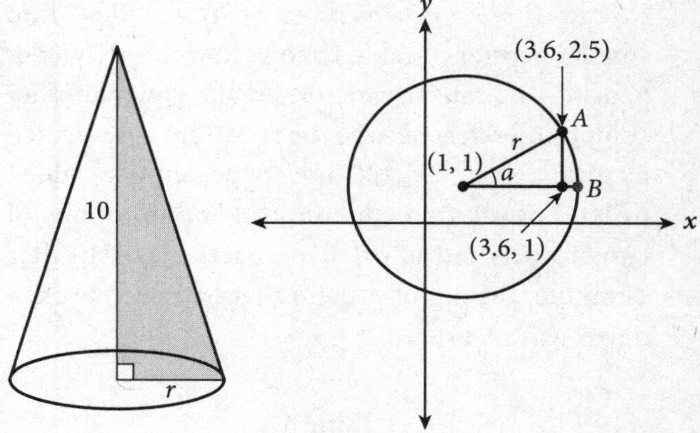

    A) $x^2 + y^2 = 9$, *Cone Volume* = 30π, AB = 2π
    B) $x^2 + y^2 = 10$, *Cone Volume* = 90π, AB = 0.5π
    C) $(x - 3.6)^2 + (y - 2.5)^2 = 9$, *Cone Volume* = 90π, AB = 2π
    D) $(x - 1)^2 + (y - 1)^2 = 9$, *Cone Volume* = 30π, AB = 0.5π

SCIENCE

Directions: After reading the passage, select the best answer to each question. Fill in the corresponding oval on the answer sheet. You may refer to the passages while answering the questions.

Pepsin is an enzyme in the human stomach that *cleaves* (break down proteins from food into smaller peptides). Table 1 shows how the activity of pepsin—the rate at which it breaks down another compound referred to as the substrate—is affected by pH. In each case, 100 units of pepsin were added to 1 ml of solution containing 1 mg/ml of one of two proteins and adjusted to a particular pH. After 1 minute, the mg of protein that had been broken down was measured.

Table 1

Solution	Substrate	pH	Activity (mg/min)
1	Protein 1	3	0.9
2	Protein 1	4	0.6
3	Protein 1	5	0.3
4	Protein 1	6	0.0
5	Protein 2	3	2.4
6	Protein 2	4	1.6
7	Protein 2	5	0.8
8	Protein 2	6	0.0

Table 2 shows that the optimum pH varies greatly from enzyme to enzyme. In each case, 100 units of the enzyme were added to 1 ml of a solution containing 1 mg/ml of Protein 2, as in Table 1. However, if other proteins or other enzyme and protein concentrations had been used, only the maximum activity would have changed. The optimum pH is a fundamental characteristic of the enzyme.

Table 2

Enzyme	Maximum Activity	Optimum pH
Pepsin	3.2	2.0
Trypsin	0.6	8.0
Urease	5.0	6.5
Glycine Oxidase	0.2	8.5

Figure 1 shows the effect of pH on the activity of an enzyme.

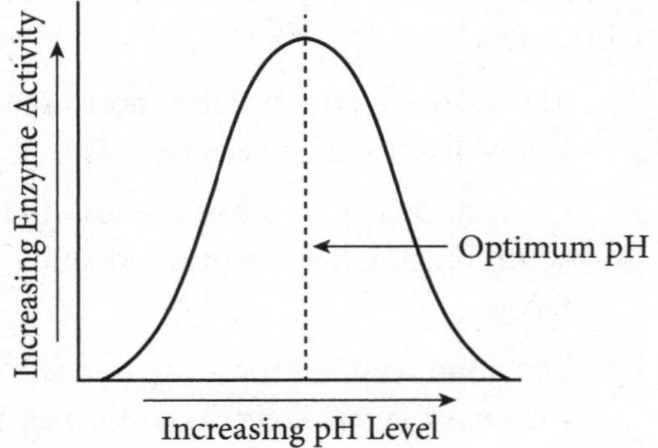

Figure 1

15. Two students are asked to design an experiment to investigate the effect of temperature on the activity rate of enzymes. Student 1 recommends using Protein 1, Pepsin at a pH of 2.0, and three different temperatures: 10°, 20°, and 30° Celsius. Student 2 recommends using Protein 1 to test Pepsin in three ways: Pepsin with a pH of 1.5 at 15° Celsius, Pepsin with a pH of 2.0 at 15° Celsius, and Pepsin with a pH of 2.5 at 20° Celsius. Which student has designed a better experiment?

    A) Student 1 because it is more efficient to adjust the temperature in 10-degree increments.

    B) Student 1 because by changing only one variable, it is easier to gauge the variable's effect on the activity rate.

    C) Student 2 because it is designed to provide more information than Student 1's experiment.

    D) Student 2 because they already know how pH affects the activity rate.

16. Based on the information in Table 1, as the pH increased, the activity of the pepsin

    A) increased only.

    B) decreased only.

    C) increased and then decreased.

    D) decreased and then increased.

17. When 100 units of pepsin are added to a solution containing 1 mg/ml of Protein 1, the enzyme's activity is measured at 0.45. Based on the results in Table 1, the pH of the solution is likely to be closest to which value?

    A) 3.5

    B) 4.0

    C) 4.5

    D) 5.0

18. According to the information in Table 2 and Figure 1, which of the following conclusions can be made about the rate (mg/min) at which 100 units of pepsin cleave (break down) Protein 2 when the pH is 1? The rate will be closest to

    A) 4.0 mg/min

    B) 3.2 mg/min

    C) 2.4 mg/min

    D) 1.2 mg/min

19. Which of the following factors in Table 1 could NOT have been directly controlled by an experimenter?

    A) The activity (mg/min) of the enzyme

    B) The substrate protein

    C) The pH of the solution

    D) The amount of enzyme added

20. Which of the following graphs best represents the Enzyme Activity curve for the enzyme Urease?

A)

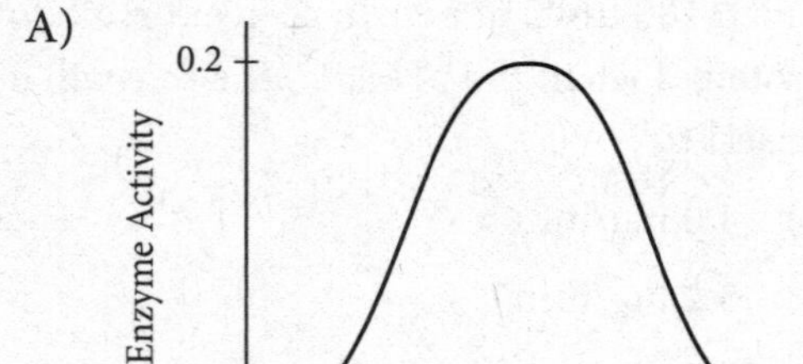

B)

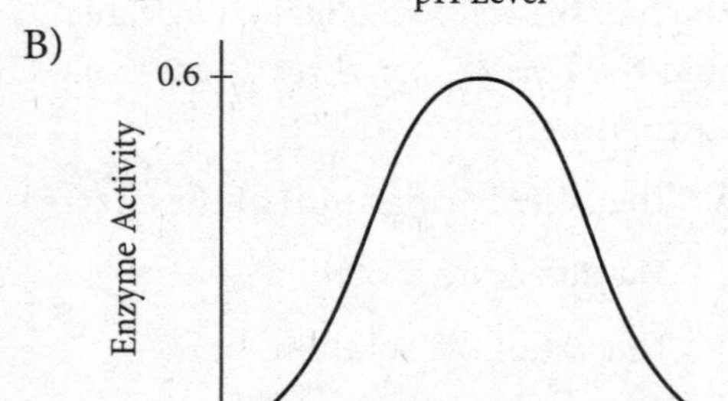

C)

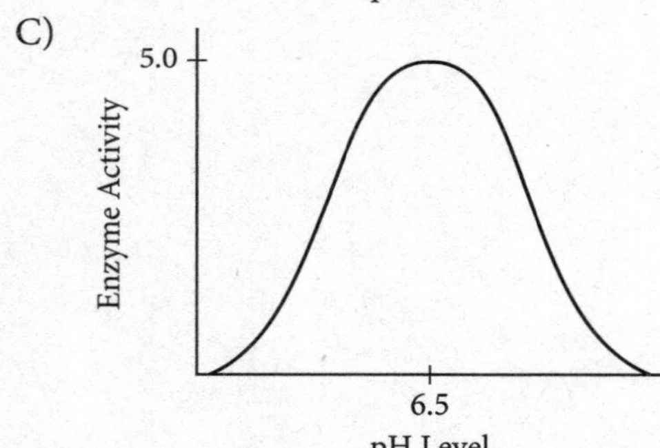

D)

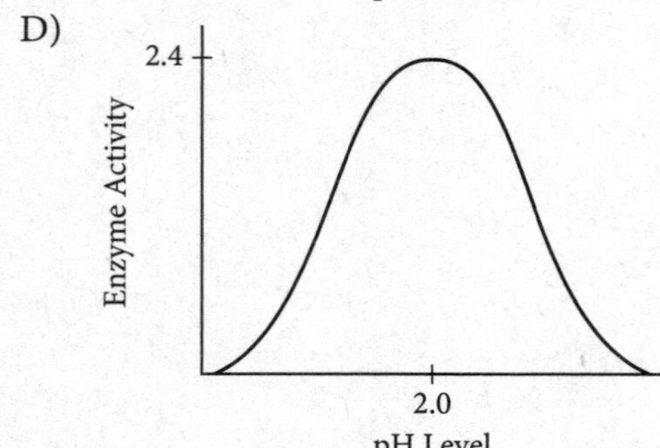

IF YOU FINISH BEFORE TIME IS CALLED, YOU MAY CHECK YOUR WORK ON THIS SECTION ONLY. DO NOT TURN TO ANY OTHER SECTION IN THE TEST. **STOP**